LAW AND SOCIAL
TRANSFORMATION
IN INDIA

Law in India is a series aimed at scholars, students, and law professionals, whose engagement with the law, especially in South Asia, reaches beyond standard black letter law towards an understanding of how law and legal institutions have an impact upon, and in turn are affected by, society as a whole.

Series advisors:
UPENDRA BAXI, RAJEEV DHAVAN, MARC GALANTER

Founding advisor:
LATE S.P. SATHE

OTHER BOOKS IN THE SERIES

SUDHIR KRISHNASWAMY
Democracy and Constitutionalism in India
A Study of the Basic Structure Doctrine
(Oxford India Paperbacks)

RINA VERMA WILLIAMS
Postcolonial Politics and Personal Laws
Colonial Legal Legacies and the Indian State

FLAVIA AGNES
Law and Gender Inequality
The Politics of Women's Rights in India
(Oxford India Paperbacks)

ROBERT LINGAT
The Classical Law of India
(translated and edited by J.D.M. Derrett)
(Oxford India Paperbacks)

ARVIND SHARMA
Hinduism and Human Rights
A Conceptual Approach

B. SIVRAMAYYA
Matrimonial Property Rights
(Oxford India Paperbacks)

RONOJOY SEN
Articles of Faith
Religion, Secularism, and the Indian Supreme Court
(Oxford India Paperbacks)

LAW
–IN–
INDIA
SERIES

LAW AND SOCIAL TRANSFORMATION IN INDIA

Oliver Mendelsohn

OXFORD
UNIVERSITY PRESS

OXFORD
UNIVERSITY PRESS

Oxford University Press is a department of the University of Oxford.
It furthers the University's objective of excellence in research, scholarship,
and education by publishing worldwide. Oxford is a registered trademark of
Oxford University Press in the UK and in certain other countries

Published in India by
Oxford University Press
2/11 Ground Floor, Ansari Road, Daryaganj, New Delhi 110002, India

ISBN-13: 978-0-19-809847-8
ISBN-10: 0-19-809847-2

Typeset in 9.5/13.2 Minion Pro
by Excellent Laser Typesetters, Pitampura, Delhi 110 034
Printed in India by Thomson Press India Ltd.

To my daughters,
Emma and Rebecca

CONTENTS

PREFACE

The experience of putting together a collection of my writings on Indian law has been both pleasurable and troubling. The pleasure has come from the sense that some of my colleagues have seen sufficient merit in my published work to suggest that there would be value in collecting some of the papers together in a volume. I am particularly grateful to Professors Upendra Baxi and Marc Galanter for suggesting this publication to Oxford University Press. Both these scholars have been a source of inspiration for many years to me personally and to many other scholars in their own (and indeed other) fields. Upendra Baxi, old friend as well as colleague, had offered to write a Foreword for the present work but was unfortunately struck by illness before this came about.

The troubling aspect of the experience has been seeing the limitations of my own writing in the face of the importance of the subject. I can only hope that the work presented here does at least a little to sharpen that sense of importance.

After a professional lifetime of doing fieldwork in India, I have been the recipient of assistance and kindness from innumerable people. I will not attempt to make even a start on listing these people here. Instead, let me mention a very few friends from my earliest years of doing work in India. P.C. Mathur of the University of Rajasthan was, from the beginning, a good friend and a great guide to Rajasthan. S.D. Muni was another early friend in Jaipur. In 1980, I met activist and writer, Madhu Kishwar. Madhu remains both a friend and a great inspiration. I also wish to mention the late Dharma Kumar, one of the most intellectually passionate human beings I have met. Of course, there are many others in India whom I feel just as warmly connected to.

The only other person I will mention by name here is Marika Vicziany, both colleague and wife. She has been a help to my work in numerous ways, not least in goading me to action.

Melbourne   OLIVER MENDELSOHN
July 2013

ACKNOWLEDGEMENTS

Oliver Mendelsohn gratefully acknowledges the following publishers for their kind permission to allow him to republish, in this collection, articles or chapters originally published in the specified journals and books.

Cambridge University Press for:
Oliver Mendelsohn, 'The Pathology of the Indian Legal System', *Modern Asian Studies* 15(4) (1981), pp. 823–63.
Oliver Mendelsohn, 'The Transformation of Authority in Rural India', *Modern Asian Studies* 27(4) (1993), pp. 805–42.
Oliver Mendelsohn and Marika Vicziany, 'The Question of the "Harijan Atrocity"', Chapter 2 in *The Untouchables: Subordination, Poverty and the State in Modern India* (Cambridge: Cambridge University Press, 1998, pp. 44–76).

Tulika Books for:
Oliver Mendelsohn, 'How Indian is Indian Law?', in Mathew John and Sitharamam Kakarala (eds), *Enculturing Law: New Agendas for Legal Pedagogy* (New Delhi: Tulika Books, 2007, pp. 132–57).

Thomson Reuters for:
Oliver Mendelsohn, 'From Colonial to Post-colonial Law in India', Chapter 15 in Veronica Taylor (ed.), *Asian Law through Australian Eyes* (Sydney: LBC Information Services, 1997, pp. 297–315).

Taylor & Francis for:

Oliver Mendelsohn, 'The Indian Legal Profession, the Courts and
    Globalisation', *South Asia: Journal of South Asian Studies* 28(2)
    (2006), pp. 301–20.
Oliver Mendelsohn, 'Life and Struggles in the Stone Quarries of
    India: A Case Study', *The Journal of Commonwealth & Comparative
    Politics* 29(1) (March 1991), pp. 44–71.
Oliver Mendelsohn, 'The Supreme Court as the Most Trusted Public
    Institution in India', *South Asia: Journal of South Asian Studies* 23
    (Special Issue) (2000), pp. 103–19.

Hart Publishing for:

Oliver Mendelsohn, 'Law, Terror and the Indian Legal Order', Chapter
    5 in Christoph Antons and Volkmar Gessner (eds), *Globalisation
    and Resistance: Law Reform in Asia since the Crisis* (Oxford: Hart
    Publishing, 2007, pp. 157–78).

INTRODUCTION

Oliver Mendelsohn

This volume represents a collection of my more considered articles and chapters on Indian law. I have not edited these pieces and so they remain as they were when initially published. Inevitably, this means that the older pieces were published when the perspectives and state of knowledge of Indian law were considerably different from today. The obvious question, then, is whether it is worth republishing old writings. Fortunately, this was not my decision to make, in the sense that it was the editors of the series and the publisher who proposed the volume.

After re-reading the contents presented here, I can now see a couple of possible justifications for this exercise. First, though the practice and many of the preoccupations of Indian law have changed greatly over the years, many of the fundamental questions about the system persist. As the majority of the chapters reproduced here are quite consciously addressed to these fundamental questions, their arguments may be seen to have some continuing relevance to present-day debates. And secondly, it may be useful for students of Indian law to see how a body of work on the subject has developed over a period of years. Certainly this development has not proceeded according to any plan: it has come about as one question has led to another. It may be helpful in this introduction to explain some of these links between the chapters and the physical and intellectual circumstances that have given rise to the work.

If I were to try to sum up my objectives in an analytical list, it would read something like the following. First, I have been concerned to explore the way in which the British constructed new legal forms, institutions and processes in India; secondly, to inform myself of just how these elements actually worked in India; thirdly, to see how the introduced system of justice supplanted or coexisted with forms and processes that predated the European incursion; and lastly, to shed some light on the still emerging character of Indian law in what is now a quite dynamic period in its development. Overall, this collection has a stronger preoccupation with the sociology of contemporary Indian law than its history. I am not, by discipline, an historian and I have ventured into history in order to understand the present (and, indeed, the future) of law in India. Throughout, I have looked at law more from the perspective of society than from within the system of law itself: the work may be classified as the sociology and historical sociology of law in India, rather than either legal scholarship or the history of law. I have been interested in what part law has played within Indian society.

The above list can serve as an abstract summary of my work, but I suspect that it does not convey much of a sense of what I have actually been doing. With that sense in mind, let me now try to explain the way my work has come about in a more narrative fashion.

When I began thinking about my doctoral thesis at the University of California in the late 1960s, I had some ideas about Indian law that now seem quite naïve. The time was little more than twenty years after Indian Independence, and I think I had almost instinctively adopted a romantic view about Indian institutions. It seemed to me then that the legal system built by the British in India must be 'foreign' to that society and therefore of questionable value and durability. It was such feelings—they were more feelings than thoughts!—that decided for me that the newly instituted *nyaya panchayats* would be at the centre of my thesis. These were part of the *panchayati raj* scheme that was mentioned in the Constitution of 1950 and had progressively taken shape in the 1960s. The panchayats were an effort to build a hybrid form of village and local governance that was supposed to revive patterns of local governance that had roots in the pre-colonial past. Nyaya panchayats were a sub-set of the general panchayats and were designed to provide an accessible, quick, cheap and 'authentic' justice that would provide an alternative to the dilatory, expensive and seemingly ineffective courts.

Before I left for field work I had an exchange of letters with Marc Galanter, already the leading American student of the Indian legal process. I have, by now, mislaid the old letter, but I do recall Marc saying that he 'hoped' I would situate my study of nyaya panchayats within the wider field of Indian legal practice. This advice proved both influential and prophetic. I based myself at the University of Rajasthan for about eighteen months and after considerable casting about, I determined on a village (really a small township) that was a sub-district centre. I spent about six months living in this village, known as Behror, and I have returned there a number of times since. In addition to housing a nyaya panchayat, Behror was the seat of several magistrates' courts.

It did not take me long to find that the nyaya panchayat of Behror was not the answer to the legal problems of the villages in the surrounding area. This was not because of any failing of the chairman of the nyaya panchayat, with whom I remained friends until his death many years later. There were a number of forces working against the panchayat, including its confined jurisdiction and the active hostility of the lawyers who were banned from appearing before it. Moreover, it soon became clear that the nyaya panchayat was scarcely more indigenous than the courts were. These legal panchayats were a form of 'alternative' justice—alternative dispute resolution as it is now known in the West and also in India—that was not particularly thought through or firmly based at that time. Fortunately, for my doctoral thesis, I had plenty of other material to work on.

So I quickly turned to studying the courts and also non-state processes within the village of Behror as well as some nearby villages. So far as the courts were concerned, I wanted to look at the kinds of disputes that were coming to them and just how they were being dealt with. My methods were pretty simple. I made myself known to the magistrates and to the officials who kept records, wrote up court decisions, compiled statistics and the like. These contacts allowed me to gather some basic information on the case load the courts were dealing with. Secondly, I spent a lot of time with the lawyers who sat around endlessly—particularly the less successful of them—in the dusty courtyard of the magistrates' complex in Behror. Usually through

the lawyers, I was able to meet litigants when they came to court for a
hearing. These litigants proved to be the richest source of understanding
of the village disputes that were giving rise to litigation and criminal
prosecution in the courts. I had to collect much of the material by
travelling (on my motorbike) to the village where the litigants lived
and talking to as many of the participants in the dispute as I could.
Thus the first chapter in this collection discusses at considerable
length the multiple court cases involving one particular litigant,
whom I have called Jagat Singh.[1] This case study involved a number of
meetings with Jagat Singh, including a stay of several days at his village
some kilometres away from the courthouse. I filled out gaps in the
narrative on a return visit a couple of years later. Through a number
of such case studies I was able to build up a picture of the litigation of
the period in the sub-district courthouse of Behror (which I originally
called Haripur, for reasons of confidentiality that later seemed
unnecessary).

Very early in this field work, I stumbled across a piece of knowledge
that has been fundamental to much of my understanding and writing
about Indian law. Perhaps I should not have been so surprised by this
'discovery', since much of it was known to generations of British judges
and administrators and many Indians with practical knowledge of the
legal process. But in my own defence, this information had over the
years become somewhat obscured in the post-Independence discussions of the Indian legal system. Thus, I found that the overwhelming
majority of civil disputes, and even criminal cases, in this part of rural
Rajasthan had their origins in a dispute over agricultural land. There
were civil, criminal and 'revenue' magistrates in Behror, and the greater
part of the work in all three jurisdictions arose from disputes over
agricultural land. A dispute over the ownership or control of land was
sometimes expressed in multiple cases over a period of years, even generations. The most common criminal prosecutions were for assault and
theft: the assault charges seemed typically to arise from physical fights
over land, and the theft charges tended to concern crops taken from
land in dispute. It became clear from case studies that criminal charges
were frequently pursued out of a tactical and punitive approach by
the parties to the land dispute. This pattern was broadly characteristic
of the court load across India at that time, and I later found (through
historical work on court reports and official records in the former India

Office Library and in Indian archives) that this had been so for more than a century before I encountered it at the beginning of the 1970s.

The predominance of land as the subject of litigation in the Indian courts stands in contrast to the ambitious formal reach of the legal system built by the British in India. The edifice of Anglo-Indian law, including the great legal codes for civil and criminal matters, was in the mind of the British Raj the great centrepiece of their civilizing mission of the nineteenth century. And the conceptual breadth of their substantive laws was sufficient to govern a great modern society. Yet it was overwhelmingly matters to do with landed property, not anything else, that dominated the work of the judicial institutions the British established in India. It took more than another century for the practice of Indian courts and most legal professionals to broaden out so as to begin to match more closely the potential that resided in the formal body of laws transferred to and later created in India.

If the practical narrowness of the Anglo-Indian courts was extraordinary, so was the mess that they seem to have made of a great many of the cases that came before them. The disputes often seemed never-ending rather than resolved by decision of the court. And there seemed to be more cases than was reasonable in the circumstances (though how this was to be measured was never made clear). For the great majority of British judges—there were rare exceptions—the fault was laid at the feet of the Indian litigants. 'The litigious Indian' was a regular postulate of British judges trying to explain what they saw as an overuse of their courts and an unwillingness to accept adverse decisions.

So why was it agricultural land and not, say, family relations, that became the dominant subject of litigation throughout the colonial period and the first decades of Independence? And why did the cases often seem to turn out so badly? The basic answer to these questions lay in the scheme of taxation and administration of land that the British imposed on India. Largely without intention or even understanding, the British *caused* the legal system they were so proud of to be dominated by disputes over land. While the British were blaming Indians for perverting what they saw as their great gift of British justice to India, the litigants were really acting on a more or less rational basis to protect or claim 'their' land. They had little option but to go to court over a land dispute, and this was unlike virtually any other issue in their lives. What the British had brought about in the nineteenth century was still profoundly at work in the courts of Behror I encountered in the early 1970s.

Not only did land disputes dominate the courts established by the British, but they also shaped the whole character of the Indian judicial process. People would fight with great strength and persistence to preserve what they believed were their rights in relation to land. This was the foundation upon which lawyers and other legal professionals could assert their own interest, which was prolongation and proliferation of cases. Over time this professional ruthlessness and exploitation of litigants developed into a culture that so repels many observers of (and, indeed, participants in) the Indian court system. This historical formation (or deformation) of the Indian legal process remains critical to an understanding of even contemporary legal behaviour in India.

Another early revelation of my field work in Behror was the claims of corruption in the courts. I was frequently told about the bribe taking of magistrates, not to mention of the officials who demanded small sums for the supply of documents and services that were officially without cost. One of my informants even identified a man whom he claimed was the go-between for litigants who sought to bribe a particular magistrate. Inevitably, it was impossible for me to work out just how widespread the corruption of magistrates really was. What would constitute evidence of bribery, other than the confession or conviction of a bribe giver or taker? Nor has this task of measuring 'corruption' in the judiciary become much easier in subsequent years. With only a few exceptions, the High Courts of the States have retained a generally solid reputation for integrity (if not always efficiency and effectiveness). And one of the chapters in this collection sets out a case for the Supreme Court of India as being the most trusted of all public institutions in India, particularly in the context of a widespread criminalization of representative politics. On the other hand, there remain persistent complaints—not least from elements of the legal profession itself—that the decisions of some lower judicial and quasi-judicial institutions are not always determined by the merits of the matter before them. Such perceptions have contributed to dissatisfaction with the courts in general. There is a special intolerance among ordinary people for any perceived lack of probity in the judiciary above all other institutions. The anti-corruption movement of recent years suggests that this is an issue that will not go away for the courts.

I puzzled away at the question of dissatisfaction with the courts throughout my stay in Behror, and while I was writing up my doctoral dissertation. I could see that the official courts were 'popular', in the sense that they were richly used by some of the people from the villages surrounding the courthouse. Despite the attempt to build alternatives like the nyaya panchayats, it was the new institutions not the courts, that had failed. But equally, it was inescapable that the courts were far from satisfactory in the justice they dispensed (or failed to dispense). The sufferings of Indian litigants seemed worse than that of litigants in most other places, though admittedly litigants do tend to suffer unreasonably just about everywhere. More than forty years later I can still see the torment in the face of a farmer who felt he had been trapped in the legal system for countless years without any gain. He begged me to help him; given that I was a complete outsider, this was a sign of how desperate he was. In the face of this desperation it was impossible to be 'philosophical' and pretend that the system was working as well as could reasonably be expected.

In addition to the effort to understand the basis and process of litigation, I applied myself to trying to find just who exercised power and authority throughout the particular village in which I was living. I also asked questions in other villages I travelled to. I was particularly interested in what are known in the literature as 'caste panchayats'. The post-Independence fieldwork of some anthropologists, notably M.N. Srinivas, had pointed to these caste councils as trying to resolve certain disputes of a kind that did not usually go the courts. And by the time I started looking at the question of caste panchayats, I already knew that courts were used mainly in relation to land matters. So I was interested to see whether many of the other disputes in the village came before the caste panchayat. What I found was that the lower the position of the caste in the ritual hierarchy, the more likely it was to have a functioning council broadly conforming to the (often quite vague) descriptions of the caste panchayat in the literature. By common consent, the ritually lowest community of Behror was the Sweeper caste, and this community's council was the most active of all such bodies in the village. Leaders of this community, both locally and in an extended geographical network were active in trying to raise the status of the community. Part of this activity was directed to trying to keep the community's inter-personal disputes within the community itself, so as to avoid a possible damage to their collective reputation.

Several other communities, including the Meenas (legally a tribe rather than a caste), and the Dhobis or Washerfolk, were able to relate cases from the recent past where a community council had deliberated on marital disputes and sexual misconduct within the caste community itself. But these were isolated cases and not typical of caste authority of the period, even for the ritually lower communities. It was clear that caste was still a critical element of village life in multiple ways, not least in the regulation of marriage that still took place almost invariably within the caste. But any authoritative local or regional functioning of councils or individuals enforcing caste norms in the name of the community seemed by then to be rare. And in the case of the middle-ranking castes—including the Ahirs as the dominant landholders—and the ritually superior castes, such action was non-existent. If someone from these castes failed to live by generally accepted rules of morality and community tradition, the collective community had no capacity to force the deviant to comply. Thus, the Brahmin community of Behror had been able to tell me about a case in the 1930s of a Brahmin man cohabiting with a Chamar woman. The community outcasted this man, and it was only some years later that he was readmitted to Brahmin society after ceasing his delinquency and performing appropriate expiation. Although the Brahmins would be similarly outraged if such behaviour happened today, they would lack the resolution to confront the delinquent in the same authoritative way. This and other examples suggest that there has been a waning of organized caste authority in Behror and presumably in many other villages throughout India, though it has to be conceded that we know remarkably little about how caste norms were enforced in the past.

Even the Sweepers of Behror, the most organized of all the castes, had the sense that time was not on their side. They recognized that economic progress would tend to threaten their own coherence. The community had already been forced to negotiate an internal conflict that involved the outcasting of one of their own and his subsequent suit for defamation against them. This conjunction of primordial sanction and modern court action in the one case serves to demonstrate the fragility of caste authority today.

Despite this, I became convinced after this fieldwork that it was wrong-headed to insist that the state was now the only possible basis of legal authority in India. It seemed to me that identification of 'legal authority' was a matter of empirical discovery rather than definitional logic. Such an approach has come to be called, perhaps somewhat pompously, 'legal pluralism'. Thus, while the modern state has great advantages in the assertion of its authority, this does not mean that other forms of legal or law-like authority cannot and do not exist side-by-side with the authority of the state. I am aware of the vagueness of this proposition and the difficulty of comparing the exercise of state authority through the courts with the sometimes more 'organic' authority of structures constituted in society (whether 'civil' or 'traditional' society). But this is not the place to pursue these and other conceptual questions about the idea of the state.

In framing these few remarks about legal pluralism, I have in my mind a particular case I collected during my stay in Behror. This was a case that came before the council of the Dhobis, and it is set out in Chapter 2. It was a complicated dispute about widowhood, remarriage, dowry and the ritually prohibited bride price among the Dhobis of the region. The whole case was heard and determined without resort to or interference from outside the caste. I concluded the case study with the following remarks:

> It would be difficult to argue that the above case does not represent a process of 'law' at work, despite the fact that it was conducted outside the institutions of the state. The process was decisional, binding, and has the general appearance of judicial action…. I know of no comparable example to be found in contemporary Britain, France or Germany. Nor could similar examples easily be found in the US, Canada or Australia—except, importantly, among the indigenous peoples of these settler societies. Among the latter peoples, there may indeed by forms of contemporary legal ordering that are broadly analogous to that of the dhobis of Rajasthan. But what makes India different from these settler societies is that, at least in conceptual terms, the example of the dhobis' tribunal is not exceptional. Thus there is no apparatus of state that could readily have been approached by the dhobis for resolution of their problem, even if they had wanted to….

This passage is drawn from a quite recent chapter in which I returned to the theme of legal pluralism that I first encountered on the ground during my fieldwork in Behror. Thus, Chapter 2 discusses the disparate examples of caste panchayats in Behror; dispute settlement among diamond traders in Mumbai; sweepers in Dharavi, the largest slum area of Mumbai; and the nineteenth and early twentieth century attempt to enforce the 'customary law' of Punjab in the Chief Court of Punjab. The conceptual tone of this chapter is exploratory rather than declamatory but what underpins it is a sense that there are a great many situations in India where there are active efforts to confront disputes by reference to authorities constituted outside the structures of the state. It was my early fieldwork in Behror that drew me many years later into this research in Mumbai and into the now often overlooked legal experience of Punjab.

After my doctoral field work from 1971 through 1972 and a shorter period in 1974, I began to think seriously about the position of the Ahirs of Behror. This was the largest land-owning community of both the village and *tehsil*, or sub-district, of Behror, and it should have answered the description of 'the dominant caste' of the anthropological literature. M.N. Srinivas had been the first to use this term in 1955 and some years later it was adopted by Louis Dumont among others. Basically, the proposition was that economic power in 'the Indian village' arose from control of land; and secondly, that this economic power was translated into political power and even something so profound as legal authority throughout the village. Characteristically it was Dumont who propounded this view with the greatest clarity and simplicity. He wrote that 'contemporary observation shows that there are three main organs of justice: the caste panchayat, the panchayat of the dominant caste, and the official courts'. Of these three dispensers of 'justice', Dumont was clearly identifying the dominant caste as the principal authority of village India.

When I tried to fit the Ahirs of Behror into this framework, I failed. Although this caste was by far the largest landholder among the thirty-one castes of the village, it lacked the power to govern the other castes or individuals in the village. In short, it lacked the attributes of a 'dominant caste'. The Ahirs did have more local political power than any other community and this reflected the centrality of landholding in the life of the village and wider region. But the economic and political power of the Ahirs fell far short of the awesome authority of the 'dominant caste' described in some of the anthropological literature.

This led me to the broader inquiry reported in Chapter 3 of this collection, 'The Transformation of Authority in Rural India'. My conclusion there was *not* that the Ahirs were an exceptional case in being dominant landholders without possessing the wider attributes of a 'dominant caste', *nor* that that concept was itself a myth. The argument was that Srinivas, Dumont and others were articulating a concept at the very historical moment that it was ceasing to be capable of summing up power relations in rural India as a whole. In short, it seemed to me then—and the evidence is even stronger now—that the authority of the most powerful communities of village India has declined. The economic and political power of these communities is still great, but this can no longer be translated into a dominance that could sometimes be described as 'legal' or 'juridical' in nature. There is now far too much resistance on the part of economically and socially subordinated groups to allow the old kind of total dominance. This has constituted a critical, albeit non-revolutionary, transformation of rural India, and it has come about from a multitude of causes. Clearly the greatest single cause has been the advent of electoral democracy.

If 'the dominant caste' of Srinivas and Dumont no longer exists, this says something quite profound about the pattern of 'law', 'justice' or 'legal pluralism' in village India today. Thus, I have already noted that the work of the courts in rural India was overwhelmingly concerned with issues arising from agricultural land during the period of my own village fieldwork as late as the mid-1970s. The number of such disputes has greatly contracted since that time, but my impression is that they have not been replaced by any fast-growing alternative sources of litigation. True, there does seem to be a considerable increase of diverse litigation initiated by the state but this seems not to have made good the shortfall brought about by the decline in litigation over land. In short, my impression—there is an urgent need for more research on this matter—is that litigation is seriously contracting in rural India. This means that the courts are a declining, not growing, presence in the Indian countryside, despite the ever-decreasing authority of once dominant castes and the waning of the already residual authority of caste panchayats. In other words, there has been no simple Weberian transfer of authority from society to the state.

What does all this mean? Does it mean that the Indian countryside is lapsing into anarchy in the face of all this declining authority?

I strongly doubt this is the case, though social order sometimes seems largely absent in much of the 'Naxalite affected' belt of eastern and central India. Perhaps more generally, this social change means that in some ways Indian villages are becoming more like small or even large congregations of people in countries of the first world. In the latter societies, patterns of authority are not always visible or easy to detect, and there is also considerable evidence of the decline of litigation too. This does not necessarily mean that the state is less powerful in those societies than it was at some time in the past, nor that there is an absence of forms of authority constituted outside the state. The same can be said about India too. It remains an important task of research and reflection to work out just what is happening to 'authority' or per- haps even 'legal authority' in a society like rural India.

My work on 'the dominant caste' led to another body of work that occupied me for some years—the status of India's 'Untouchables' (now more often known as Dalits). The connection was the relations I had seen between the various Untouchable castes of Behror and their social superiors, including the Ahirs. There was also another path leading to this work. I have drawn attention above to my finding that much of the violence that came before the courts of Behror had its origins in disputes over agricultural land. This insight led me to look more gener- ally at agrarian violence in India. I was warned by several people that this was too broad a focus of study, and they proved right. But I had soon worked out that a disproportionate number of violent incidents in the countryside involved people from the lowest, the Untouchable, castes. Many of these incidents came to be called 'Harijan atrocities' in the 1970s, and they appeared to be growing in number. To abbreviate this story, the focus of my study now became the Dalits, Harijans or Untouchables, an aspect of which was the violence they were involved in. This apparently increasing violence was quite different from the sort I had heard about in Behror some years earlier. It was no longer violence between individuals or families but political violence, and it had its roots in profoundly unequal social arrangements. I was joined in this work by Marika Vicziany, and our major publication was *The Untouchables: Subordination, Poverty and the State in Modern India.*[2]

Chapter 4, 'The Question of the "Harijan Atrocity"', is drawn from the above work. A consideration of violence involving 'Harijans' (a term for Untouchables or Dalits made popular by Gandhi but now fallen into disuse), the chapter is less directly focused on the official legal system than are the other chapters in this collection, but is closely linked to the discussion in Chapter 3, 'The Transformation of Authority in Rural India'. The common theme is the decline in deference paid by subordinated Indians to their economic and social superiors and their increased willingness to resist. The central argument of Chapter 4 is that this violence has been growing over a period of decades and that it represents a bitter reaction on the part of some higher-caste Hindus to the increased resistance of Dalits. The more the Dalits have challenged the economic and social order, the more they have provoked violent reaction. The concrete issues have been the struggle for control of agricultural land and, perhaps as important, the demand for social respect. These are the perspectives argued in Chapter 4 through the analysis of a number of examples.

The revolt of these subordinated communities has played a major part in bringing to an end 'traditional India', however that is conceived. Old authorities have lost their hold on village India. And the courts that were at the centre of governance during the British rule have been sidelined in this transformation. Thus the demands of the Dalits are only to a limited extent admissible in a court of law, even if poor people could make the imperfect courts work in their interest (and pay the bills of the lawyers). Perhaps more often than not, landless labourers do not have a legal right on their side in claiming land. And while it is true that Dalit activists have occasionally sought to enforce Indian anti-discrimination legislation, overall they have seldom turned to the courts to better their condition. Instead, for decades now and in many States of India, they have adopted direct political action, sometimes violent action, to prosecute what they see as their rights. To a large extent this can be seen as the basis of the 'Naxalite' or revolutionary movements in States like Bihar, Madhya Pradesh and Andhra Pradesh. So from a historical perspective, the mode of action in relation to disputed claims to agricultural land has shifted from the courts to politics. This is an enormous change for a modern legal system that has been dominated by litigation over agricultural land since its inception some two centuries ago.

The remarks in this Introduction have thus far touched on four of the chapters in this collection: Chapters, 1, 2, 3 and 4. Chapters 5 and 6 take up the theme of litigation and the legal profession in urban India, particularly Mumbai (formerly called Bombay). They are again based on fieldwork, including extensive interviews with advocates, solicitors and judges in Mumbai and to some extent in Delhi too. This study has coincided with a progressive shift in the balance of litigation from the villages to the cities of India. It also coincided with increased globalization of India's economy following new policies of liberalization enacted from the early 1990s.

Clearly, agricultural land has never been the preoccupation of the courts in Mumbai, for many decades now the largest city in India. Urban property is by far the dominant source of litigation in Mumbai today, particularly the issues surrounding the scheme of rent control that has been in place in urban India for many decades. The matter of rent control is complicated, but what is important here is that it has created two classes of people whose interests are diametrically opposed—the landlord and the protected tenant. Mumbai has some of the most expensive real estate in the world and the rents paid by tenants protected under rent control legislation are a fraction of the rents prevailing in the commercial market. So it is in the interest of the tenant to hang on to the rented premises like grim death, while the landlord strives mightily to oust the tenant or at least to charge them a more realistic rent. This perfect clash of interests is ineluctably dumped on to the courts, which have found themselves virtually impotent to resolve the situation. Any other subject of litigation in Mumbai has for many years been tiny relative to the flood of litigation arising from rent control. All the players—tenants, landlords, lawyers, judges and the myriad 'advisers'—know that they are participating in a gigantic game, the winner of which is measured by the size of the payout.

There is a close parallel between the contemporary legal situation of Mumbai—the problem has been present in other Indian cities too—and the question of agricultural land in the courts throughout India for more than a century. The parallel is that the courts have had foisted upon them the structural conflict caused by deep interventions into economic life on the part of the state. In the case of agricultural land, those interventions amounted to a legal and administrative transformation that grossly unsettled land relations for a century-and-a-half. This caused an avalanche of court cases that shocked and puzzled the mainly British judges in charge of the courts before 1947. In Mumbai of the last several decades, and increasingly as the value of property has risen dramatically, the courts have been similarly swamped by cases arising from the unrealistic rent control laws. So the broader argument underlying some of the articles in this collection is that the distortions of the Indian legal process so widely identified and criticized at home and abroad have to a deep extent been created by particular and major state interventions into economic life. The 'due process' courts established by the British have had to try to make sense of the economic and social disruptions caused by other branches of the state, and the result has often not been pretty. It is these profound disruptions, not the culture or personality of the Indian population, that account for many of the special difficulties of the Indian legal process.

Rent control litigation seems now to be on the wane, since there have been important reforms to the legislation as part of the larger scheme for liberalization of the Indian economy. The legislation is now less favourable to the tenant and rather fairer to the landlord; over time, this should result in fewer disputes between the two parties. But, since the legislation does not alter the law with respect to property already under the regime of rent control, except for large corporations, reduction in the volume of disputes and litigation has been slow. But it does seem that at last some rationality is coming into the management of property in Mumbai, without any obvious detriment to the poorer citizens of Mumbai who were the presumptive but not the actual beneficiaries of rent control. In turn, this will surely bring about some major alleviation of the terrible imbroglio that rent control inflicted on the judicial process of the city. There are some small signs that the new dispensation is marginally more beneficial to the pavement and slum dwellers of Mumbai—something like half the population of the city. But the project of housing the poor of Mumbai is far larger than clearing away the detritus left by ill-conceived laws controlling rents.

One of the perennial problems identified by critics or even chroniclers of the Indian legal system is that of 'arrears' in the courts. Every year the government produces statistics that identify the number of cases lodged, disposed of, and carried forward. What the statistics of recent decades appear to show is a growing mountain of cases before a court system that is utterly unable to come to grips with the sheer demand for litigation in India. It appears as if there is a litigation explosion happening in India. In fact, the situation appears to be the exact reverse of this. Overall, the uptake of litigation seems to be declining rather than growing. While 'arrears' of undecided cases are indeed growing all the time, the causes have to do with the behaviour of the legal profession and the incapacity of the courts to discharge their workload. If the number of cases instituted every year is greater than the number disposed of—this seems to be the norm throughout India—then 'arrears' enjoy an annual jackpot.

Chapter 6 also considers at some length the changing character of the legal profession, particularly in Mumbai. The change is in the character and salience of firms of what in Britain are called 'solicitors' or lawyers who generally do not appear in the courts. Over India as a whole, a large majority of lawyers are 'advocates' or litigators rather than solicitors. These advocates are engaged usually directly by clients to initiate and defend civil action and criminal prosecution, and in most cases there is no solicitor or attorney briefing the advocate. Nor do many Indians go to a lawyer to order their affairs, such as to draw up a will or seek assistance with a commercial matter. It was only in Bombay, Calcutta and Madras, as opposed to virtually everywhere else in India, that there was a separate branch of the profession known as 'attorneys' (later called 'solicitors'). In the nineteenth century most of these lawyers were British in origin and they tended to have an association with British business houses operating in India. Often, unlike the advocates, the attorneys and solicitors were organized in firms rather than operating as individual practitioners. Over the last couple of decades and in the context of liberalization and globalization of the Indian economy, some of these firms have been transformed into corporate law firms along the lines developed over the last half century in the US, Britain, Australia and elsewhere. The rise of such firms is discussed in this chapter, and there is a case study of one firm in particular.

There is no doubt that the rise of the firms—above all in Mumbai but also in Delhi and in Bangalore—represents a major change in the overall character of legal practice in India. The transformation of some of the old firms of solicitors and now the rise of new firms too are a direct consequence of the opening up of the Indian economy to greater trade and investment opportunities over the last twenty years or so. The leading firms are now connected to the global practice of law and business in a way that is worlds apart from the parochial practice of litigation in the dusty small towns and the cities of India. Indeed, the gulf is so great that sections of the profession have become alarmed that their jobs will be threatened by an influx of foreign lawyers as part of the apparatus of global capital. Curiously, some of those who have been most vocal in their opposition to the intrusion of foreigners into Indian legal practice are advocates, even though it is almost unthinkable that foreign lawyers would contemplate appearing in the highly specialized world of the Indian courts. Most Indian solicitors take the view that foreign lawyers actually deliver them work rather than take it away. And they also know that a multinational firm provides something of a bridge for them to participate in a globalized legal practice. It is fair to say that the new character of Indian law firms represent the most dynamic part of the Indian profession. Certainly, many of the best law graduates are drawn towards a career in these firms rather than what they identify as the often dispiriting world of litigation.

Chapters 7 and 8 are about 'public interest' or 'social action' litigation—the latter is the term favoured by Upendra Baxi, one of its progenitors—that was born in the late 1970s in the Supreme Court and later in the High Courts of the States. This litigation has gone through a number of phases over now more than 30 years, beginning with petitions arising from issues of social justice and civil rights including the plight of prisoners under trial, the squalid condition of gaols, the rights of the mentally ill in state institutions, and the rights of pavement dwellers in Bombay. In later phases it took a particular interest in official corruption—including that of a former Prime Minister, Narasimha Rao—and environmental issues.

Chapter 7, 'Life and Struggles in the Stone Quarries of India', is a case study of stone quarry workers in Faridabad, near Delhi. A majority of these workers were Dalits, and many of the other workers tribal Indians. It was the social origins of these workers that drew me into this study as part of the larger work on Dalits. The centrepiece of the chapter is the 1984 Supreme Court case of *Bandhua Mukti Morcha* v. *Union of India and Others* (the Bonded Labourers case). This case was initiated as public interest litigation (PIL) by Swami Agnivesh, simultaneously Arya Samaj monk, union organizer, and politician, and represents one of the great victories of PIL in India. Bhagwati J. handed down the main judgment of the Supreme Court, and it was highly favourable to the workers on the question of whether they were 'bonded' labourers in the meaning of the Bonded Labour System

(Abolition) Act, 1976. Pursuant to the judgment, some hundreds of the stone quarry workers were declared 'bonded' by the relevant government official and were 'liberated' and 'returned' to their apparent place of origin in Rajasthan. The State government was ordered to 'rehabilitate' them so as to secure their future.

Unfortunately, the concrete results of the stunning legal victory were less of a triumph. On a conceptual level, the chapter is critical of the lead judgment of the court for its approach to identifying the condition of 'bonded labour'. The national and State governments are also seen to be less than effective in supporting the bonded labourers who had been liberated as a result of the judgment. Over the succeeding months and years, many of the liberated workers ended up back in the Faridabad quarries for want of any secure employment in the place where they had been taken to live. The chapter does not take a general position on the effectiveness of public interest litigation, of which the Bonded Labourers case is a leading example. But it does argue that great court victories on behalf of some of the most subordinated Indians will not be translated into a solid change of life circumstances without the dedication of major resources by government and other organized forces of good will. Legal activism cannot move social mountains just through words, even if the words are spoken by the highest court in India.

Chapter 8, 'The Supreme Court as the Most Trusted Public Institution in India', is a consideration of the achievements of PIL as a whole. By the year 2000, the date of publication, it was clear that PIL had become a major part of Indian law. The chapter is included here despite the fact that it is quite a short piece and by now only a past milestone in the quite lengthy history of social action litigation. Perhaps it warrants republishing here only because there is so little serious publication on this form of litigation from either a legal or sociological perspective. The purpose of the chapter is to provide a short narrative of some of the more salient streams of public interest litigation and the way in which the Supreme Court and to an extent the High Courts of the States have transformed themselves from the late 1970s. In important ways, these apex Indian courts have become courts of the people. This has been an extraordinary transformation of courts, particularly the Supreme Court, whose early years were at least partly characterized by devastating opposition to redistributive land reform.

The new role of the Supreme Court as the ultimate court of the people has not been without its critics. Inevitably there have been complaints that the Court has usurped the role of the legislature, particularly when it hands down decisions with major implications for government spending. But perhaps there has been less complaint about judicial activism in India than there would be if there were an apex court in a Western democracy as proactive as the Indian court. Indira Gandhi's Emergency of 1975–7 had shocked lawyers to their core, and the subsequent judicial inventiveness has to be seen through the prism of that shock. The Court proved able to move from a concern with classic civil liberties to addressing some of the worst of India's social, environmental and governance problems. To an extent never before seen in India, the Court has joined the press as a searchlight into the abuse of human rights. Quite plausibly, some have argued that this form of court action has been instrumental in the very survival of Indian democracy in the years following the Emergency of the 1970s. What is less clear is just how many material victories the courts have actually secured for the most marginalized and subordinated Indians. Much more work of the kind undertaken in Chapter 7 needs to be done in order to make a secure assessment of the impact of the Court on practical conditions in India.

The final chapter in this collection, 'Law, Terror and the Indian Legal Order', considers the issue of anti-terrorism legislation and enforcement in the context of the US-led 'War on Terror' following the terrorist events of '9/11' in New York. Although this chapter is directed more towards legal policy than other chapters in this collection, I have included it here because of its discussion of the important dialectic between libertarianism and authoritarianism in independent India. This tension is clearly of great significance in the development of the Indian legal system. Empty valorization of Indian law will do no good to its future.

India has been a strong partner of the US in this War on Terror for a couple of reasons. First, India has suffered a great deal of terrorism from different quarters in the years since Independence; and secondly, it suited the right-wing, Hindu nationalist BJP Government of the time to find new international allies in the Indian fight against terrorist acts committed by Muslims—whether they were Indian, Kashmiri or Pakistani Muslims, between whom there was often no distinction made. This chapter traces some of the history of terrorism in India over a period that goes back more than half-a-century, and describes the legal regime constructed to enforce the legislation. The stance of the chapter is wary of the loss of civil liberties entailed in this legal regime, though of course it is sympathetic to the Indian concern to confront terrorism with resolution. Loss of civil liberties in the fight against terrorism is scarcely a phenomenon limited to India, but this loss is a matter of concern wherever it occurs.

Finally, of course, it has to be said that a collection of articles such as the present one cannot do justice to the whole phenomenon of law and legal process in India. For many centuries, long before the British period, India was deeply imbued with law in a whole variety of modes. The creation of the Anglo-Indian legal order and then the developments of post-Independence India have greatly enriched, and complicated, that pre-colonial legal life. In a very small way, I have been trying to understand that large process in the articles re-published in this collection. My hope, rather than my expectation, is that this collection might inspire some fresh interest in the study of one of the world's most fascinating legal systems.

Notes

1. I called the article 'The Pathology of the Indian Legal System'. I now look at this title without any affection, since it could be read as disrespectful. I certainly did not intend this. What I was trying to come to grips with was just why many of the litigants and ordinary citizens of India seemed to regard the judicial process with attitudes including horror. Outside observers sometimes shared these attitudes, no matter how sympathetic to India they were. It would be turning history back to change the title in this republication.

2. Oliver Mendelsohn and Marika Vicziany, *The Untouchables: Subordination, Poverty and the State in Modern India* (Cambridge: Cambridge University Press, 1998).

I

THE PATHOLOGY OF THE INDIAN LEGAL SYSTEM*

The Indian court system is by all accounts unusual.[1] The proceedings are extraordinarily dilatory and comparatively expensive, a single issue is often fragmented into a multitude of court actions, execution of judgments is haphazard, the lawyers frequently seem both incompetent and unethical, false witness is commonplace, and the probity of judges is habitually suspect. Above all, the courts are often unable to bring about a settlement of the disputes that give rise to litigation. So great are these failings that the Indian judicial process can reasonably be seen as a 'pathology' of a legal system.[2]

The roots of the pathology have not been subjected to so intense a study as the symptoms, and most European observers have been content to account for the system in terms of a litigious disposition in the Indian people. There have been two attempts to mount a more systematic explanation of the special nature of the Indian judicial system; the purpose of this paper is to give a third account. The argument is not that the two existing views are entirely false, but that neither is sufficient to explain the way in which the Indian judicial system has developed.

* This chapter is a reproduction of the article published in *Modern Asian Studies* 15(4) (1981), pp. 823–63. I am now less than enthusiastic about the title, since it might be thought by some to be disrespectful. The title reflected the attitudes of many litigants and ordinary observers of the time, and it would be re-writing history to change it now.

Bernard Cohn sees the problem (which he never empirically identifies at any length) to be rooted in the character of Indian peasant society. Indian peasants have failed to accept the very basis of the court system and have therefore abused its processes:

> It is my thesis that the present attitude of the Indian peasants was an inevitable consequence of the British decision to establish courts in India patterned on British procedural law. The way a people settles disputes is part of its social structure and value system. In attempting to introduce British procedural law into their Indian courts, the British confronted the Indians with a situation in which there was a direct clash of the values of the two societies; and the Indians in response thought only of manipulating the new situation and did not use the courts to settle disputes but only to further them.[3]

The British legal system is based on the idea of equality but 'North Indian society operates on the reverse value hypothesis: men are not born equal, and they have widely differing inherent worth'. Indian peasant society is dominated by status values as opposed to the contractual values that predominate in European society. Moreover, the Indian village is a multiplex social world in which people are bound together in a variety of relationships; these are ignored by a court concerned only with the issue of the moment. The Indian peasant values compromise rather than decisive victory, which is the rationale of the British courts. The result of this comprehensive clash of the values and structure of Indian society with the introduced legal system could only result in a fundamentally flawed judicial process.[4]

Robert Kidder has contested Cohn's argument.[5] Unlike Cohn (and most other observers of Indian courts), Kidder does not start from a judgment that the courts are basically unsatisfactory. He adopts a functionalist, putatively value-free perspective, which rests on the assumption that conflict is endemic to all societies and that the way of acting out conflict will vary with the society.

For Kidder, the central problem is to account for the variance between the 'norms' of the judicial system and the character of the practical judicial process. He argues that

> if formal legal provisions are not having their intended impact on the relations between litigants, the explanation lies in the relationship of those provisions to the social structure of the judicial system rather than their incongruity with indigenous values.[6]

Kidder, then, wants to explain the special character of Indian litigation by reference to the internal workings of the judicial administration itself, rather than by a clash of indigenous Indian values with those of the British-based courts. He argues that the judicial process in India is best conceptualised not as adjudication but as 'negotiation', and that an understanding of the nature of this process will account for the features of litigation that are commonly thought unsatisfactory:

> the skills developed by the various specialists of legal administration and the interest structure which has evolved within and around the bureaucracies of legal administration have produced a maze of such intricate and unstable practices and relationships that the legal system cannot provide predictable, decisive, final outcomes through knowledge of, and appeal to, 'the law' in Bangalore.... The social process of litigation has produced a mechanism for prolonged negotiations based on a utilitarian manipulation of every resource, both personal and organisational, made available by the court system.[7]

In short, the courts cannot provide quick, decisive outcomes because they have become immensely complex social systems in themselves.

Kidder does not confront Cohn's thesis squarely. Granted that the legal administration has developed in a way that works against rapid adjudication in favour of one party or the other, we are left with the problem of explaining why this is so. Kidder has remarkably little to say about this. He alludes to the multiplex relationships of Indian village society as a fruitful source of disputation. But he argues that there is nothing especially Indian about such relationships; they also exist in western societies, where they can complicate litigation in the same way they do in India. And in one unclear passage, Kidder observes that the 'factual ambiguity' common in land disputes can produce unusual complications in litigation.[8]

Insofar as Kidder has attempted an explanation of the phenomena he notes, he has been thrown back towards Cohn's argument. Kidder's main difference with Cohn is his rejection of the idea that Indians have acted out a root-and-branch rejection of all the courts stand for. But if this point is severed from the argument, Kidder is saying something not incompatible with Cohn's account. For both writers there is something about the nature of village society in India which deflects the courts from delivering the kind of justice they theoretically stand for.

Kidder merely adds the point that it is possible to find the same kind of deflection in lower-order western courts; and he declines to be judgmental about the process of Indian litigation, since for him protracted judicial proceedings represent a way of achieving 'self-definition' in a complex social order.[9]

This paper follows both Cohn and Kidder in arguing that the structure of village Indian society has pushed the court system into its peculiar mould. And the paper accepts Kidder's argument that the problem is not one of a clash of values, or at least not the comprehensive clash of values that Cohn identifies. But the burden of the argument presented here is that there is a missing factor which can largely account for the pathology of the Indian legal system: land. Overwhelmingly, the courts have been concerned with land disputes and it is the character of land relations in Indian village society which has both inhibited the western-style courts from effectively settling these disputes and shaped the judicial administration itself. The pathology of the judicial process in India is ultimately inexplicable without an understanding of the concrete issues of litigation. To simplify, the courts have been unsatisfactory institutions because they have been charged with resolving a uniquely entrenched class of disputes.

The first part of this paper is a case study which exemplifies some of the structural problems of Anglo-Indian justice. The second part attempts to locate these problems in an historical context and to spell out a more general account of Indian litigation.

I. The Case of Jagat Singh

The History of the Conflict

Jagat Singh was in 1972 involved in at least ten cases in the courts of Haripur, in Alwar District of Rajasthan, and he has an extensive history of litigation.[10] All the cases centre on land he possesses in or near his village. For years Jagat Singh has been resisting the efforts of his kin and neighbours to gain control of parts of this land. The struggle has been waged through a variety of means, including physical force and litigation.

In 1965 Jagat Singh retired as a Major in the Indian Army and he immediately set about fulfilling a longstanding ambition to become a full-time farmer in his ancestral village, rather than settling into the superannuated urban life that most of his fellow officers choose. He now occupies over 200 acres of cultivable land in his own and the adjacent villages. Only about one-quarter of this land is ancestral property; the rest he bought from fellow Rajput landholders in three neighbouring villages. The manner in which he inherited and acquired this land is important in understanding the conflict.

Jagat Singh's ancestral lands are part of an original block of 125 acres owned by his great-grandfather. This man had four sons, each of whom succeeded to one-quarter of the estate. One share was extinguished by the death of one of the sons and Jagat Singh has succeeded to two of the remaining three shares; his father and he himself were the sole heirs of their generation, and the other share came through his adoption by a childless first cousin of his father. The remaining share is greatly subdivided: the initial shareholder had five sons, thereby reducing the share of his heirs to one-fifteenth. The succeeding generations have also been greatly productive of male heirs; one of the five sons had six sons and another had two. Thus today the one-third share of the estate is divided between a very large number of Jagat Singh's kinsmen.

By 1945 his inheritance of almost 85 acres was complete. The holding, however, was greatly fragmented and he sought to consolidate it through exchange with his kinsmen. They refused to cooperate with him out of a belief that he would cheat them in the exchange, so Jagat Singh turned to other Rajput landholders in an effort to build a farm that could support his family in comfort. In 1947 he managed to buy very cheaply 157 acres of cultivable land and 63 acres of pasture from his own and two neighbouring villages. By the end of 1947 he had become what was for the area a very large landowner, possessing 230 acres of cultivable land and 63 acres of pasture. For what is now more than thirty years, Jagat Singh has been waging a ceaseless battle to retain these lands.

The disputes and litigation fall into two categories, which mirror the two ways in which he acquired his land. The first category is disputes within Jagat Singh's own family: these have been the most durable and serious disputes. The second conflict has been with cultivators who were one-time tenants on land he bought or who still work lands adjoining his own.

Chronologically, the disputes with the non-kinsmen were the first to develop in earnest. Jagat Singh's purchase of the lands immediately gave rise to disputes with the tenants who had worked the land by sharecropping or other arrangement. A condition of many of the purchases was the removal of the tenants prior to payment. Where this was not the case, Jagat Singh's first effort was to eject the existing tenants as a precaution against land reforms which might deliver land to the actual tillers of the soil. In all, Jagat Singh was able to retain about two-thirds of the land he had purchased. The other one-third went to tenants either by court decision or by his capitulation in the face of the reform legislation enacted in a series of measures beginning in 1949. Between 1950 and 1953, two of Jagat Singh's disputes with the tenants were fought to the level of the High Court of Rajasthan. In both cases the decision went against him. Generally speaking, those longstanding tenants who strongly resisted their ejectment and defended Jagat Singh's court suits were able to retain their status as tenants and eventually succeed to full proprietary rights. The many tenants who did not appear in court were ousted virtually by default.

For many years now Jagat Singh's chief adversary has been one Raghbir Singh, a first cousin of his father. Most of Jagat Singh's kinsmen in the village are descended from Raghbir Singh and he commands the support of the whole family except Jagat Singh's nuclear group. The dispute between the two men has an inherited dimension, since there was ill-feeling between Jagat Singh's father and his two uncles on the one hand and Raghbir Singh on the other. Jagat Singh can give no explanation for this, other than to note the frequent fractiousness among Rajputs and to impute jealousy to Raghbir Singh in the face of the greater prosperity of his father and uncles.

Jagat Singh's personal situation was a favoured one from the beginning. He received a superior education and joined the Army as an officer. His own children have been similarly successful. In contrast, Raghbir Singh and his descendants are either illiterate or minimally educated. Almost all of them have had to remain in the village and depend on the 35 acres of mediocre land that is their patrimony. It is in this context of poverty and prosperity within the one family that the dispute must be placed. Jagat Singh's lands have been a painfully tangible expression of his social superiority and, more importantly, they have represented a vehicle by which Raghbir Singh's group might be able to better their poor condition.

Although with hindsight the conflict seems to have been almost inevitable, it was slow to develop. The period between the end of the major struggle with the tenants in 1953 and Jagat Singh's retirement from the Army in 1965 was comparatively free of disputes simply because Jagat Singh could exercise no more than sporadic superintendence of his land. He was unable, for example, to prevent his kinsmen from grazing a flock of two hundred goats on the tasty thorn bushes that grow on his land. But there were at least two issues that came to a head in this period. The first arose from Jagat Singh's attempt to sell 20 acres of his land to a fellow Army Officer. The plot was distant from his other fields and could therefore be disposed of with profit. It was part of the ancestral property and still registered in joint names, so the sale required the consent of the kinsmen or partition of the whole family property. The kinsmen refused to give their consent and, indeed, claimed the land as theirs. In retaliation, Jagat Singh made an official report that Raghbir Singh had fraudulently been collecting a State annuity of Rs 50 for some twenty years. The annuity was eventually stopped and Jagat Singh went on to instigate court proceedings which resulted in the wrongdoers having to repay Rs 800 to the state. They were forced to sell some of their land to meet this payment.

A second family conflict before 1965 entailed protracted litigation. Jagat Singh claims that while he was away on service he had habitually extended various aids to Raghbir Singh through the agency of his wife, who was resident in the village—chiefly grain and money when the crops failed. But since the debts were not being repaid, Jagat Singh stopped the loans. He states that in retaliation his kinsmen came to his house and threatened his wife with violence unless she continued to lend them assistance. In order to protect her, Jagat Singh sought a court order that the kinsmen cease their intimidation. The case dragged on for a number of years until Jagat Singh dropped it as, he says, a conciliatory gesture.

The struggle intensified almost immediately after Jagat Singh's return from the Army. The stance of both parties rapidly became entrenched, Jagat Singh refusing to yield the slightest portion of his property and Raghbir Singh determined to wrest land from his kinsman that he believed was rightly his own. The years between 1965 and 1974 can be seen as one continuous struggle which is focused from time to time on a particular issue. I will sketch some (not all) of the individual disputes.

One of Jagat Singh's first efforts on his return was to turn out the goats that had grazed on his land for over fifteen years, and from 1965 to 1967 there was a running battle over this issue. The dispute was pressed through physical confrontation, although there does not seem to have been any actual exchange of blows. Jagat Singh was finally successful in repulsing the invading goats, perhaps through having worn out his opponents by his obvious intransigence. But another dispute in 1965 took a more violent turn: as an incident in one of the several disputes over field boundaries, Raghbir Singh's party demolished part of a mud wall separating fields occupied by the different parties. The action occasioned a serious physical clash with *lathis* (wooden sticks) and both sides sustained injuries. They each instituted criminal proceedings for assault against the other, and seven years later, the cases were still pending. The dispute over the boundary was not, of course, settled by the fight—five years later it again broke into violence.

In physical confrontations, Jagat Singh's party is the weaker. Raghbir Singh controls in his family a number of able-bodied men who are themselves vitally concerned in the ongoing dispute, since part of the stake is the use of much-needed land. The family group has also been aided on occasion by other groups within the village who have been prejudiced against Jagat Singh through their own disputes with him. Jagat Singh, on the other hand, has remained an outsider in the village and can physically depend only on his eldest son. His career and outlook set him apart from the other villagers and he takes little interest in village affairs. Even his dwelling lies outside the village, since he prefers to leave his large house in the village to his son and daughter-in-law in favour of living with his wife in a rudimentary shed in the fields. But in spite of his relative weakness, both prudence and his own disposition have sometimes impelled Jagat Singh to engage in physical resistance. Any loss of possession could only be repaired by physical action at a later time or by lengthy and expensive litigation in which there would be no certainty of success. Moreover, his own disposition makes him less than reluctant to chastise his opponents physically. Force and litigation are often complementary rather than alternative modes of struggle for Jagat Singh. But overall, his preferred method of conflict is through the state legal structure, where his greater resources and understanding lend him a distinct advantage over his opponents. His favoured tactic is to use the state legal system to raise the costs of opposing him—through framing cases of criminal assault or breach of the peace, for example. He is usually the aggressor in the legal system, whereas in the village he is constantly on the defensive. The intractability of the struggle owes much to the advantage that each side enjoys in a different arena of conflict.

One of the most complex of the long chain of disputes occurred in 1967, and it illustrates some of the strengths and weaknesses of Jagat Singh's position. In 1965 the land revenue settlement officials collected their information from Jagat Singh's village, and he states that one of their mistakes was to omit some 63 acres of pasture land from his holding; the land was noted as pasture common to the village as a whole. Jagat Singh was later able to have this determination overturned in the courts, since he was able to produce a sale deed for the land. But he deliberately neglected to execute the favourable judgment; he reasoned that he could retain at least partial use of the pasture without further swelling his formal holding to the point where it would become a prime target for confiscation under the land ceiling laws. He has no intention of abandoning his claim to the land; the law allows him a number of years to execute a judgment, and he intends to wait for a more propitious time to do this.

The pasture land again came into contention in 1967, when the kinsmen began to push their cattle through Jagat Singh's cultivated lands in order to reach it. Raghbir Singh claimed that in so doing he was simply trying to make use of an established right-of-way, whereas Jagat Singh disputed the existence of a path and complained that his lands were being damaged by the unauthorized practice. The dispute was taken before the statutory *gram panchayat*, the legal authority for pronouncing on public ways. The panchayat found in favour of Raghbir Singh—Jagat Singh complains that the *sarpanch* sided with his kinsmen for his own ends—and in the face of Jagat Singh's intractability, the matter was taken up with the head official of the administrative subdivision. He in turn referred the matter to the local police inspector, who duly inspected the site and found that a right-of-way did exist. Jagat Singh complains that the inspector wrote his report and promised to report favourably on any subsequent effort of Raghbir Singh to force the way in return for a payment of Rs 220. No fight ever eventuated on this issue since Jagat Singh succeeded in his appeal to the magistrate against the finding of the panchayat; the final decision was that there was no right-of-way for the cattle. So although Jagat Singh had failed at the village, his persistence through the legal structure was finally rewarded. This is one of the rare occasions in which he was placed on the defensive both in the village and in the official world.

These, then, are some of the individual disputes in the long conflict between Jagat and Raghbir Singh. There is every indication that the conflict will persist, since neither side demonstrates any disposition to moderate its stance and each has the expectation of further conflict. Whenever Jagat Singh walks between his fields and the village, he straps a revolver to his side and his son goes armed with a wire-bound *lathi*. He has lost what he says was his previous willingness to help people less fortunate than he is, since he has learnt that 'in life one usually harvests only trouble from good deeds'. But amid regret for the passing of his bucolic dreams, his present situation is not without its compensations. He finds village life dull compared with his Army days, and the dispute does at least have the merit of a diversion. It is a kind of game, a deadly serious game of point and counterpoint, and also a game from which he can derive some amusement. He views the institutions of the law as bodies that can be manipulated to provoke continuous irritation to his opponents. Indeed, his enthusiasm for the law is such that one lawyer speaks of him as 'the perfect litigant'. He has quite rightly seen that entanglement in the legal system is far more of a nuisance to his kinsmen than to himself, and that he can use the system to offset his physical inferiority.

Raghbir Singh's party is equally committed to the struggle but they do not share their kinsman's enthusiasm for it. Since Jagat Singh's return to the village they have suffered a net loss; they have lost benefits they enjoyed in the past and gained nothing in return. The legal unsoundness of their claims and their poverty rule out the courts as a habitual mode of attack. Only rarely do they make an appearance in court. Very occasionally they have used the legal structure in an offensive capacity—to frame assault charges—but otherwise they have simply exploited Jagat Singh's difficulty in controlling a large tract of land with only his son as a reliable physical support. Their perception of the conflict is less sophisticated than Jagat Singh's but on occasion they, too, act out a (joyless) game in which points are scored by harassing one's opponent. They know that they can at least succeed in denying Jagat Singh the capacity to enjoy his lands in peace.

It is superfluous to discuss at any length the numerous disputes between Jagat Singh and villagers other than his family in the years since 1953. But we can note that many of them have been over encroachments by neighbouring cultivators. In 1965 and 1971 two separate disputes of this nature broke into physical fights and on the second occasion the police consented to Jagat Singh's demand that his opponents be prosecuted. He later dropped the charges in return for a written apology lodged with the court. The gesture did not spring from any real spirit of reconciliation but from a calculation that he had harassed his opponents to the point where they will be reluctant to trouble him in future. He notes that a magistrate has chided him for litigiousness, but he has no intention of heeding such criticism. It is a question of right and wrong.

Comment

This study does not purport to be typical of contemporary disputes and litigation in the area from which it is drawn, let alone for other regions of India and other times. It is atypical in the complexity of Jagat Singh's situation and in the profuseness and longevity of the litigation. But at the same time it is not unrepresentative of structural problems of Anglo-Indian justice both now and in the nineteenth century past. The inconclusiveness of litigation in relation to the basic conflict is certainly characteristic of litigation over land in India. And at the level of *process* it displays characteristic traits, such as the harnessing of litigation in tandem with direct action, the intertwining of civil and criminal actions, the slowness of the judicial process and the imaginative exploitation of judicial opportunities. In this sense it represents a good starting point for a more general discussion of Indian courts.

As to this case itself, the primary question to be asked is just why the courts have been unable to resolve the most deep-seated conflict, the one within the family. Why does the family conflict now produce court cases which are only incidents in a continuing struggle rather than points of resolution? If we pursue Cohn's logic, we should conclude that the problem lies in the attitudes of the litigants towards the courts. Jagat Singh could be seen to be so assertive and litigious a personality as to have needlessly burdened the courts and fatally injured their capacity to resolve the conflict. In turn, Raghbir Singh might be taken to have acted out his rejection of the values of the courts by ignoring the courts wherever possible and taking direct action, which confounds the most fundamental principles of Anglo-Indian justice. I want to argue that this is not a useful perspective on the judicial process revealed in the present case.

There can be no doubt that Jagat Singh has been marvellously productive of litigation. His criminal prosecution and suits for injunction are particularly good evidence of his judicial fecundity, and it would do no violence to the word to call him litigious. But if a principal criterion of litigiousness is the extravagance of litigation and the triviality of the cause, then Jagat Singh does not qualify. Although various motives have entered into his judicial career, he has never lost sight of the fundamental aim of protecting his own and his immediate family's livelihood. He has only instituted those legal actions which he calculates to be either necessary or desirable for maintaining his position. And there is nothing in the case to suggest that his calculations have been either wrong or irrational. His occasional enjoyment of the conflict is nothing more than light relief in a grindingly serious business.

Indeed, much of Jagat Singh's litigation has been a response to the very failure of the courts to settle his disputes. He initially approached them as a means of securing a quick victory and he is on occasion almost wistful at finding himself still embroiled in the system. So, while his character and resourcefulness have helped create and sustain litigation, it would be misleading to see in his disposition the reasons for the courts' failure to settle the conflict. Jagat Singh has done no more than take limited advantage of institutions that strike him as defective in their incapacity to provide him with the protection that his legal entitlement merits. Moreover, much of the character of the litigation has not been of his own making. The dilatoriness of proceedings and the technicalities of procedure have not always been promoted by him, nor have they always worked in his favour.

The ineffectiveness of litigation can more plausibly be attributed to the failure of Jagat Singh's opponents to accept their faulty position at law. While at almost every point Jagat Singh has been careful to satisfy the rules of the Anglo-Indian legal order—he has always, for example, insisted on the execution of written documents attesting his land purchases—his kinsmen opponents have often contested litigation without the benefit of evidence that will prove acceptable to the courts. They have kept their chances alive through refusing to act out the assumptions underlying the judicial system: unfavourable judgments are either ignored or treated as temporary setbacks to be countered by whatever means are at their disposal, including physical force. In fact, violence appears not so much a consequence of a breakdown in justice as an ordinary feature of the conflict. In the eyes of the disputants, physical force seems to exist in the same universe as judicial action.

But Cohn's argument can give no real insight into the actions of Raghbir Singh and the other opponents of Jagat Singh. It is true that their actions fail to correspond with the expectations underlying the judicial order, but the ground of this is not a cultural or narrow psychological distaste for the courts. Their attitude to the courts is as instrumental as is Jagat Singh's. But unlike him, they have seen that the courts do not in the main represent a useful opportunity structure in their struggle to appropriate 'their' land. Hence, they have done their best to ignore them. Nor can the courts be seen as having provoked an irrational stand in Raghbir Singh's party. Their initial actions rested on a quite reasonable hope that they could divest Jagat Singh of some of the land in dispute, and even after thirty years of failure they can still hope that eventually they will inherit the earth. Jagat Singh's burden is becoming no lighter with his advancing years and a political climate increasingly hostile to large landowners.

If Cohn's thesis cannot account for the present case, then nor can Kidder's. His discussion does not so much as speak to the material in this case study, since his analysis is confined to the judicial process narrowly construed. If we tried to apply his views here we would have wrongly to concede that the material conflict is not the key to the judicial inconclusiveness. Moreover, most of the active conflict does not even take place in the court—Raghbir Singh hardly ever attends. Clearly, the heart of the case lies in the village and we would grasp only a pale shadow if we concentrated on the court process.

Our own account of the case proceeds from material factors. We can reduce the complexity of the background to the conflict to several such factors. First, we can note that all those who have fought for the land have had some intimate connexion with it: ancestral history, prior tenancy, and the possession of neighbouring and poorly demarcated fields have given Jagat Singh's opponents a sense of entitlement to parts of his land. No claimant has made a bid that is totally without justification, though it may not be one acceptable to the court. That there are so many people who have claimed an interest in the land is largely attributable to the number and depth of disruptions in its social setting.

At least four major disrupting factors can be identified. The first is Jagat Singh's inheritance of two-thirds of the family's ancestral lands. The effect of this was to reinforce a gap in prosperity which had already divided his father and uncles from their kinsmen in the village. The second disruption was Jagat Singh's purchase of a large block of land in 1947. This act both widened the economic division within the family and, more importantly, brought Jagat Singh into conflict with the then tenants of the land. It is scarcely conceivable that such a radical deprivation of the tenants' livelihood could have been effected without causing serious animosity. The third disruption was the revenue settlement, which played an indirect part in the cattle-path dispute and led directly to disputes and litigation with neighbouring cultivators. A fourth factor was the return of Jagat Singh from army service in 1965 with a determination to end the encroachment on his land by kinsmen and neighbours. His return hardened into physical reality his displacement of old interests and his rise to the status of the largest landholder of the village.

Beyond these material factors, there are elements of individual psychology and culture which have also shaped the conflict. It is not a case of exclusively economic calculation by perfectly rational actors. Aside from the unusually tenacious character of Jagat Singh himself, the conflict has been fuelled by a pre-existing family feud. It would be wrong to see the conflict as a feud which has conveniently and incidentally been expressed in a dispute over land; this is not the way it appears to the disputants themselves or to this observer. Rather, problematic social relations have been enlisted to deepen what is basically a conflict over land. From this and other cases we can draw the conclusion that the more intimate the relations between villagers, the deeper they can explore their difference over material issues. This perspective goes some way towards explaining the more serious nature of the disputes within Jagat Singh's family. Family relations are peculiarly 'multiplex' and they often serve to entrench and ramify a dispute beyond the bounds of a similar material conflict between socially more distant people.

The economic interests of the disputants, their belief in the Tightness of their cause, the social complexities—these are the basic reasons for the failure of the courts to resolve this particular case. But we are not compelled to regard the courts as a total failure. They have played an important part in helping Jagat Singh retain the land that is his by legal entitlement. He would scarcely have been willing to use them so assiduously if they possessed no utility. Moreover, it could be argued that had the courts not been there, the conflict would have been acted out through more systematically uncivilized means. Still, none of this serves to blunt the fact that the conflict is no closer to resolution after thirty years of judicial consideration.

Could the outcome have been any different if the courts had acted differently? Could they have been more successful if they commanded a more powerful enforcement agency? Enforcement is generally a difficult matter for Indian courts, but in this particular case they have (albeit slowly and inefficiently) secured compliance with most of their judgments. What, then, if they had made a real attempt to bring the parties to a compromise, such that the whole basis of the conflict was removed? They would in this way have met Cohn's objection that they are out of kilter with indigenous authorities, which are said not to single out one incident in a conflict but to address the whole affair and to try to restore harmony on the basis of compromise. It can be conceded that a measure of material satisfaction may well have induced Raghbir Singh to give up his struggle, at least temporarily. But what incentive would Jagat Singh have had to give up any of his land? For him harmony is a minor value when it is opposed to legitimate self-interest, and his standard of legitimacy is the law of the land. He would have been prepared to make only the most minor concession to his opponents, so minor that it would scarcely have satisfied them. But again, we should resist seeing the problem as stemming from Jagat Singh's particular personality. On a structural level, it would be almost impossible to graft a compromise model of justice on to a land system founded on the principle of apportionment according to finite legal principles. Either one is or is not entitled to particular property in dispute. Jagat Singh is simply acting out the legal model in claiming what is his by right.

Ultimately, then, the failure of the courts in this case is not something which can be attributed to the personality of the litigants or the culture and procedures of the courts themselves. The failure must be connected to problems in the structure of land relations. The second part of this paper will attempt to broaden and deepen, particularly historically, the discussion of problems raised in this case study. We will then be in a position to confront the views of Cohn and Kidder more directly.

II. The General Problem of Anglo-Indian Justice

Land Disputes as the Basis of Litigation

Before the close of the nineteenth century, Britain had furnished India with legal doctrine and judicial procedures sufficient to a great modern economy.[11] In practice, however, the judicial system implanted by the British and inherited by independent India has always reflected the concerns of what is overwhelmingly a peasant society. The great majority of court cases have had to do with the use, ownership and profit from agricultural land. This is true for all three jurisdictions of the courts: civil, criminal and revenue. The only other large bloc of cases has been suits brought by moneylenders and merchants for the repayment of simple money debts.[12] While there have been important changes in the pattern of litigation over the last century, the predominance of land as the subject of litigation has remained constant.

What is the reason for the dominance of land as a cause of judicial action? The obvious answer is that land is bound to be the most contentious issue in a peasant society. Unfortunately, this answer is more obvious than illuminating. The question masks what are really three distinct inquiries: why has land come into dispute in India, why have the disputes ended up in the courts, and why has there been so little litigation over matters other than land?

The first question is not at all easy to answer, partly because land may be valued for a variety of ends, including livelihood, power and status. The effect of British dominion over India was to render impossible the highest level of conflict, viz., the effort by individuals or clans to carve out new kingdoms by force.[13] But what the British did not accomplish was the reduction of land conflict in general; indeed, it is probable that there was more dispute over land after the coming of the British than there had been before.[14] These disputes can be seen to fall into two categories. The first category is perennial disputes which survived British intervention and includes succession issues caused by the death of a landholder; the intrusion of an outsider (often through marriage) into the village community; resentments stirred by the adoption of an heir by a landholder; instability caused by desertions of land during droughts; and a landholder's inability (through infirmity, a too-small family, a too-large holding or sundry other reasons) to impose full physical control on his land. In circumstances such as these, it has been common to find multiple claimants to the one piece of land.[15]

The second class of disputes had no precedent in pre-British India, since it was contingent on an ideological and administrative revolution which changes the very basis of land tenure in India. The British administration injected into India an alien, western conception of property and artificially reconstituted land relations in conformity with it. The new scheme of land tenure was at once the direct cause of a vast number of disputes and also the basis for practical developments that entailed further deep and widespread conflict over land.

Both these classes of land conflict—the 'traditional' and the British-inspired—have been generously expressed through litigation since the nineteenth century. The logic of this litigation is substantially the same in both cases and is bound up with the transformation of Indian land relations by the British. Despite the seeming digression, we are forced to consider the basis of this transformation; without this, no more than a superficial understanding of Indian litigation is possible.

The Formal Basis of the British Land Administration

The root of the changes engineered by the British was a concern to formalize and simplify land tenure in India.[16] The new ruler encountered an imprecise, legally ambiguous agrarian situation in which it was often difficult to find a single 'owner' of land. Rather, land was shared in a bewildering variety of ways between three categories of competitors: the cultivators of the land, the controllers of the cultivators (often known as zamindars or intermediaries); and different levels of what can be called 'the state'. Ceaseless competition between these categories and even within them—between large and small intermediaries, for example—meant that the agrarian situation was highly fluid. What seems to have been at stake was not ownership of land as a unitary physical entity, but interests in land, it was possible for multiple and legally imprecise interests to co-exist in relation to a single plot of land. This situation could be tolerated by successive rulers of India because, by and large, their interest was in collecting a share of the profits of agriculture. It was of little importance to them to legislate the question of 'ownership' of land.

A similar pragmatism on the part of the new British rulers soon yielded to systematic attempts to define the tenure of land in India. Thus for the British the pragmatic question, 'from whom will we collect our revenue demands?' gave way to the very different question, 'who is the proprietor or owner of land, such that he has the duty to pay the revenue demand?'[17] This question was not the product of mere naïveté or passion for abstract logic. Behind the conceptual engineering were a variety of motives, but above all the concern to maximise revenue for the state. Once the identity and duties of the proprietors had been fixed, the exchequer of Company and, later, Crown would be secure. The recognition of title as a transferable commodity would underpin the invariability of the revenue demand; agriculture would develop through the inefficient yielding title to the efficient, and the government would always receive its handsome due.[18]

Who, then, were the legal proprietors of land? Throughout North India this question was answered in favour of intermediaries, in the sense that nowhere was there a systematic effort to give title to the actual cultivators.[19] But the 'intermediaries' varied between an individual who controlled hundreds of villages to a corporate group in control of a single village. The standard of recognition differed over both time and region; how far the variance was justified by tenurial reality remains an open question. In the West and South the *ryotwari* system of proprietorship was said to recognize actual farmers rather than intermediaries, but most of the proprietors were landlords rather than tillers of the soil. The flexibility of these attempts to answer the almost unanswerable was grafted on to an arbitrary scheme whose premise was refusal to take Indian land tenure on its own terms.

By virtue of having embarked on the effort to identify and define the rights of the proprietors of land, the British revenue authorities were logically committed to the further task of specifying the nature of non-proprietorial interests. If the zamindars and landlords were the owners of the land, then what was their legal relationship to the people who cultivated it? By the latter part of the nineteenth century this further question had been worked into a complex edifice of tenancy legislation. The various and imprecise customary relationships yielded, at least in theory, to legal relationships in which the rights and duties of both parties were clearly defined. The landlord's right to rent and the ejectment of delinquent cultivators was secured, while one class of tenants—'occupancy' tenants—was afforded legal protection against excessive rents and arbitrary ejectment by the landlord. The tenancies of this class were declared to be property susceptible of alienation and inheritance. The remaining tenants—the great bulk of the cultivating population—were accorded no rights at all in the land they worked.

The tenancy legislation was the last great addition to the formal structure of land relations in British India, of which the barest sketch has been given here. What had begun as a concern to secure the financial base of British rule in India had burgeoned into an enterprise that changed the very structure of land relations. Irregularity, imprecision and custom had yielded to a regular, clear and formal scheme of rights and duties in relation to land. For the first time, a ruler of India had used its authority to define the very concepts of ownership and tenancy, and to apportion land among the population in conformity with its definitions. This had been done through a monumental series of revenue 'settlements', which had also entailed a vast scientific study to specify the productivity of land and hence the revenue that could be levied from the designated owners. The scheme had immense consequences for the countryside, not the least of which was the creation of a staggering quantity of frequently intractable litigation.

The Causes of Litigation during the British Period

Given the attention that has justifiably been paid to the British land system, we have a surprisingly incomplete picture of litigation over land through the century and a half of British rule. This relative ignorance notwithstanding, a kind of conventional if contradictory wisdom grew up to account for what seemed to be the ready reception of British law by the rural population. On the one hand British officialdom could look with intense satisfaction on what seemed to be a popular recognition of the merits of British law. At the same time there was a suspicion— sometimes a conviction—that Indians had over-indulged themselves in litigation, either because they were a quarrelsome, litigious people or because they had somehow missed the point of litigation.

But not every official was content with the conventional view. One nineteenth century magistrate in Bengal noted that,

> the complaints of these people are seldom or never litigious. I have seen some conspiracies supported by false evidence; but suits simply litigious, brought forward merely from the quarrelsome disposition of the prosecutor, are not common.... Out of one hundred suits, perhaps five at the utmost, may fairly be pronounced litigious....[20]

The useful suggestion here is that the conventional view erred in attending to the form of litigation without an appreciation of the purposes of the litigants themselves. In more technical terms, the error was selection of a too narrow unit of analysis. The more we concentrate on external judicial behaviour and the less on purpose, intention and motivation, the more prone we are to see a 'litigiousness' in India. There can be no controversy that 'conspiracies supported by false evidence' and an unusually high level of judicial gamesmanship were rife in India, and that these helped to undermine the official aim of Anglo-Indian justice—settlement of disputes according to definite law within a finite period of time. But it is quite another claim that Indians were prone to institute or prolong litigation out of motives unconnected with a substantial conflict. This claim is generally false and since the conventional view subscribes to it, we would do better to avoid speaking of Indian judicial behaviour in terms of 'litigiousness'. While not completely inapposite, the label creates more confusion than illumination.

As a psycho-cultural stereotype, 'the litigious Indian' cannot account for the incidence, nature or style of Anglo-Indian litigation. The concept fails, for example, on simple logic: if litigious personality were the mainspring of litigation, we should expect to find court actions stemming from every category of dispute endemic to village society— marital conflict, for example. In fact, land disputes have been shown to account for the great bulk of litigation. Moreover, the diagnosis of a litigious Indian personality assumed a general over-resort to litigation without designating a yard-stick for measuring what was a 'reasonable' quantum of litigation. Was the standard to be that of Europe, in which case the *per capita* involvement in law suits may well have been low? Or was there to be a notional standard for a country of the particular social profile of India? The question of the relevant standard was persistently ignored.

Any satisfactory explanation of Indian judicial action must proceed from a clear understanding of the material causes of litigation. Thus, what the British had done was to draw land relations more tightly into the web of government than any other facet of social life. They had singled out land relations from all other social relations—labour and marriage, for example—and successfully asserted a claim to regulate them. This claim entailed not only legislative and executive intervention but also the right to adjudicate disputes over land. The Indians, for their part, were prepared to use the British courts because they could see an advantage in so doing. They saw no such advantage in disputes about issues other than land, though the formal scope of the courts was sufficient to cover these disputes. Had the British intervened in, say, marital relations as deeply as they had in land matters, then it is likely that marriage would have been a greatly litigated affair too.[21] What follows is a working out of this perspective through consideration of several of the leading issues in land litigation of the British period. The examples are selective—they do not purport to exhaust even the principal types of litigation.

An overwhelming proportion of litigation before Indian independence was intimately related to the quantum of land revenue demanded by the British authorities. In very simple terms, the burden pressed so hard as to impoverish many proprietors and at the same time to drive them into pressing their sub-proprietors and tenants equally hard. This pressure tended to lead either directly or indirectly to law suits. A good example of this can be seen in the problem of mass transfers of title. The early revenue settlements occasioned the transfer of an almost incredible proportion of land. In the Banaras region of the North-West Provinces, for example, nearly half the land went to new owners in the years 1801 to 1806.[22] The transfers owed almost entirely to the high-pitched revenue demands of the Company, the non-payment of which provoked compulsory sale of the defaulter's land. In practice, the transferee was often unable to translate his formal title into physical possession, and the fledgling courts were sometimes—just how often is unclear—enlisted as a means of acting out the conflict between the purchaser and the incumbent.[23]

After about 1820 the early form of compulsory sales was abandoned but the phenomenon of mass transfers was soon continued through a new means. The heavy revenue demand and increased agricultural costs (sometimes associated with irrigated cash crops) were now leading an unprecedented proportion of zamindars to borrow money from professional moneylenders and affluent fellow zamindars. Rural credit was available as never before, largely because of legal innovations that worked to the advantage of the creditor. In 1855 the usury laws were abandoned out of fidelity to the most modern laissez-faire European thought. And through a series of court decisions and legislation, including the Civil Procedure Code (1859) and the Transfer of Property Act (1882), land was made newly vulnerable to the ambitions of moneylenders. A mortgagee of land was extended the same rights to foreclosure and judicial sale as a mortgagee in Britain, rights which seem not to have existed in pre-British India. The effect of such court orders was to transfer the mortgaged property, either to the lender (in the case of foreclosure) or to a purchaser (in the case of judicial sale, though this purchaser might well be the lender himself). Even where a loan had not been secured against the zamindar's land, the latter could now be judicially attached and sold in order to discharge the zamindar's debts. In short, the refinement of legal doctrine (and the sheer increase of courts) had ensured that the judicial apparatus would become the most powerful means of acquiring title to agricultural land.[24]

It was not the case that every moneylender moved to divest his zamindar creditors of their land. For the 'pure' type of moneylender, as opposed to the zamindar-cum-speculator, the object was often to perpetuate an advantageous loan arrangement. The transfer laws could be used as a threat to ensure a steady flow of interest payments and the threat executed only if payments ceased or dwindled to an uneconomic level. But in the instance where a moneylender of whatever category did invoke the judicial transfer machinery, the logic of the approach was hardly mysterious. Application for a foreclosure decree, judicial sale or attachment and sale was simply the perfection of a logic that underpinned the whole loan transaction. The moneylender had acted from the first on the basis of the capitalist conception of property that had been introduced by the British. In going to court, he was simply making use of the available enforcement machinery.

The incumbent acted on a quite different, a traditional, set of values. He may have known the risks of entering into a mortgage or other heavy borrowing arrangement but he was quite unprepared to accept the consequences of his act. Whatever expedients he had been forced into, he regarded the land as rightfully his. The profuse exchange of land for money notwithstanding, no regular market in land was ever established in the nineteenth century. Commercial calculation was all on the side of the purchaser or mortgagee; on the other side were desperate measures taken to stave off disaster. Where it occurred, loss of land was almost always a thoroughly involuntary event that overtook the impoverished zamindar. How could he agree to be robbed of his livelihood, status, identity? How could his heirs agree to this?

Intransigence on the part of the incumbent led directly to a highly problematical judicial process. The threatened zamindar invariably cast around for means of avoiding his own displacement; he did not set out to choose means that conformed to the 'rule of law' but simply to discover an effective means. This he might find in the court system or the village itself, or in both. The court system abounded in opportunities to thwart what might have seemed an open-and-shut case for the purchaser or mortgagee. And the zamindar stood ready to defend his land physically, where this seemed prudent. In short, and through mechanisms described below, the depth of feeling in the incumbent represented a challenge to the orderly working of the judicial apparatus. The courts laboriously struggled with a problem that was ultimately beyond their competence.

The revenue burden was even more directly related to what was by far the largest category of suits which had land as their immediate subject, viz., rent suits. Landlords were forced to pass the demand down the line, thereby inevitably incurring a problem of enforcement. The most common form of rent suit—as much as 99 per cent of the whole category—was for arrears of rent with or without a demand for ejectment of the delinquent tenant.[25] The remaining rent suits had to do with claims for enhancement of rent by the landlord, claims to occupancy status by tenants, and a range of other tenancy problems. In a great many instances the landlord employed the judicial remedy as merely an adjunct to self-help within the village.

The tenancy issue was also directly related to the problem of mass transfers of title to land. A very high proportion of the transfers did not result in any physical dispossession. Rather, the auctions and judicial pronouncements created what was in effect another interest in land.[26] The incumbent zamindar was left in possession but was now obliged to treat the purchaser as a landlord. This arrangement must have suited many of the new proprietors, particularly the fresh class of commercial speculators who lacked any knowledge of agriculture. But these new proprietors tended to run into difficulties in enforcing their rent rights against tenants who continued to see themselves as zamindars. Often they had little alternative but to turn to the courts.

But much of the conflict following the revenue settlements was not the result of any British policy calculated to push land relations in a particular direction. Rather, it was a simple consequence of the almost defeating task of preparing a 'record of rights', a register of titles to all the land in a given region. Free exchange of land within the villages, formal or informal partitions of joint holdings, imperfect boundaries between fields, the fact of household or village servants often culti-vating land free of rent, and the ambiguous, sometimes meaningless, distinction between landlord and tenant—these were some of the problems that made preparation of the record of rights a frequently arbitrary affair that violated the practical scheme of tenure. The dif-ficulty was compounded by the quality of the personnel enlisted to draw up boundaries and assign plots to particular owners and tenants; the complaints about the capacity and honesty of many of these minor officials were so persistent as to be impossible to discount.

Many of the mistakes of the settlement were corrected before it was promulgated, or soon after. But in many instances, the assign-ment of holdings provoked conflict where there had previously been harmless ambiguity. The beneficiaries of the settlement were happy to accept their fortune; indeed, bribery quickly became a common means of ensuring a favourable assignment. But those who believed they had a greater right to the land in question were now faced with permanent extinction of their claim. Rationally, they had to contest the settlement decision, and they turned to the courts in great numbers.

Judicial challenge to the record of rights was renewed with every fresh settlement.

The litigation flowing from traditional land disputes was somewhat different in character. Here it was not a case of disputants operating on different standards of entitlement; merely the translation of an old kind of dispute to a new forum. But the two classes were alike in the logic of the litigants. Like the auction purchaser who lacked possession, these disputants were responding to the opportunities offered by the courts. The willingness to take the judicial option was in part a function of the absence of an institutional alternative: there appears never to have been regular adjudicative control of land disputes in India. The basic solvent of such conflict had always been more-or-less naked power. The village was a world of super- and sub-ordination, and in a dispute between an economically (hence politically) dominant individual or group and a subordinate, the will of the former was likely to prevail. The process was ordinarily not of a kind that could be termed 'juridical'.[27] Disputes between relative equals occasionally attracted the judicial intervention of a princely outsider, but this was essentially an *ad hoc* event. And while custom played a crucial role in the day-to-day ordering of economic life, it was ultimately unenforceable in the face of opposition from a dominant party in the village. Overall, a practical if precarious economic order was possible without the existence of a concrete judicial structure.

Establishment of the courts injected a wholly new element into agrarian conflict. Old sources of power and coercion were by no means rendered obsolete but their efficacy was now suspect in certain situations. The courts represented a quite fresh opportunity structure for both outsiders and villagers. It now seemed possible to secure victory by means other than simple *force majeure*. But by the same token, the capacity of the courts actually to deliver 'justice' was qualified by the old village processes. Willingness to litigate did not preclude resort to other forms of struggle. Litigants chose the weapon(s) most suited to the struggle and their own situation.

The logic that dictated litigation was absent in most disputes where land was not the matter in contention. The myriad marital disputes and petty village quarrels are a good example. Importantly, the authorities had attempted far less to regulate these incidents of social life. Even the fragmentary efforts to overrule custom tended to be half-hearted. Thus, efforts to fix the minimum age of marriage seem not to have been implemented with any degree of seriousness. And while the body of written Hindu law was now administered by the regular courts, this was of limited scope and mainly invoked in relation to landed property. In short, the British gave remarkably little encouragement to litigation which did not involve a substantial property issue.

This restraint served to keep alive the traditional authorities at or near the village level. There was no invariability to either the structure or quality of authority throughout village India but, as a generalisation, it can be said that standards of behaviour within marriage, the caste community and the village as a whole were enforced and disputes adjudicated by a range of interlocking authorities including village headmen, dominant castes and individual caste panchayats. These bodies seem to have been strongest—sometimes exercising a clear juridical authority—in relation to the very disputes that had failed to engage the attention of the British. For instance, an individual caste had both a strong corporate interest in enforcing its own laws and customs and the capacity to do so through more-or-less regular tribunals with a range of sanctions, including outcasteing. While the British ultimately contributed to the erosion of these traditional authorities, in the short run they seem to have imposed their will on law-breakers much as before. Even today, some of the traditional bodies continue to exercise a calculable, if greatly diminished, authority. But significantly, they take no part at all in land disputes.[28]

In sum, there was nothing uniquely Indian about the popular response to the Anglo-Indian courts. The origins of most litigation lay in a land structure deeply disrupted by the British administration. There was a clear and not obviously irrational logic in the decision to go to court: whether plaintiff or defendant, the claimant was acting out of calculated self-interest. His logic was materialist, rather than rooted in a unique culture or psychology. He was not uncomprehending, mischievous nor enacting a quarrelsome disposition. It is true that not every litigant conformed to the character assumed in the formal model of the new justice: the model pre-supposed a willingness to comply with a decision of the court, whatever it might be. Many litigants, the physical incumbents above all, were quite unwilling to concede the validity of any decision that took away 'their' land. But there was nothing 'Indian' about this psychology. It was a case of peasants casting around for means of avoiding their own downfall.

The Causes of Litigation in Independent India

Within a framework marked by continuity, there have been important changes to the pattern of litigation in India over the last thirty years. There is now less litigation in absolute terms than there was in the nineteenth century or first half of the present century and, therefore, far less relative to population.[29] The great change has been the virtual disappearance of rent litigation as a result of land reforms; other suits have declined in more modest numbers.

Post-independence land reforms had the stated goal of giving land to the tiller, but achievement has fallen ludicrously short of this ideal.[30] At the same time, the scheme has had a considerable impact on agrarian life. The major change goes by the general name of 'zamindari abolition', a measure which was implemented by the various States during the decade after 1947. The scheme had the effect of abolishing what was largely a formal and financial tier in the rural hierarchy; it stripped property rights from those (zamindars *et al.*) who were intermediaries in relation to the collection of state revenue from land. North and East India were in effect converted to the *ryotwari* system of land tenure prevailing in the West and South; the state was brought into a direct revenue relationship with every individual proprietor of land, now called proprietary tenant or a synonym for this.

In most States the change brought about very little direct redistribution of land and certainly failed to do away with widespread landlordism.[31] The rights of the long-established and legally protected tenants (the occupancy tenants) were in effect made absolute in relation to their land. This entailed no physical transfer of land: it was in essence a formal legal change. Tenants with inferior rights, usually called tenants-at-will—these constituted a majority of the tenantry over India as a whole—were *not* converted into proprietary tenants in most States. While the zamindars lost their right to collect revenue on behalf of the state (for which they were handsomely compensated), they were certainly not stripped of all rights in land. The ex-zamindars were allowed to retain those lands (usually termed *khudkasht* or *sir*) which they had worked with their own hands (an occurrence limited to very minor zamindars), by hired labour or through periodic lease in return for a share of the crop or a cash rent. In some areas this extremely loose formula allowed the ex-zamindars to retain a large proportion of 'their' lands; legally, they became proprietary tenants of the land, in the same way that their former occupancy tenants became proprietary tenants. None of this helped the majority tenants-at-will. Indeed, many of them were positively harmed by zamindari abolition. Where the tenants were weak, they were frequently ejected from land that the zamindar sought to claim as *khudkasht*.[32]

Zamindari abolition did not occasion the flood of litigation that attended nineteenth-century 'reforms' of the land system of India. Where tenants were relatively strong, the zamindars quickly realised the futility of trying to dislodge them through judicial action. And where the tenants were weak, they could be ejected by direct action; they themselves were too poor and timid to use the machinery of the courts, no matter how strong a case at law they might have had. Overall, zamindari abolition greatly reduced the quantum of litigation in India. There were only 579 rent suits in Bihar in 1972, compared with tens of thousands of such cases in any pre-independence year.[33] The explanation for this is very simple: the state has replaced the zamindars as direct collector of revenue and there is now no ground for the old-style rent suit, which was intimately connected with the levy imposed on the zamindar by the state. The remaining rent suits are of a kind familiar in landlord–tenant relations in the West. Nor has the state taken over rent (more properly, revenue) suits from the zamindars. An effectively reduced revenue demand and a more benevolent attitude to the farmers have meant comparatively few judicial claims for revenue by the state. The reduced demand has worked to dry up litigation in another way too. Impoverishment of title-holders by the intolerable revenue demand and the consequent enforced sales, mortgages and litigation are now largely a thing of the past.

But a later measure in the reform package has provoked a considerable quantity of litigation, since its potential for redistribution has been far greater than that of zamindari abolition. Beginning in the fifties, the various States enacted legislation specifying a 'ceiling' on the amount of land which could lawfully be owned by an individual or family. Surplus land was to be redistributed to the landless or to poor tenants. The early legislation was studded with loopholes reflecting a general lack of political will on the part of national and state governments. But from the late 1960s and particularly the 1970s, the legislation has been amended to give it more bite, and implementation has become somewhat more serious. The response of landholders holding parcels surplus to the ceiling has been dramatic: they have approached the courts in large numbers in order to set aside orders to divest them of land.[34] The novel aspect of these judicial contests is that they pit landholders against the state rather than against other citizens. The same phenomenon can be seen in relation to another reform measure, the effort to give the former tenants-at-will security of tenure and a guaranteed share of the produce of their land. As soon as government has become relatively serious about this measure, it has been assailed by landholders desperate to retain their traditional dominance.[35]

There remain many other causes of litigation in contemporary India, undoubtedly the greatest single one being land revenue settlements.[36] These invariably lead to thousands of suits in any District of India. The settlement tends to revive old conflicts—the drawing of boundaries between fields is a perennial problem—and create new ones. Many of the disputes are either caused or fuelled by simple errors or deliber- ate falsehoods in the new record of rights. This is the work of minor officials, many of whom are notoriously susceptible to bribery. For the rest, litigation is incidental to many small categories of land disputes of both a 'traditional' and modern kind. Thus the old problem of succes- sion (including adoption) continues to be a fruitful source of discord, as does the modern problem of sale of land; both these kinds of dispute are represented in the earlier case study. But beyond these comments, it is too early to give a definitive account of the developing character of post-independence litigation. It remains to be seen whether litigation will continue to decline; if it does, the ground will not be any reduction of tension in agrarian relations. Rather, the developing tensions are not always of a kind that can easily be expressed in civil court action. Thus, tensions arising from the growth in consciousness of poor tenants may well be expressed in political rather than judicial terms.

The Judicial Pathology

The seeming puzzle of Anglo-Indian justice is the contrast between the eminently 'rational' motives of the litigants and the nature and outcome of the judicial process, which tends to what I have termed a 'pathology'. The central failure of the courts has been their inability to resolve disputes by their judgments. Official statistics, some historical analysis and contemporary case studies reveal a picture of extraordinary judicial inconclusiveness. This can be separated into two parts, though in practice the parts are often intertwined: first, a widespread lack of enforcement of court judgments, and secondly, an unusual complexity in the process of litigation itself.

The first problem is clearly evident in rent and money lending suits, by far the largest group of cases in British India. Relatively few of these were actually contested by the defendants—poverty, ignorance and even lack of notice of the case deterred most peasants from making an appearance in court, and the plaintiffs were almost routinely awarded judgment. But a judgment debt had to be realized, and at the stage of execution a very high proportion of decrees were returned as 'wholly infructuous'.[37] In other words, the judgment debtor was either unwilling or unable to pay the debt. The plaintiff's next option was to seek court approval to attach and sell the debtor's property (including rights in land) or, more frequently, to come to some kind of accommodation with him outside the court. The plaintiffs were quick to learn that the courts could be used as a valuable resource, if not an ultimate arbiter according to the rule of law. Indeed, for the money-lender (as opposed to the straightforward zamindar) the court's incapacity to make good its judgment could be an ultimate boon; the pressure of the judgment could be used to renegotiate the loan at even more usurious rates and so bind the peasant to him in perpetuity. The judges, however, took their failure more seriously—they engaged in an annual wringing of hands over the 'wholly infructuous' column in the administration report. But it was scarcely their fault. They were being asked to provide authoritative backing to the grossest form of exploitation arising from their colleagues' revenue policies and the appetites of native petty capitalists. The peasants could only be squeezed so far at any one time.

The most remarkable example of the same problem was the chronic lack of enforcement of judgments which transferred title to land from zamindars to auction purchasers or mortgagees.[38] There were several distinct reasons for this. First, the transferee, who was a purely commercial man, had no interest in taking possession of land. His concern was merely to secure a high return on his loan, and he would invoke the judicial transfer machinery only as a last resort to make good his investment. Transfer of title must often have been only a formal stage in the decline of a zamindar and his relationship with a creditor; certainly, it was no panacea for the creditor's problem of loan enforcement. He now had to collect rent as landlord, a task no easier than extracting repayments on the original loan. The moneylender-cum-landlord would be continually forced to seek judgments against the declining and recalcitrant ex-zamindar. The judgments were not always enforceable, but over time the whole process was bound to exact a heavy toll on the incumbent. Ultimately, either he or his heirs may have been so beaten down and impoverished that it was both feasible and profitable for the lender to make a genuine transfer to a more buoyant farmer. The lender had thus been able to make the courts work for him, albeit in a roundabout way and perhaps to a lesser degree than strict legal right would have dictated.

The most bitter contests of all were those where both claimants were agriculturalists. Any judicial decree calling for the expulsion of an occupant was met with solid opposition. He would leave his land only when forced to and the ground for compromise was far more limited than in the above case. The conflict tended to be acted out on a number of levels and at a degree of intensity that might be termed 'irrational'. The incumbent, for example, might be prepared to enter into crippling loan transactions in order to maintain his fight for control of land which had been jeopardized by his previous borrowing. Both parties might use the courts in an aggressive capacity in order to raise the costs of opposition. False witness, bribery, proliferation of suits in the several jurisdictions—these were routine tactics. This kind of conflict must have given rise to much of the work of the criminal courts. The motives for instigating prosecution were revenge and, more importantly, harassment of one's opponent; it is doubtful that self-protection was a serious consideration. A considerable number of the cases were obviously sheer fabrications, though there was clearly a high incidence of physical confrontation.

The courts, though lacking an autonomous power of enforcement, could call on the enforcement mechanisms of the state—ultimately the police force. But the police were unequal to the demands made of them.[39] The British had created the most systematic police force ever known in India, but it was a bureaucratized, highly centralized force.

They were based in the great cities and provincial towns, with comparatively few outposts in minor centres of the countryside. Inevitably, they could exercise only intermittent control of agrarian conflict. Once they got to a village they could go through the motions of enforcing a judicial transfer or reaffirming the rights of an occupant, but as soon as they retired to the barracks an already violent conflict was likely to erupt in new incidents which confounded their action. Moreover, the police were notoriously susceptible to financial inducements and to intimidation by dominant groups. Poor pay and low status did little to instill in them a resolute commitment to enforce the law without fear or favour.

But the insufficiencies and inadequacies of policemen were in no sense the root frustration of the judicial system. A body of courts effective only through the routine use of force could scarcely be regarded as the custodian of the rule of law. The frequency and fruitlessness of claims for police enforcement were more symptom than cause of the judicial malaise. In any case, a ruthlessly efficient scheme of enforcement would have created as many problems as it solved. Protracted struggles were no doubt socially wasteful and intellectually unsatisfactory, but on another level they were a means of gradual adjustment to the disruptions worked by British intervention in land relations. The very flaws of the judicial system gave it some (albeit unintended) success as an anti-revolutionary instrument. An effective system of British justice in India would have tended to yield swift and total victory to those who challenged the *status quo*—the moneylenders, speculators and expansionary farmers. These were the groups which usually had legal right on their side. But the incapacities of the system afforded the parties of the *status quo*—the impoverished zamindars and tenants—room to manoeuvre. They could use their position in the village and sometimes the courts themselves to limit or forestall the judicially sponsored victory that rightfully belonged to their opponent. Had this not been the case, physical displacement and the consequent resentments and instability would have proceeded even further than they did.

Of course, not every instance of protracted and inconclusive litigation could be directly related to British land policy. The conflict over partition of great family estates was hardly an artefact of British rule, even if the incidence of partition was promoted by British policies.

What the British provided was a new structure for acting out these conflicts. We can freely concede, moreover, that motives other than simple economic interest entered into such struggles, as they sometimes did in more prosaic disputes of both a time-worn and new kind. In more general terms, Gluckman's remarks about the Lozi tribesmen are equally applicable to the multiplex world of the Indian village: a dispute about a specific thing often 'precipitates ill-feeling about many trifling incidents in the past between the parties and among their kind, incidents which may go back many years.'[40] What we need not concede is that social complications of this order were a powerful factor in any but a strict minority of the cases about land that appeared before the courts. And secondly, we should remember that socially complex disputes about land had always belonged to a category of disputes for which there was no regular means of settlement. The courts certainly made hard weather of such cases, but this was not because of any defect relative to comparable modes of dispute settlement.

Some of the sham and complexity of Anglo-Indian justice has disappeared in the post-independence world. The deliberately formal rather than physical transfer of land to moneylenders and the attendant judicial complications are no longer common; the dwindling taxation of agriculture has largely removed the condition for this development. There also seems to be a tendency to less intense resistance to loss of land on the part of large landholders. The beneficiaries of the steady decline of this class—they are rarely serious about agriculture and are in many ways anachronistic figures—are middle-peasant proprietors who buy up land piece-by-piece. This is not a process which can easily lead to bitter conflict between seller and buyer. These transfers may well harm tenants (often share-croppers) on the land, but these are people who are usually too weak to put up a realistic fight. There is certainly no lessening of competition for land—quite the reverse. But there tends to be less ground (and less financial capacity) for expressing this competition in litigation. Despite all this, the case of Jagat Singh is testimony enough that epic struggles and complex judicial activity do still occur. Moreover, any generalization for so recent a period must be strictly tentative.

Thus far I have been preoccupied with land litigation from the perspective of the village. The object has been to identify the deep-seated nature of disputes over land in order to supply the context for the narrow judicial history of land litigation. By now the dimensions of the British ambition to subject conflict over land to the 'rule of law' must be obvious. The *raj* was attempting to bring to order what was the most unruly class of small-scale conflict in agrarian India, and this at a time when, through its own intervention, the incidence of such conflict was running at an unusually high level. Inevitably, performance fell far short of ambition. The judicial system was not rejected out of hand but rather developed a character quite distinct from its rationale. It was unable to provide 'predictable, decisive, final outcomes through ... "the law"'.[41] Instead, the system came to be a forum for the stylized acting out of conflict. The beneficiaries of the system were those who learnt to put together a good judicial 'performance'. These people were in effect awarded points for their performance, points which acted as a resource in the larger struggle for land. A litigant who took the courts at face value and failed to master the rules of what was a unique game was unlikely to secure great benefit from them.

The distinctive character of the Anglo-Indian judicial system emerged through the medium of the most cherished foundations of British law, the rigorous procedures designed to promote justice. British (indeed all western-style) courts are essentially cautious institutions: they are authorized to give judgment for one or the other party—there can never be a compromise, though the winner may receive less than his claim—only after each side has had an opportunity to put its case. This principle is met in practice by complex rules governing procedure and evidence, by the right to representation by a lawyer and the capacity to appeal against an adverse decision. It is these procedures and rights which have been systematically distorted in the Indian case.

Schooled by their lawyers—a key group which flourished very early in the new order—the litigants found marvellously intricate ways of exploiting procedural opportunities. The one land dispute could become a whole series of court actions: civil, revenue and criminal. If speed of action were undesirable, opportunities for delay through adjournment were abundant. An adverse decision could be appealed to ever higher courts. False witness (positively encouraged by many lawyers) could be employed almost with impunity: the complexity of cases tended to be such that lying was virtually impossible to detect. The appearance of rival 'hand-writing experts' to prove the veracity/ mendacity of crucial documents was commonplace. And in the face of their manifold professional and financial problems, officials—land record-keepers, police, the magistrates themselves—frequently capitulated to the bribery of a desperate litigant.

Why did the litigants behave in a manner that made a mockery of the processes designed to promote justice between them? This question can be answered indirectly through another question: what reasonable alternative did they have? Each of the parties would eagerly have seized any opportunity for a decisive result in his favour. But the background to many cases meant that no such opportunity was forthcoming. Once aware of this situation, the litigant (strictly, the plaintiff) had two logical options: he could abandon the court system in favour of some other means of advancement, or he could attempt to derive some residual advantage from the courts. For many litigants, the first was no real option at all. It was only the traditionally powerful agrarian figure who could have any confidence that his cause would be successful in the village itself. And even this confidence tended to be misplaced as the second option became an institutional possibility. As a response to the very weakness of the courts, litigants and lawyers quickly learnt to exploit the system in their own interest. Very quickly systematic distortion of judicial procedures was routinized: the very structure of the judicial system came to embody the ploys and ruses of the cunning. In short, a fundamentally incompetent mode of conflict resolution had been redefined by its clients in a way that offered them some hope of ultimate success. On its own terms the court system was an abject failure; for the litigant, the system was not without redeeming value.

The successful litigant has learnt to skirt the many pitfalls surrounding the courts. Above all, he has learnt to extract some value from his 'friend' at court, the lawyer. This man is drawn (initially with the likely aid of a tout) from one of the world's most parasitic legal professions. The development of a high standard of professional legal ethics in India has been inhibited by factors such as poor legal education, a frequent contempt for the figure of the peasant, and the very desperation and hence vulnerability of the litigants. The Indian lawyer is paid only to litigate: he cannot ordinarily charge fees for mere advice. Hence, he is never reluctant to counsel court action. This structural bias towards litigation is furthered by intense competition within a too numerous profession.[42] Both client and lawyer are anxious to win their joint case, the lawyer because his business depends at least partially on a reputation for success. But the client wants a victory that is cheap and as rapid as possible, the lawyer one that is as protracted and therefore expensive as possible. Observation of the relations between lawyer and client in contemporary India suggests that in a high proportion of cases, the original cause of action is submerged at least temporarily in the machinations of a too resourceful lawyer. The problem is compounded by the habitual intervention of various other third parties—the *munshis* ('lawyers' clerks), touts, 'social workers', village politicians and sundry unclassifiable intermeddlers. Some of these perform a genuine service in smoothing the path of ignorant villagers on a daunting bureaucratic expedition. But like the lawyers (in whose pay they often are), these people tend to have an interest which cuts across the concerns of the litigant.

There is ample evidence, then, that the judicial system has become a complex social structure in itself. The various specialists in legal administration, to use Kidder's phrase, have entrenched themselves so as to be capable of operating as a force independent of the will of the parties to the dispute. Clearly, this tends to make the judicial process more unwieldy, less predictable and even less just than it otherwise might be. At the same time, neither the procedures nor the third-party professionals are the root problem of the judicial system. A large part of the reason for the emergence of such an unsatisfactory legal profession is the opportunities offered by conflicts which are essentially beyond the competence of the courts to resolve. If the disputes had been more tractable, then it is doubtful that the lawyers would have had so great a room to manoeuvre in their own interest.

Cohn, Kidder and a Third View

Kidder's analysis of the Anglo-Indian legal system is obviously quite different from Cohn's, but at one level the two converge. Both accounts rest on an assumption that the character of the judicial process can be explained in isolation from the other organs, policies and consequences of Anglo-Indian rule; we are invited to view the courts as a wholly independent institution. The present account proceeds from a denial of this assumption. What I have called the pathology of Anglo-Indian justice—essentially its inconclusiveness—was not at root a function of *a priori* attitudes to British justice as a discrete system of rules and procedures (Cohn), nor of internal developments within a due process system inherently susceptible to distortion by the participants in it (Kidder). Rather, the formal independence of the courts masked the fact that they were part of a larger administrative whole and were pre-occupied with the economic consequences of policy framed by other organs in the administration. The fate of the courts was bound up with the land structure of India under British rule. A turbulent agrarian structure was reflected in an immensely problematical judicial system. The most basic problems of Anglo-Indian justice would have beset an equally ambitious judicial system of whatever procedural and cultural complexion.

The language of Cohn's argument suggests that the function of the courts was simply to settle disputes. From another perspective, however, their function was to enforce the new definition and allocation of rights and duties concerning land. In this sense, the courts were an enforcement arm of the land administration. They were there to enforce the taxation claims of the state and to back those who acted in conformity with the new scheme of entitlement. This can be seen most clearly in the revenue courts. By the mid-nineteenth century, the jurisdiction of the revenue courts in the North-West Provinces and some other areas was to hear charges of delinquency in payment of revenue to the land administration and also to adjudicate disputes relating to the occupancy of land and the incidents of tenure, such as rent rights. The link between these two seemingly quite distinct functions was the British concern to redefine the whole legal status of land in India, so as to benefit themselves and the 'worthy' among the Indian population. The courts were in effect asked simultaneously to enforce the revenue claims of the state, to hammer home the dispossession and impoverishment decreed by the land authorities, and to bridge the divisions which had been opened up. It is no wonder that they failed in all but the first task.

Cohn is right to argue that the Anglo-Indian courts did not fit into Indian society very neatly, but the lack of fit was not as he identifies it. Initially, the courts did not fit Indian society in proportion as the new land policy did not fit; the courts were derivative institutions designed to apply this policy (the law) to individual cases. The land policy was not intended to 'fit' Indian society; it was a radical policy which aimed at the installation of something like a capitalist order in India. But the problem for the courts was that a category of Indian villager did not accept the validity of rules which worked to deprive them of land they regarded as legitimately theirs. The relevant clash was not over values to do with status and culture and between native and alien judicial procedures, but an economic clash. The courts obediently set out to give support to the party whose conception of right coincided with that of the policy makers, but they were obstructed in this by the degree of resistance put up by the other party. There was nothing 'Indian' about this resistance; it was resistance to economic deprivation. The seemingly curious effect of the courts' incapacity to cope with this resistance was that the lack of fit between administration and society was somewhat reduced; the old order could persist to a greater extent than it would have had the courts done their job, that is given support to the rising, *anti-status quo* parties which usually had legal right on their side. A class of litigants had in effect managed to disaggregate the courts from the land administration and to invest them with some of the independence that the formal model suggested.

The question of perjury is relevant in this context. There is no ground for believing that lying is more prevalent in village India than it is in any other society, and yet false witness is a notorious feature of Indian court behaviour. For Cohn, the disparity can be explained as a reaction to the alienness of the courts and a consequent willing-ness to violate ordinary canons of action. While there may be some little truth in this, overall the view lacks explanatory power. The better view is that perjury stems from a knowledge of both the dangers and opportunities inherent in the courts. Elizabeth Whitcombe quotes a nineteenth-century revenue official remarking the dramatic growth in perjury over a ten year period. At the beginning of the period, the zamindars perjured themselves rarely; ten years later they did so freely.[43] Now it is unlikely that during this time the litigants had come to see that their 'Indian' values clashed with the values of the courts. It is more plausible that the zamindars had learnt what to do in order to pursue their own interests in the courts. They had learnt that if the courts were not their natural friend, they could at least be manipulated so as not to be an effective enemy. Over time, false witness became virtually an institutionalized part of the judicial process. By now, even a novice litigant tends to realize that honesty is a luxury in the courts.

The lawyers, of course, reinforce this perception; the client is routinely coached to give evidence to suit his own case rather than the facts of the matter.

If Cohn were correct, a court system more sensitive to Indian values and processes would presumably have been more successful. Again, there may be some truth in this. Some of the litigated disputes may have been confronted more productively had the courts considered the totality of relations between the parties, or been willing to effect a compromise between them. But it is highly unlikely that greater flexibility and institutional reform could have cured the pathological aspects of the system. There were strict limits to the potential for reform. As we noted in the case study, it would have been logically impossible to replace the 'winner-take-all' principle with a commitment to bring the parties to a compromise. The whole basis of the British land scheme was a concern to define and apportion land according to strict legal right. The purchaser of land could scarcely be told that he had purchased full proprietary rights in a property but that in the event of a dispute, a court would be committed to conceding him much less than this. Moreover, there would have been little 'traditional' about such a stance; we have repeatedly noted that land disputes were not subjected to such orderly treatment in pre-British India.

Kidder has also rejected Cohn's psychology of the Indian litigant, but he has done so through reasoning which is itself open to objection. Kidder claims that far from having rejected the basis of the courts, Indians were attracted to them by the very characteristics that marked them off from native processes: 'the court system draws new customers specifically because of its ideology of legal-moral absolutes', or the principle that the party with legal right on its side is entitled to a total victory.[44] The objection to this view is its suggestion that prospective litigants evaluated the courts as an autonomous entity. Litigants appear to have approached the courts as part of a whole new land scheme, rather than as a novel mode of justice that was seen to have a normative value superior to native processes. The initiators of litigation were acting out a logical imperative, rather than opting for a kind of justice they specially trusted. Just as the British authorities had perceived that establishment of courts was the corollary of defining and allocating rights and duties in land, so disputants came to the courts for defence of rights they claimed under the new system. This is not to say that the winner-take-all principle was not attractive to many litigants, only that it was not the primary ground for going to court. The British had dictated court use by the way in which they had intervened in land relations.

The strength of Kidder's work is his description of the manner in which the 'adjudicative ideal' is displaced in the judicial system. The central weakness is the failure to give an adequate explanation for the appearance of the processes he identifies. It is not enough to point to the inherent susceptibility of due process systems to distortion by the several participants in them. Why has the same distortion not taken place in the US, Britain, France? Kidder's response is to draw on an influential short article by van Velsen in order to argue that comparable distortion has in fact taken place in lower-level courts in the West.[45] Despite the fact that this is on a strictly minor scale when compared with India, Kidder is able to discern an identical basis for these western and the routine Indian processes: 'multiplex' social relationships. This throws him back perilously close to Cohn, and suggests a level of irrationality in the average Indian litigant which cannot be sustained by empirical work. Indians are neither so self-indulgent nor so driven by lawyers that they would persist with a judicial system that offered them no material hopes.

The most telling argument against both Kidder and Cohn is that they have concentrated too little on the nature of the disputes that the courts had to contend with. To put the matter differently, both writers have neglected to stress that land relations are a crucial part of 'social structure'. If this is made clear, then we *can* say that problems within the social structure of India led directly to the worst problems in the judicial system. No doubt due process schemes of justice are peculiarly susceptible to distortion, but the extent to which the procedures are exploited will be contingent on the character of the society in question. The nature and bitterness of land disputes after the British intervention provided an ideal basis for extraordinary distortion of the Indian model of western-style justice. So, the judicial pathology is curable only by a cessation of the kind of cases that have been its principal cause. This, in turn, is contingent on changes within land relations, and we have suggested that some of these changes have already taken place. The judicial pathology appears not so marked today as it was during the British era.

Notes

1. This work is based primarily on field research in India during 1971–72, and shorter periods in 1974 and 1980. The core research was a stay of some six months in a village fictionally titled Haripur, in Alwar District of Rajasthan. Haripur is the seat of several magistrates' courts that serve the sub-District, and so presented the opportunity for observation of one of the many hundreds of local court complexes in India. It was also a convenient village for the study of dispute settlement outside the courts. For financial assistance I thank the Indian and Australian Governments, which supported me with a Commonwealth Scholarship in 1971–72, and La Trobe University for a travelling grant in 1980.

2. The sociology of both the British-based legal system of India and indigenous legal processes is at a low level of development. This contrasts sharply with the great volume of commentary on substantive law in the Anglo-Indian courts. The most systematic description of processes in the courts is in Robert L. Kidder, 'Courts and Conflict in an Indian City: A Study in Legal Impact', *Journal of Commonwealth Political Studies*, 11(2) (1973), pp. 121–39; see also Robert L. Kidder, 'Litigation as a Strategy for Personal Mobility: The Case of Urban Caste Association Leaders', *Journal of Asian Studies*, XXXIIL2 (1974), pp. 177–91; Robert L. Kidder, 'Formal Litigation and Professional Insecurity: Legal Entrepreneurship in South India', *Law and Society Review*, 9(1) (1974), pp. 11–38; Charles Morrison, 'Clerks and Clients: Paraprofessional Roles and Cultural Identities in Indian Litigation', *Law and Society Review*, 9(1) (1974), pp. 39–62; Charles Morrison, '*Munshis* and Their Masters: The Organization of an Occupational Relationship in the Indian Legal System', *Journal of Asian Studies*, XXXL2 (1971), pp. 309–28; R.S. Khare, 'Indigenous Culture and Lawyer's Law in India', *Comparative Studies in Society and History*, 14(1) (1972), pp. 71–96; Marc Galanter, 'The Modernization of Law', in M. Weiner (ed.), *Modernization* (New York, 1966), pp. 153–65; Marc Galanter, 'The Displacement of Traditional Law in Modern India', *Journal of Social Issues*, XXIV(4) (1968), pp. 65–91; and the several articles on the Indian legal profession in *Law and Society Review*, 3(1–2) (1968–9).

3. Bernard S. Cohn, 'Some Notes on Law and Change in North India', *Economic Development and Cultural Change*, 8 (1959), p. 90.

4. Ibid., pp. 79–93 *passim*.

5. Kidder, 'Courts and Conflict in an Indian City'.

6. Ibid., p. 122.

7. Ibid., p. 123.

8. Kidder, 'Courts and Conflict in an Indian City', p. 136.

9. Ibid., p. 137.

10. This study is written on the basis of extended interviews with Jagat Singh and his opponents at the courthouse and in the village itself, and interviews with lawyers and magistrates in Haripur. These interviews took place at various times in the period 1971–72 and in 1974. A short visit to Haripur in 1980 showed that the conflict was then as bitter as ever.

11. The best (though still limited) account of the growth of Anglo-Indian law is A. Gledhill, *The Republic of India: The Development of Its Laws and Constitution* (London: Steven & Sons, 1951). See also C. Fawcett, *The First Century of British Justice in India* (London, 1934); H.S. Bhatia (ed.), *Origin and Development of Legal and Political System in India* (New Delhi: Deep and Deep, 1976).

12. The revenue courts were by definition exclusively concerned with land matters. In the early part of the nineteenth century, their jurisdiction was limited to delinquencies in the payment of land revenue and disputes over revenue liability. (In Bengal and certain other areas these were within the civil jurisdiction.) Later their jurisdiction was expanded and they tended to overlap with the civil courts. On the latter problem, see Elizabeth Whitcombe, *Agrarian Conditions in Northern India* (Berkeley: University of California, 1972), pp. 205–34 *passim*.

In the criminal courts, the most common prosecutions since the late nineteenth century (when annual statistical returns became available) have been for physical violence, theft and breach of the peace. To give a random example, in 1876 in the princely State of Alwar (which had a Punjab-style land system and Anglo-Indian courts from mid-century) 4,960 out of a total of 5,913 cases covered by the Indian Penal Code (which does not deal with breach of the peace—this falls under the Criminal Procedure Code) fell into the categories of violence or theft. Reading back from my own field observations and interviews, it would appear that the great majority of these flowed from land disputes. The subject of theft allegation is very often crops on disputed land. Many of the allegations are deliberately false, and there is a steady flow of prosecutions for laying false information to the police.

Litigation in the civil courts was classified from the late nineteenth century under three heads: suits for money or movables, rent suits, and title and 'other' suits. The breakdown between these categories varied over region and, to some extent, over time. (For changes in the post-independence period, see below.) The permanent settlement areas (mainly the original Province of Bengal) had far more rent suits in both absolute terms and relative to the other categories than did, say, Punjab or Madras.

To take one year at random, Bengal in 1900 had 287,261 suits for money or movables (the former being the principal item), 284,288 rent suits and 76,976 cases to do with land title and other matters, making a total of 648,525. This excludes all appeals and also suits in the High Court and certain minor courts; the figures are from the *Report of the Civil Justice Administration for Bengal Province for 1900* (Calcutta, 1901). In Madras, by contrast, only 11,028 out of a total of 208,132 suits in 1880 were for rent (*Report of the Civil Justice Administration for Madras 1880* [Madras, 1881]). While official figures may have been accurate enough, the mode of classification of suits greatly understated the land factor. A very high proportion of the money suits were the functional equivalent of rent suits; they were brought by either full-time money-lenders or farmers cum money-lenders, people who in effect represented simply another tier in the land hierarchy concerned to maximize its share of the profits from agriculture. See the discussion below. For readily accessible material on the pattern of litigation see the *Civil Justice (Rankin) Committee Report* (Calcutta: Government of India, 1925).

13. For an interesting view of land conflict before the British intervention see Richard G. Fox, *Kin, Clan, Raja and Rule* (Berkeley: University of California, 1971).

14. Cf. L.I. and S.H. Rudolph, *The Modernity of Tradition* (Chicago: University of Chicago, 1967), p. 261: 'It seems likely that the "rise" in litigiousness was in part a statistical artifact reflecting the transplantation of disputes to a new location where they were easier to record.' It would seem that these authors pay insufficient attention to the new causes of dispute and hence litigation under British administration of India; see the argument below.

15. Commentary on the village situation prior to British rule is necessarily conjectural; available accounts lack the detail necessary for definitive statement. Nonetheless, an understanding of the 'timeless' quality of some of the conflicts observable today can be laid beside scattered comments in early British reports on India and the work of historians of mediaeval India, in order to provide a plausible outline of the pre-British situation. For the Mughal period, there is some useful material in Irfan Habib, *The Agrarian System of Mughal India* (New York: Asia Publishing House, 1963).

16. The literature on British land policy is very large. Among the most useful are W.H. Moreland, *The Revenue Administration of the United Provinces* (Allahabad, 1911); B.H. Baden-Powell, *Land Systems of British India*, 3 Vols (London, 1892); Elizabeth Whitcombe, *Agrarian Conditions in Northern India*; the various articles in R.E. Frykenberg (ed.), *Land Control and Social Structure in Indian History* (Madison: University of Wisconsin, 1969); Neil Charlesworth, 'The Myth of the Deccan Riots of 1875', *Modern Asian*

Studies, 6(4) (1972), pp. 402–21; Richard G. Fox, *Kin, Clan, Raja and Rule*; Eric Stokes, *The Peasant and the Raj* (Cambridge, 1978).

17. Moreland, *Revenue Administration*, p. 36.

18. The concept of land as a freely transferable commodity seems to have been largely unknown to pre-British India. During the Mughal period there had been occasional instances of zamindari rights being sold but such transactions were not an ordinary feature of agrarian life. The most common mode of land acquisition seems to have been inheritance, conquest or expansion into vacant lands. See Habib, *Agrarian System of Mughal India, passim*.

19. See Moreland, *Revenue Administration*; Bernard S. Cohn, 'Structural Change in Indian Rural Society 1596–1885', in Frykenberg, *Land Control*, pp. 53–121; Whitcombe, *Agrarian Conditions in Northern India*; and M.F. O'Dwyer, *Final Report of the Alwar Settlement* (n.p., 1901).

20. A magistrate at Midnapore, quoted in Rudolph and Rudolph, *The Modernity of Tradition*, p. 261.

21. It is well known that in parts of Africa the British courts were heavily preoccupied with matrimonial matters. This was presumably a consequence of the British intervention into domestic relations regarded as uncivilized, in contrast with a general policy of non-intervention in Indian marriage.

22. An official report cited in Cohn, 'Structural Change in Rural Indian Society', p. 69.

23. The disparity between formal transfers and dispossession has been remarked by a number of officials and historians, among them Cohn, ibid., p. 89, and Whitcombe, *Agrarian Conditions in Northern India*, p. 227.

24. For a fuller discussion of the 'modernization' of the legal machinery in the late nineteenth century, see ibid., Chapter 5.

25. Of 93,289 rent suits in Bihar in 1914, 92,494 were for arrears of rent. This was a typical figure. *Report of the Civil Justice Administration 1914* (Patna, 1915).

26. W.C. Benett, a settlement officer in Gonda, put it thus: 'The result of all these transactions is the creation of a number of concurrent interests in the same soil.' Quoted in Whitcombe, *Agrarian Conditions in Northern India*, p. 227.

27. C.f. Bernard S. Cohn, 'Anthropological Notes on Disputes and Law in India', *American Anthropologist*, 67(6), Pt II (1965), pp. 82–122.

28. The anthropology of Indian law is at a primitive stage of development: M.N. Srinivas, *Caste in Modern India* (Bombay, 1962), p. 118. These comments are based on my own field work and the scattered material in published work. For a summary of the latter, see Cohn 'Anthropological

Notes', also, Louis Dumont, *Homo Hierarchicus* (Delhi: Vikas, 1970), pp. 167–83.

29. For example, in Bihar in 1912 there were 56,939 suits for money or movables, 96,508 rents suits, and 22,570 title or 'other' suits, making a total of 176,017. The figures for the same categories in 1972 were 22,758, 579, and 17,923, making a total of 41–60. *Civil Justice Administration Reporttor* 1912 and 1972 (Patna, 1913 and 1979).

30. For a guide to the literature on recent land reforms, see P.C. Joshi, *Land Reforms in India* (Bombay, 1975). Daniel Thorner, *The Agrarian Prospect in India* (New Delhi, 1976), is still the best introduction to the subject.

31. Ibid., pp. 31–51.

32. There is still a marked lack of empirical studies of the land reforms. These comments are largely based on interviews with land officials in Bihar and West Bengal, February–May, 1980. See F. Tomasson Januzzi, *Agrarian Crisis in India: The Case of Bihar* (Austin: University of Texas, 1974).

33. *Civil Justice Administration Report* (Patna, 1979).

34. There are no available statistics. However, interviews with officials in Bihar and West Bengal in 1980 suggest that there are many thousands of such cases in the High Courts of these two States. Most of them have reached the High Courts direct, without appeal from lower courts, by the device of a writ petition. The argument is that there has been a breach of a fundamental right guaranteed by the Constitution. The favourite peg, until it was recently abolished, was Article 31 of the Constitution, the 'right to property' clause.

35. This is particularly true of West Bengal, where the Communist Government's *Operation Barga* (a drive to register the names and plots of sharecroppers) has provoked widespread panic among landholders. Source: interviews and observations in West Bengal, April 1980.

36. This is based largely on discussions with revenue staff and interested parties in Alwar District, 1971–72.

37. For example, 36,235 of 98,730 execution proceedings (40 per cent) were returned as wholly infructuous in Bihar during 1912. Moreover, another 15,429 cases met with only 'partial satisfaction'. Source: *Civil Justice Administration Report* (Patna, 1913).

38. See note 23.

39. For a useful discussion of the problems of police in the countryside see L.I. Tomkins, *Report on the Reorganisation of the Police of the Alwar State* (Lahore, 1912).

40. Max Gluckmann, *The Judicial Process among the Barotse of Northern Rhodesia* (Manchester, 1955), p. 19.

41. Kidder, 'Courts and Conflict', p. 123.
42. The size of the profession is quantified and set in comparative perspective in Marc Galanter, 'The Study of the Indian Legal Profession', *Law and Society Review*, 3(2–3) (1968–9), pp. 201–17.
43. Whitecomb, *Agrarian Conditions in Northern India*, p. 216.
44. Kidder, 'Courts and Conflict', p. 124.
45. J. Van Velsen, 'Procedural Informality, Reconciliation and False Comparisons', in M. Gluckmann (ed.), *Ideas and Procedures in African Customary Law* (London: Oxford University Press, 1969).

2

HOW INDIAN IS INDIAN LAW?*

The question in the title of this chapter is impossibly broad, but my hope is that struggling to answer it may prove instructive. Let me begin the discussion with another, semi-rhetorical, question I have often been asked in professional or social situations outside India: 'Indian law is basically the common law, is it not?' My standard answer to this question is something like, 'Yes, but there are important differences in the way it works.' Any person with a substantial understanding of Indian law will know that this answer avoids far more than it illuminates. It is reasonable enough to argue that the single most important influence on the character of contemporary Indian law is the legal concepts and overall approach adopted first in Britain and later in other English speaking territories. But equally, the Indian legal system can certainly not be described as simply the common law in an Indian setting. This is what I want to try to unpack in this chapter, through looking at a number of approaches to law in India.

It is easy enough to locate the 'Indianness' of the way in which the official legal system of India works. The organization and characteristics of the legal profession; the subject matter of litigation; the processes of

* This chapter was originally published in Mathew John and Sitharamam Kakarala (eds), *Enculturing Law: New Agendas for Legal Pedagogy* (New Delhi: Tulika Books, 2007), pp. 132–57. I thank Marika Vicziany, as usual, and Upendra Baxi for commenting on the draft of this chapter. I am particularly indebted to Professor Baxi, who dissected the piece in his familiar manner (simultaneously devastating and supportive). I know that this published version has not met his criticisms but I am still thinking about them!

the courts; the behaviour and expectations of litigants—these are some of the matters explored over many years (albeit by too small a group of socio-legal scholars). These studies have illustrated the distinctiveness of the official Indian legal system, which for many decades has been very far from a 'foreign' or 'colonial' system. But these are *not* the perspectives explored in the present chapter, except in passing. Here, I wish to open up some rather more fundamental questions as to the distinctiveness of Indian law.

Legal Pluralism

The system of law established by the British and carried on by independent India holds itself out as the sole legal authority in the country. In this respect, the Indian legal order simply mirrors the official stance of any other modern legal regime. This pretension to legal monopoly is everywhere a myth or a fiction—we know this comprehensively from 30 years of law and society scholarship, and indeed from much earlier thinkers like Henry Maine.[1] In perhaps every developed political society, there is much law-like activity that takes place outside the apparatus of the state and, conversely, within that apparatus, much of the activity resembles processes in the world outside.[2] The decision to name as 'law' only what happens in official institutions reflects the drive of nineteenth-century legal positivism and also the appetites of the modern nation state. In the case of India, the claim to monopoly of law by the state is especially weak.

The practical ambit of Anglo-Indian law was always narrow: aside from the administration of criminal justice, the Indian courts were dominated by issues surrounding landed property.[3] This is not to say that the British project of transferring law to India was not an ambitious one or that there were not important cases in their courts concerning issues other than land; rather, it is to note that, in quantitative terms, litigation over land dwarfed all other civil cases. For the most part, the great flow of social relations went unregulated by the law and the courts of colonial India. And to a large, if now diminishing, extent, this remains true of the post-independence period too.

For example, the British did not seek to bring marriage and its incidents under the umbrella of the state. Births, deaths and marriages were not required to be registered. A limited legislative regime was provided for marriage and divorce among the relatively small Christian and tiny Parsi communities but not for the dominant Hindus or Muslims.[4] The enactment and dissolution of marriage and disputes to do with children and marital property remained overwhelmingly a matter for agencies constituted without reference to the state. After independence, marriage among Hindus was officially regulated for the first time under the Hindu Marriage Act 1955 but, until recently, this has changed behaviour very little. Even now only a tiny minority of people, overwhelmingly in urban situations, and probably women more than men, resort to the courts in family matters.

A glimpse of the apparently traditional world of authority in matters of marriage dispute can be found in the following case I collected during field-work in Behror, a sub-division of Alwar district in Rajasthan, in the mid-1970s.

A Dispute among the Dhobis (Washerfolk)[5]

Two sisters, one of them blind, had been married to one dhobi man.[6] Within three years of the wedding, the man had died, leaving the sighted sister with a small child. The two widows returned to their father's household. Widow remarriage is the norm among dhobis and a second marriage was successfully arranged for the sighted sister, while the blind sister and the small child were left with the parents/grandparents. As part of the second marriage arrangement, the new husband paid Rs 350 to the parents of the bride in a transaction witnessed by several men from communities other than the dhobis. When the parents of the deceased first husband found out about this transaction, they became angry. They said that the money was properly theirs as *jagra* or compensation for the loss of their daughter-in-law's services.

The affair was considered serious by the dhobis, since it appeared that the transaction constituted the prohibited practice of bride price (as opposed to the approved practice of dowry payable by the parents of the bride). Accordingly, on the occasion of the next community funeral, a meeting was convened to consider the case. The meeting found that the new husband had indeed paid bride price, tantamount to purchasing the woman, and because of the seriousness of the breach of caste rules, he and several of his relatives were to be outcasted.[7] For their part, the parents of the bride succeeded in avoiding punishment on the grounds that they had accepted the payment as a contribution towards the costs of maintaining their daughter's child and her blind sister rather than as a payment for the woman herself.

The outcastes felt harshly treated and they sought a special meeting to reconsider the affair. (My informant used the language of the state in describing the process: he referred to ordinary community meetings at the time of weddings or funerals as the 'lower court' and special meetings as the 'high court'). The meeting was duly convened on the understanding that the appellants would pay the considerable cost of a meeting at which some 400 people from widely dispersed locations would attend. This time the appellants argued that the sum paid was indeed *jagra* but that the compensation had been paid to the wrong person; it should have been paid to the father of the deceased husband. It could not be maintained, therefore, that the new husband and his father had not paid compensation in defiance of caste rules or that they had paid bride price instead. But the meeting was not satisfied with this argument: why had none of the elders been consulted about the proper practice, and why was payment witnessed by people from other communities and not by dhobis? The matter was turned over to five respected dhobi elders. These men deliberated and issued judgment that the new husband be fined Rs 350, Rs 300 of which was to go to the father of the deceased husband and the remainder to the community representatives for their expenses. The other outcastes were each fined Rs 11. All were readmitted to the caste upon payment of the amounts.

A notable aspect of this dhobi case is the evidence of widow remarriage and polygamy. The former practice has traditionally been forsworn by many high castes or castes pretending to high status, the Brahmins above all. The dhobis' liberal position on widow re-marriage happens to be in line with the Hindu Widows' Remarriage Act 1856, one of the few legislative interventions of the British designed to bring about more 'civilized' family practices.[8] Until recently, arguably, the dhobis' tolerance of polygamy was also in conformity with the law. The British made no serious effort to prohibit polygamy among Hindus.[9] It was left to the Hindu Marriage Act 1955 to render polygamy clearly unlawful for Hindus, though the effect of this prohibition on practice remains unclear. Beyond the matter of legislation by the colonial and independent authorities, the dhobi case is a simple pointer to the great plurality of Indian practice in family relations.

The dhobi case is also an example of the workings of what is called in the sociological literature, 'the caste *panchayat*'.[10] By the time I collected this and a number of other cases in the early 1970s, only some of the lower castes of Behror still had any ongoing processes that could address disputes within their community.[11] Many such cases appear to have been taken up because they involved behaviour seen as adverse to the reputation of a caste actively seeking to improve its reputation. In the case among the dhobis, it was the charge of payment of bride price that produced such resolute action. Bride price is an emotive issue throughout Hindu India: there is widespread self-righteousness about families denying themselves the proceeds of 'selling' their daughters. It may be that the latter practice is associated with Muslims, though on the sub-continent Muslims themselves have tended to move towards the Hindu practice of dowry rather than bride price. So this is the context of the dhobis wanting to separate themselves emphatically from the proscribed practice of bride price.

It would be difficult to argue that the above case does not represent a process of 'law' at work, despite the fact that it was conducted outside the institutions of the state. The process was decisional, binding, and has the general appearance of judicial action. The case is also remarkable by the standards of other contemporary nation states possessed of highly developed legal institutions, even if one concedes that law-like activities outside the state apparatus are characteristic of all those societies. This is not a case of tentative decision-making on a matter of family relations while nervously looking over the shoulder at the official legal system—decision-making 'under the shadow of the law', to use Marc Galanter's phrase.[12] Rather, the panchayat of the dhobis was squarely and seemingly with perfect confidence in its own legitimacy resolving a complex and important issue that had arisen in relation to the community's rules for the arrangement of marriage. It is clear from this one small case that the modern legal order of India has left space for legal action by parties outside the state in a way that has no simple analogue in most other nations with a highly developed legal order.[13]

I know of no comparable example to be found in contemporary Britain, France or Germany. Nor could similar examples easily be found in the US, Canada or Australia—except, importantly, among the indigenous people of these settler societies. Among the latter peoples, there may indeed be forms of contemporary legal ordering that are broadly analogous to that of the dhobis of Rajasthan. But what makes India different from these settler societies is that, at least in conceptual terms, the example of the dhobis' tribunal is not exceptional. Thus, there is no apparatus of state that could readily have been approached by the dhobis for resolution of their problem, even if they had wanted this. If, inconceivably, the dhobis had gone to court over this matter, just one of their problems would have been the evidence of 'traditional' but now unlawful polygamous marriage. Although there is now a single family law applicable to the dhobis and to all other Hindus in India, we have noted that very few Indians in fact approach the courts for resolution of family problems according to this law. The Indian state is in practice content to leave family law to anybody that can assert authority over such issues, though the number of such bodies is declining. True, and whatever the past situation, the Indian state does not now lend legitimacy to the activities of 'customary' bodies like the panchayat of the dhobis. But nor has it taken action to de-legitimate these bodies. It just ignores them, leaving their vitality to be determined by forces other than the legal apparatus of the state.[14] The dhobi case was not typical of dispute processes in Behror even 30 or 40 years ago, when it took place. At that time, and even more so today, there were very few communities in Behror that had the coherence to resolve a serious dispute surrounding community rules so neatly. Yet this is not to say that the case is an isolated one that lacks any more general relevance. To what extent, then, does the case among the dhobis represent a form of justice that was previously characteristic of Indian village life? Secondly, can we proceed analogously from this case to formulate more general propositions about Indian patterns of 'dispute settlement' or 'law' or 'justice' that hold good for India today? Before we address these questions directly, it will be useful to say something about 'Hindu' law, since this represents another and more celebrated body of law than any legal process to be spelled out of cases such as that of the dhobis above.

The Question of Hindu Law

The most discussed body of distinctively Indian law is generally known by the name 'Hindu law'. Today, Hindu law usually appears as a body of principles of 'personal' or family law embodied in statutes (many of them passed by independent India) and associated case law. 'Muslim law' consists of rules on the same subject matter but the difference is that, for political reasons, there has been no codification of this law, the greater part of it remaining to be found in cases. The courts that interpret and apply Hindu and Muslim law are the ordinary Indian courts. So 'Hindu' and 'Muslim' or 'Islamic' law have, in formal terms, become simply sets of principles dealing with matters such as marriage, inheritance and adoption. From this perspective, Hindu and Muslim laws are two among many classificatory subjects of law within the overall legal system of the state and are thus analogous, say, to criminal law or the law of contract. The relative impact of this Hindu and Muslim law is often seen to be shrinking as other areas of law, concerning direct foreign investment, for example, proliferate and develop greater significance.

It is now commonly accepted that the British transformed and—this is perhaps more controversial—substantially degraded Hindu and Muslim law in India, and that this process was considerably furthered by post-Independence codification of Hindu law.[15] Whatever they were before the arrival of the British, Hindu and Muslim law were certainly not a limited set of substantive laws within a far wider state legal order. This said, there is now a stirring of argument to the effect that Muslim and particularly Hindu law are no longer to be seen as mere historical relics. Hindu law, it is argued, is now rising from the ashes of the legal holocaust that was Anglo-Indian law.[16] So one recent work argues at great length that Hindu law is currently undergoing a vigorous 'postmodern' revival.[17] While Menski endorses Derrett's position on the decline of Hindu law under the British and the early post-independence regimes, he suggests that over the last couple of decades, the Indian courts have been engaged in a little noticed reformation of Hindu law which has revived its relevance and utility. We will return to this proposition towards the end of this chapter.

Menski seemingly calls his own position 'postmodern' by virtue of his rejection of what he calls the 'positivism' and 'modernism' brought to bear upon Hindu law for centuries. His argument is that the colonial authorities and early postcolonial elites attempted to create a legal order under the state that was oblivious or contemptuous of practical differences in the customary law followed by different communities in India. The root fallacy underlying the British approach was a complete misunderstanding of the nature of Hindu law. That body of law was never comparable with law in the west. Contrary to what the British policy makers of the late eighteenth and nineteenth centuries thought, there were no 'codes' of law to be found in Hindu India. Manu, the presumptive author and eponymous title of the most celebrated text of Hindu law, was not a 'code' of law that was ever enforced in pre-colonial India.

Shorn of Menski's language of 'postmodernism', there is general agreement on this central proposition of his work. To borrow a memorable phrase from Robert Lingat, 'the classical legal system of India substitutes the notion of *authority* for that of legality'.[18] The great texts of Hinduism, including the Dharmasastras such as Manu, can be seen to have underpinned the idea of a Hindu legal order, but they did not represent textual codes to be enforced by courts. Lingat and others have argued that the highly variable custom of different communities must have been a more fertile source of social rules than were the great texts. Lingat tries to link these disparate sources (text and custom) in the following summary:

> This conception would have ended in a complete divorce between reality and law, had not the law revealed by the Sages been profoundly based in the traditions and aspirations of the Hindu world. It is careful to explain that wherever it cannot conquer custom remains queen. But custom's triumph by no means diminished the authority of the law. It can only fetter the application of the latter, perhaps only for a time. No rule is really legitimate and finally sanctified until it conforms to that law.[19]

So for Lingat, even highly variable custom derives its ultimate authority from the Hindu text.

Despite his agreement with scholars like Lingat as to the essential unenforceability of the Dharmasastras, Menski's account of the classical Hindu period is somewhat distinctive. He insists that the ideal form of Hindu law involves no external authority at all but consists wholly in self-regulation by individual Hindus. It is only with the breakdown of self-regulation that the morally inferior but more efficacious external legal authority needed to be constructed. For Lingat, by contrast, Hindu law only became truly 'law' once the commentators and digest makers of the medieval period had done their work sufficient for it to be enforced by the institutions of the state. Menski criticizes this approach as 'positivist', by which he means that Lingat has unwarrantedly conceived of law as essentially, indeed exclusively, a creature of the state. This criticism seems to have some validity to it, though Menski himself is sharply vulnerable to criticism that his own account of the classical Hindu approach leaves law completely undefined. If law is self-regulation according to principles derived from revelation and associated traditions, then where does law begin and end? How is law to be distinguished from religion or morality? There is no hint of an answer to these questions in Menski's work.

A different approach again is taken in some recent work by Donald R. Davis Jr. He takes issue with the proposition endorsed by Menski and others to the effect that Hindu law is an example of natural law thinking. In conformity with almost all recent approaches to Hindu law, Davis sees 'the Dharmsastra texts not as codes of black-letter law to be applied by judges'.[20] Rather, they are 'textbooks of materials, hypotheticals, and systematizations pertaining to a legal system'.[21] These materials must be accorded their full weight by the persons authorized to expound them—people trained in the Vedas, not judges—but there is no process of appealing to the authority of the Sastras over any principles applied in actual cases. So complete is the separation between the religious and moral precepts of the scriptures and the content of custom that Davis categorizes the Hindu system as one of legal positivism rather than natural law:

> Whereas natural law theory is concerned to maintain the superiority of natural law in the face of expedient concessions to social facts in the form of unjust laws, Hindu jurisprudence admits the superiority of social facts in the determination of *dharma* and law, despite any contravention of Vedic 'natural law'. This is the essence of legal positivism.[22]

There is

> legal recognition even of acts that violate rules of Dharmasastra, when those acts have already been accomplished in fact. Part of the legal interpretation here involves taking certain rules as advisory 'oughts' rather than mandatory 'musts'.[23]

Inevitably, Davis faces the objection that the language of legal positivism sits poorly with the unquestionable moral authority of the Dharmasastras within Hindu law. 'Hindu law' cannot exist as an idea or a putative legal system in the absence of the Sastras as ultimate authority within the system. On the other hand, Davis' invocation of the language of legal positivism makes dramatically clear how different the Indian scene was from medieval Christian thinking about the connection of human law and the law of God. He is clearly right to lay such heavy emphasis on the marvellous pragmatism of the Hindu legal system, a pragmatism which operated side-by-side with a powerful set of precepts to which everyone was rigorously subordinate. This is the point of Lingat's statement that the classical Hindu law embodies a conception of 'authority' rather than 'legality'. The core texts and principles of the Hindu order have unquestioned authority, but this does not mean they constitute a black-letter compendium to be applied by courts under the state or the great diversity of tribunals within civil society.

Whether blinded by their own legal tradition or out of deliberate concern to change India—both these outlooks are discernible on different issues and among different policy makers—the British approached Hindu law in a spirit quite alien to its previous development. They assumed that texts such as Manu were enforceable codes of law and set about appointing jurisconsults steeped in such texts to advise the British judges of 'the law' to apply in 'personal' matters that were to be governed by Hindu or Muslim law respectively. Eventually the courts were emboldened to dispense with their advisers and proceed to expound Hindu and Muslim law according to their own understandings. Not the least contradictory aspect of this enterprise was the building of a body of binding judicial precedents of Hindu law, an enterprise previously unknown to India.

But to repeat an observation stated rather than argued above, the material issues of litigation in colonial India were overwhelmingly matters to do with agricultural land. Such material disputes were presumably the context in which most matters of Hindu law arose—issues of inheritance, including adoption, for example—and they cannot have constituted a statistically large part of this litigation over land. In short, the actual impact of 'Hindu law' as manufactured and dispensed by the courts of British India was unlikely to have weighed very heavily on the people of India conceived as a whole. Again, this conclusion can be no more than stated baldly in the present context.

The Question of Customary Law

This short discussion of Hindu law may help frame the case of the dhobis of Behror discussed above. It is clear that the customs of the dhobis are far apart from the ideals enunciated in the Dharmasastras—the dhobis' practice of polygamy and positive endorsement of widow remarriage are examples of this. On the other hand, our discussion suggests that Hindu law left great scope for differentiation of social practice and the development of independent patterns of authority and dispute processing throughout Indian society. So it is not merely the modern Indian state that has been remarkably 'hands off' relative to social practice, but also 'Hindu law' itself.[24]

Thus far we have provided a single example of law-like activity outside the confines of the state, though we have insisted that the courts of the state have been preoccupied with a narrow range of material matters. We have foreshadowed trying to answer the question of whether any generalization can be attempted on the basis of the one case drawn from the dhobis of Behror. In fact, there has been remarkably little attempt to generalize about the whole world of law or legal authority in India. Louis Dumont, with his characteristic clarity and boldness, is an exception. Dumont sums up the situation of post-Independence India thus: 'Contemporary observation shows that there are three main organs of justice: the caste panchayat, the panchayat of the dominant caste, and the official courts'.[25]

Although he uses the term 'justice', it would seem that Dumont is treating this term as a synonym for 'legal authority' or even 'law'. This imprecision in nomenclature is common to those who try to analyse the operations of the legal instruments of the state, chiefly the courts, side-by-side with structures constituted by civil society.

In Dumont's account, the 'official courts' are sufficiently self-explanatory but the other two bodies need brief explication. 'Caste panchayat' is the decision-making council within an individual caste, of which there are many hundreds throughout India. In Dumont's conception the caste panchayat deals with matters internal to the caste and which are conceived to affect the interest or reputation of the caste.[26] Clearly Dumont would regard the dhobi case as an example of the caste panchayat at work.

'The dominant caste' is a term invented in the 1950s by the sociologist M.N. Srinivas, who argued from fieldwork in southern India that there were certain castes that were 'dominant' mainly by virtue of their 'preponderant economic and political power'.[27] For Dumont, it was control of land by a particular caste that was the sole constituent of 'dominance'.[28] This dominance reproduced at the local level the pre-colonial dominance of the king over a more extensive level of territory. While the power of the king has been taken over by the Indian state, the dominant caste retains power in the village. So, in a conceptual and partly practical sense, the dominant landholding communities were and are the 'kings' of their villages. Their power includes the capacity to dispense a certain amount of 'justice': 'the notables of the dominant caste are often entrusted with the arbitration of differences in other castes or between different castes, and they can exact penalties for unimportant offences.'[29]

This is not the place to subject Dumont's argument to close analysis, though it can be said that the schema is outdated (in relation to the idea of the dominant caste) and also insufficiently subtle or complete to be readily accepted.[30] What remains helpful about Dumont's outline is that it points us firmly towards a conception of legal authority in India that is plural rather than unitary; that is part local and part more territorially extensive; and that is composed of institutions and structures that arise both from the state and within civil society. To this complexity we will need to add the fact of historical and to some extent continuing influences exerted by the Hindu and Muslim legal systems.

What is also useful in Dumont's scheme is his avoidance of the term 'customary law' or even 'custom', since my own view is that these concepts often distort, more than they illuminate, the study of Indian society and law. True, this is not always so. Thus there would be no obvious distortion of the dhobis' case to describe it as 'customary law' in operation. I have already stated that the process in that case had all the marks of 'legal' or 'judicial' process if one leaves aside the fact that it proceeded completely outside the institutions of the state. And it is clear that the decision-making body was 'customary' or 'traditional' in its makeup. Moreover, what was in issue was the apparent 'custom' of compensation being paid by the family of a bridegroom who sought to marry a widow. Where the participants differed was over who was the proper recipient of the compensation. But even in this case there was no readily available body of substantive 'customary law' that could answer the question at issue. Rather, the decision-makers fashioned a judgment of considerably creative jurisprudence. So even here we need to be careful about applying the label 'customary law' so as not to give the impression that there was a cut-and-dried body of principles available for simple application.

The Particular Case of Punjab

The heyday of Indian 'customary law' talk was the second half of the nineteenth century and it flourished particularly in relation to the province of Punjab, finally absorbed into British India in 1849. Punjab was the arena for a revived (from the early decades of the century) contest between the conservative, Romantic and paternalistic school of British administrators and legal reformers influenced by the Utilitarianism of Bentham and James Mill.[31] It might be said that over India as a whole, the winner of this contest was the latter group, since Macaulay's Indian Penal Code was finally enacted in 1860 and a number of other law codes followed. But 'the Punjab system' of administration represented at least a partial victory for the conservatives, who were greatly concerned to prevent the disintegration of 'the village community'.[32] It was largely in relation to this latter concept that the discourse of 'customary law' developed.

Much later, in 1915, the then Lieutenant Governor of Punjab, Michael O'Dwyer, summed up the attitude to 'customary law' in Punjab thus:

> The problem before us in the Punjab is unique. Other Provinces in India have as a rule, the Dharma Shastras and the various commentaries on them for the Hindus and the Shariyat and the Hadis for the Muhammadans.... Here we have elected to be governed by custom. We have no body of feeling that condemns our tribal customs as a whole as antiquated or unsuitable. No desire for uniformity, no sense of injustice is involved in the maintenance of the existing system. Our function is therefore to uphold, not to destroy.[33]

The legislative basis of this election to recognize custom was the Punjab Laws Act (1872). The critical part was section 5:

> Decision in certain cases to be according to Native law.—In questions regarding succession, special property of females, betrothal, marriage,

divorce, dower, adoption, guardianship, minority, bastardy, family relations, wills, legacies, gifts, partitions, or any religious usage or institution,
the rule of decision shall be:

(a) any custom applicable to the parties concerned, which is not con-
    trary to justice, equity or good conscience, and has not been by
    this or any other enactment altered or abolished and has not been
    declared to be void by any competent authority;

(b) the Muhammadan law, in cases where the parties are Muham-
    madans, and the Hindu law, in cases where the parties are Hindus,
    except in so far as such law has been altered or abolished by legisla-
    tive enactment, or is opposed to the provisions of this Act, or has
    been modified by any such custom as is above referred to.

By virtue of this section, 'applicable' custom could trump the Hindu
and Muslim law as declared by the courts in other regions of India. This
was, on the face of it, a momentous change of legal approach for at
least this province. It maintained and provided firmer legal foundation
for an administrative and judicial approach that had already been pursued in Punjab for at least 20 years. Following the formal annexation of
Punjab to British India in 1849, Lord Dalhousie had issued a Despatch
in which he stated that as Governor-General he 'would wish to uphold
Native institutions and practices so far as they are consistent with the
distribution of justice to all classes....' But he also noted that with a
couple of exceptions 'there is no portion of the country which will not
be benefited by the gradual introduction of the British system at the
earliest possible period.... (T)hese directives may have been said to
have been the ultimate basis of the observance of customary law from
1849 to 1872.'[34]

Punjab was perhaps a particularly favourable case for the recognition of 'customary law'. More than for many parts of India, Punjab
could be seen as composed of what were termed 'tribes', albeit these
tribes were for the most part settled in villages and practising agriculture. Indeed, recognition of the customary law of the Punjabi villagers
proceeded mostly in relation to the principles by which *land* was either
shared out or held in common. This preoccupation with land simply
echoed the refrain of the British administration throughout India,
dependent as it was on the taxation of agriculture. But here, in Punjab,
the effort was to attend to the 'customary law' by which land was
managed. To this end, and as part of the land settlement operations,[35]

the official records were filled out with answers to a set of standard questions about matters such as inheritance rules (affecting women, including widows, for example), tenancy, admission of outsiders to the 'village community' (of landholders, not including tenants), principles for sharing the 'waste' land utilized for grazing and other purposes, rules for the rotation of crops, and so on. In addition to the material collected for individual villages (known as the *wajib-al urz*), a record of tribal customs that affected numbers of villages (called *riwaj-i am*) was also compiled.

This is not the place for a full consideration of the Punjab experiment in the recognition of customary law. What is relevant in the present context is a cluster of deep problems in the British encounter in Punjab. First, we can point to the simplistic and ultimately false notion of 'the village community' implicit in much of the British consideration of 'customary law' in Punjab. When the British administrators/scholars of the period talked in terms of 'the village community', they meant the landholders. These were the only people of regular interest to the administration, except in its criminal jurisdiction, since they were the people from whom land revenue (the principal form of taxation) was levied. Other communities often became virtually invisible in British accounts. A century later Dumont and other scholars rightly dismissed the notion of 'the village community' with its mute but nonetheless audible denial of differentiation, domination and subordination within the perhaps typically multi-caste villages of India. The 'village community' of British imagination was largely coterminous with the 'dominant caste' of post-independence anthropology, including that of Dumont. This left a great number of subordinate castes out of account, a statistical majority of the population.

There was also a deep contradiction in the British effort to enforce customary law through their own courts. If there were such a thing as customary law, then it must have been enforced by indigenous institutions (whether within civil society or 'the state') prior to the British arrival. Logically the British administrators of Punjab must have known this, but they wasted no effort in puzzling over any mechanisms by which this may have proceeded. There was a sound enough logic to this lack of official curiosity, since in policy terms the issue was irrelevant. The administration of Punjab was not qualitatively different from that elsewhere in British India; it was merely that in Punjab, the British

were prepared to recognize custom as the source of law regarding certain issues in their courts, as opposed to the hybrid Hindu and Muslim
law they recognized (and partly created) in the other provinces. But
from the perspective of society in Punjab, this studied ignorance of
the structures of customary lawmaking or enforcement (as opposed to
the substantive rules) made for a profound falsification of the whole
enterprise of 'customary law'.

The closest the British came to recognizing the problem of how
custom was created and sustained was in the debate on the merits of
codifying custom in Punjab. Following definitive recognition of custom
as a source of law in the Punjab Laws Act 1872, there was considerable
discussion as to whether the next appropriate step was codification.
C.L. Tupper, an official greatly influenced by Maine and his ideas of
evolutionary jurisprudence, was the most energetic promoter of codification. Tupper's view was that society in Punjab was not sufficiently
evolved to benefit from the systematic application of British law. In
order to sustain the prevailing custom he proposed that it be codified
where possible and that the code be admitted to the courts as a 'rebut-
table presumption'.[36] Such a measure would both preserve custom
and simplify the task of the courts. But this was not the view of the
then Lieutenant Governor of Punjab, Sir Robert Egerton. His views
were presented in a letter from the Secretary of the Government of
Punjab to the Government of India in 1881, and are worth quoting at
some length:

> [C]ustoms arose under a state of social life governed by many inter-
> dependent conditions. Tribal customs are appropriate, and should be
> enforced so long as the conditions remain unimpaired, and so long as
> they are suited to the expectations and views of justice of the members
> of the tribe; but the tendency of our administration is to dissolve the
> tribal bond and to give free scope to individual energy. New conditions
> are thus created and new expectations raised. The process is gradual,
> but sure; and though the Lieutenant-Governor does not desire to hasten
> the decay, he would not propose any measure which would prolong the
> existence of a custom for a longer time than is necessary to prevent the
> dislocation of the society which has been governed by it.... (D)irectly
> any attempt is made to legalize a custom, its virtue as a custom is lost....
> As soon as the impress of the Legislature is stamped upon such customs,
> they become to all intents and purposes unalterable records of a state of

things which may continue or may change, while a change in the body of substantive law thus formed is very difficult to effect without the pressure of an influence which a social revolution only could exercise.... Instead of codifying customary law, Sir Robert Egerton would prefer to leave the enforcement of it to the courts as at present.[37]

This passage offers two connected views of custom. First, Egerton makes clear that his and the British Government's overall preference was 'to dissolve the tribal bond' in favour of unleashing 'individual energy'. Tribal custom was therefore only to be tolerated as an interim measure. Connected to this was his view that codification of custom would freeze it, preventing its change unless it became quite grossly out of kilter with the present constitution of society.

The views of Egerton and others prevailed and the customs of Punjab were never formally codified, though codification was again seriously contemplated as late as 1915. On the other hand, a de facto form of codification gradually asserted itself through a standardization and homogenization of customs as they were recorded in villages and districts of Punjab.[38] And a companion standardization was asserted through the Chief Court of Punjab, which operated from 1866 until 1947. The Court's findings as to applicable custom became precedents for future cases, and inevitably what was created was a new Anglo-customary law for Punjab that paralleled the Anglo-Hindu and Anglo-Muhammadan law throughout India. Whatever customary law in Punjab might have been before the British, it must have been quite different from the creature of the British administration over a period of some 80 years.

This discussion of customary law in Punjab may seem something of an excursus but the reason for it is that this side of the Anglo-Indian law story has been considerably forgotten. And whatever the flaws in the British approach in Punjab, there was more than a kernel of validity in their discovery of customary law there. The British were clearly correct in their recognition that matters of what were called 'personal law' elsewhere in India were largely regulated by the communities of Punjab themselves. Of course, this was true not just for the land-holding communities that monopolized the attention of the British but presumably for all religious categories—Hindu, Sikh or Muslim—and for all castes or tribes.[39] To say this is not to suggest that the communities or the villages were self-governing 'little republics', in Metcalfe's famous phrase—this romantic British depiction left totally out of the account the habitual, not episodic, involvement of regional and even imperial rulers in the lives of the villages.[40] It also incorrectly conflated village and tribe or caste. And it ignored the profound influence exerted by Hindu and Muslim law. But what the Punjab materials do make clear is the plural ways in which authority was asserted prior to and even after the British arrival.

This is a convenient point at which to turn back to the questions posed after the discussion of the dhobis' case. I observed that there were few caste communities in Behror of 30 years ago still capable of taking up disputes within the community, as the dhobis had done in that case. If we put this observation alongside the discussion of the British treatment of customary law in Punjab, it seems clear that over time there has been a major decline in the capacity of communities to govern themselves (or, to use the other language encountered in the literature, administer 'justice' [Dumont's phrase], 'settle disputes', constitute 'juridical' authority,[41] dispense 'customary law', and so on). We lack evidence to verify Dumont's claim that authority in rural India was shared by three parties: the king (and later the courts introduced by the British), the dominant caste and the caste panchayats. It seems almost certain that Dumont has oversimplified a complex and fluid set of social arrangements across both region and time. But equally, Dumont seems to have generally been travelling in the right direction in his claims (albeit dressed as fact). At, say, the turn of the nineteenth century, the landholding communities of Punjab and most other places of India seem to have been what Srinivas and Dumont much later called the dominant castes, and such communities clearly exercised disproportionate power in the villages. To a considerable extent they governed themselves—the 'customary law' discovered by the British in Punjab comprised some of the understandings and processes whereby these dominant landholding castes managed their own affairs. The landholders also governed their subordinates to a large extent. Sometimes this latter power might well have amounted to 'juridical' authority, in Cohn's language. These same communities were often bolstered in their authority by connections with regional rulers, or kings; sometimes the two came from the same clan or lineage (or 'tribe', as the British tended to call such social formations). But these clans or dominant castes were not omnipotent, and they must often have left space for the inward-looking actions of caste panchayats, such as the dhobis of Behror.

By now, the patterns of social governance in rural India can no longer be epitomized with even approximate accuracy in the short-hand manner attempted by Dumont. To state somewhat baldly what I have argued in detail elsewhere, the dominants have largely lost the capacity to impose anything like 'juridical authority' on their subordinates in the countryside.[42] This does not mean that the dominants have totally lost their power. Rather, the relationships between the most powerful elements in the countryside and their dependents or subordinates have changed. In other words, the subordinates are no longer prepared to accept the domination they once had to. They may still be weak and dependent economically but they are citizens of a democracy with the right to vote. Political competition has often taken the place of oppressive domination. Among the many factors that have brought about change in the relationships in the countryside, perhaps this advent of democratic politics is the most significant.

Alongside the change in power relations between what Srinivas and Dumont called the dominant castes and their subordinates, there has been a prolonged and deep erosion of coherence within seemingly most of the multiple communities of the Indian countryside. Caste communities in the villages, whether dominant or subordinate, habitually report an inability to protect their norms through the imposition of punishments such as outcasteing. Only those at the very bottom of the hierarchy regularly show continuing coherence. This suggests that the example of the dhobis of Behror cannot now be generalized to any great extent. There has clearly been a significant growth of individualism brought about by factors such as temporary and permanent migration to towns and cities, increased education, the spread of mass media and film, the globalization of opportunity, and so on. But do all these changes amount to a complete destruction of the group basis of life in the Indian countryside? And what can we say about such issues in relation to the cities, which contain a fast growing proportion of the Indian population? This is what we need to turn to now, near the end of this chapter.

From 'Customary Law' to Legal Pluralism

The examples in this chapter have been directed to the development of an account of Indian law, authority or dispute settlement—these terms have largely been run together—that emphasizes the vitality of processes outside 'the state' (itself a problematic term in the Indian historical context). This is not because the importance of the official legal system of India is discounted here; it is the great legal system of Asia, and is becoming more significant all the time. Rather, I am concerned to try to locate what I take to be the particular genius of Indian society for authority, sometimes amounting to 'legal' or 'juridical' authority, to be constituted in civil society rather than by the state. But I have argued that some of the old patterns of coherence and group assertion within civil society have been weakening over time. We are certainly long past the time when it would be plausible to talk of rural India as marked by the rule of 'customary law'. *A fortiori*, presumably, the cities of India cannot be marked by the rule of custom. And yet it seems to me that there remains a profound current of group organization within many areas of Indian social and industrial life, including in the cities. With this perspective in mind I recently conducted some research, scarcely more than preliminary, into patterns of dispute processing in some diverse communities, mainly in Mumbai, but also in Delhi. It may be useful to say something about these inquiries.

The Palanpuri Diamond Merchants

One community I looked at was the diamond merchants. The diamond industry has been a considerable Indian success story over the last several decades. India now processes the overwhelming majority of the world's rough diamonds, and Indian traders have come to be leading players in the global diamond industry. The first Indians began trading in Amsterdam and Antwerp—the latter is still the most important trading centre in the world—as early as the 1930s, and they have now reportedly taken majority control of this trade away from other communities, chiefly Jews.[43] The leaders of the Indian diamond industry come overwhelmingly from one community of some 4,000 to 5,000 households of Jains in the village of Palanpuri in northern Gujarat.[44] These are the people who have come to dominate the Indian and now the whole world's manufacture (cutting and polishing) of diamonds. Latterly, they have leveraged this position into a majority share of the post-mining trade in diamonds.[45] The Palanpuris' success has been so great that by now they can no longer supply sufficient labour even for the trading and management level of the Indian industry, and this has opened up opportunities to others, including collaborators/competitors from Kathiawad in southern Gujarat.

The Palanpuris see themselves as a tight-knit community. They compete with each other during the day but have a common social life. Marital alliances between the richest Palanpuri families of the diamond industry are frequent. Their self-image is of a highly functional and ethical community, well able to regulate themselves through a pattern of mutual trust bolstered by the steadying hand of respected figures within the community. They attribute much of their success to this mutual confidence within the community. Naturally, on occasion disputes arise amongst the Palanpuris. There are many points at which such disputes can occur in the diamond trade: substitution of inferior diamonds can take place in physical exchanges; diamonds may be stolen or simply lost; insolvencies occur; and there are often questions as to price payable. Some of the disputes are common to just about all manufacturing and trading industries, whereas others arise from the particular nature of the diamond industry. Thus the physical circumstance of trading in tiny packets of immensely valuable stones leads to great potential opportunity for fraud and theft and, conversely, the demand for high levels of trust between the participants as an alternative to expensive and perhaps ineffective external security measures.

The Palanpuris pride themselves on usually keeping themselves out of court. They are by now quite professional in their dealings, taking care over the drafting of business documents such as approval memoranda and consignment notes. In the event of disputes arising, they are able to enlist pressures including fear of loss of face in order to bring recalcitrant disputants or malefactors to agreement. Given the smallness of the Palanpuri community, they are all specially dependent on retaining the trust of their fellows. This is said to act as a spur to reasonableness and compromise in disputes. On occasion, someone (always a man) respected both for his business credentials and as a community figure is enlisted as a third party to help resolve a dispute.

Such involvement does not usually take the form of an official third party. For example, in one case, a Palanpuri broker had lost a small packet of diamonds, worth some Rs 150,000, entrusted to him by a Palanpuri trader. This loss was accepted as a genuine misfortune. Although the small-scale broker was willing to make good most of the loss, he wanted to retain Rs 25,000 of his capital to enable him to carry on his livelihood. A respected Palanpuri diamond manufacturer was called in to assist in the settlement, and after some five hours of talk he was able to get the trader to propose the sum of Rs 125,000 compensation as if it was his own suggestion.

In another case a young Palanpuri trader had made significant losses and in an attempt to cover them, he lost more; he could only meet 25–30 per cent of the shortfall. The same business figure as in the case above was consulted, and he managed to get the creditors to see that the statement of remaining assets was genuine. While the trader agreed to sell his wife's ornaments and his house, the majority of the debt could still not be paid. This outcome was accepted by the creditors, not all of whom were Palanpuris.

In a third case involving the same business figure, one of his relatives came to propose that he mediate a dispute in which the relative was himself involved. The prospective third party agreed to assist, but told his relative that he would show him no favour. The relative went away and did not come back. This example was said to illustrate the standards of fairness and honesty that underpin the success of the Palanpuris' management of their business operations in India and now worldwide. The Palanpuris see their industry's standards as now under attack, since they do not see the Kathiawadis as possessing the same high standards of morality as they themselves have. The Kathiawadis were originally employed as diamond cutters, mere workers, and are said not to have attained high levels of education. This gathering diversity within the industry is seen as a challenge to the Palanpuris' preferred way of running affairs.

Of course, self-management of disputes within a particular business community is not peculiar to the Indian diamond industry; we know from Stewart Macaulay's early work on contract enforcement that informal dispute processing is the hallmark of much commercial organization even in the US.[46] And within the world diamond industry, there are more striking examples of self-management of disputes outside India. Thus, the diamond industry of New York is dominated by Orthodox Jews, and Richman notes that these traders 'have systematically rejected the court and state-created law to enforce contracts and police behaviour'.[47] Richman argues that the Jewish merchants of New York have been able to accomplish this despite the high value and portability of the products and also the preference of the trade for credit sales rather than simultaneous exchange. Both the latter circumstances would ordinarily tend to increase theft, fraud and general non-performance of contracts. The critical factor that has offset these temptations is the fear of loss of reputation within the Orthodox Jewish community. In a word, few of the participants in the diamond industry will risk the ostracism within their religious community that would result from any business malfeasance. There appear to be some points of convergence here with the conduct of the Palanpuri Jains.

Some Other Examples from Mumbai and Delhi

The Palanpuri diamond traders are only one among a number of Indian commercial groupings that can be seen to have made attempts to regulate their affairs with a firm eye towards avoiding the courts. For example, there is an active mercantile association among the traders in the wholesale cloth market in Delhi. This association elects office bearers (called *panchas*) and one of their principal tasks is to try to resolve disputes between the traders themselves and between traders and certain customers. There are particular incentives to keep commercial matters out of court, including an incentive that arises from the universal practice of keeping two sets of account books. While the motive for this (as in almost every country on earth) is tax avoidance, one of its by-products in India is to provide a powerful disincentive to going to court. Thus, typically at least, one of the parties cannot afford to produce to the court the evidence locked in different account books—to do so would invite the tax authorities to take action.

Within the association of cotton merchants of Maharashtra based in Mumbai, there are frequent exercises in conciliation and mediation rather than formal arbitration. Disputes can arise over the quality of cotton and the terms of the contract. Such disputes are particularly likely to arise in contracts for 'forwards' and futures, since there may well be a discrepancy between the quality of cotton sought and the quality delivered some time later. There are thousands of agricultural markets across the country at which cotton is sold, as well as smaller marketing centres. Sometimes it is necessary to go to a farm to verify quality. If a dispute does arise, it may be handled in different ways and with the intervention of different third parties. Sometimes the machinery of government—the District Officer (Collector), for example—is enlisted to help settle a dispute. But sometimes higher-level, more formal, dispute resolution within the merchants' association is necessary to sort the matter out.

If we turn from commercial organizations to residential communities in the large cities, it is possible to see similar patterns in village India. For example, in the Dharavi-Matunga Labour Camp complex of Mumbai (often dubbed the world's largest slum) there are communities that replicate caste communities elsewhere in India. Thus, there is a community of some 300 Valmiki or sweeper families in Dharavi, almost all of them originally from Haryana. Some of them have been in Mumbai for more than 50 years. What had led me to look at this community, and to mention it in the present context, was familiarity over many years with the relatively large Valmiki community of Behror, which is geographically close to the area in Haryana from which the Dharavi Valmikis have migrated. 35 years ago in Behror, the Valmikis had the most active caste panchayat of all the castes of the village. Their special motivation arose from their position as the ritually lowest caste in Behror and the ambition to try to improve their status. In Dharavi, the community has a *samiti* or organization comprised of elected (male only) *panchas* and some respected elders. This *samiti* is said to be active in resolving disputes within the community, as well as making representations regarding their living conditions within their oppressively crowded quarter.

The above examples of group organization and actual dispute settlement in urban India, mainly Mumbai, are no more than suggestive. What they suggest to me is continuing patterns of willingness, for various reasons, to organize in groups that to a highly variable extent are prepared and capable of intervening in conflicts within the group. Sometimes the basis of the group is what Geertz called primordial affiliation (the Palanpuris and the Valmikis fall into this category),[48] while at other times the primary basis seems to be a common industrial or commercial situation (the clothsellers of Delhi, the cotton merchants of Maharashtra and, again, the Palanpuri diamond merchants). The motivations of the groups are not always the same either, though desire to avoid the courts is strong among the commercial groups. It may be that these examples are no more than straws in the wind but I have raised them here because I have the impression that they may be connected with patterns of community organization that characterized village India in the past. True, a number of these examples are scarcely unique to India. But this does not of itself falsify the idea that the Indian situation is specially productive of a particular kind of group organization that involves the construction of patterns of authority or, sometimes, pathways to cooperation and compromise. It seems to me to be social structure and material self-interest rather than any psychology of abnegation that might account for such a propensity, if it exists.

Menski, Hindu Law and Legal Pluralism (or 'Customary Law'?)

In the earlier consideration of Hindu law, I foreshadowed returning to Menski's claim that something of a 'postmodern' reformation of Hindu law is at work in India today. Menski's argument is that there has been an effective judicial abandonment of the modernist vision most plainly stated in Article 44 of the Constitution, which looked towards the enactment of a uniform civil code for Indians of all communities and religious traditions. For Menski, enactment of such a code would have spelled the end of Hindu law. The code has not been enacted and conversely, from the late 1970s:

> Hindu law was increasingly reconstructed by an activist judiciary to revert to a more outrightly pluralist shape, emphasizing situation-specific justice over certainty of legal rules, and thereby giving new respect to Hindu law's customary plurality and internal diversity.[49]

From these beginnings a new hybrid postmodern law has gradually emerged, particularly from about 1988:

> Postmodern Hindu law remains at present characterized by the uneasy coexistence of official formal sources of state law and continued adherence to informal value systems which are extremely diverse, are anchored in religion, culture, and social reality, and may be instantly

called upon in situations where conflicts arise. In fact, before any matter goes to court, it may be resolved in the informal sphere. Formal recourse to law is neither the only, nor necessarily the most appropriate method of solving Hindu law disputes.[50]

In Menski's account, the gap between the world of formal state law and the pluralistic social world has increasingly been bridged by the courts. The judges have declined to impose the legislative Hindu law in a mechanistic, modernist, uniform way. They have attended to the specificity of social situation and, in the process, have crafted a far from consistent but more appropriate Hindu law. Menski argues that this postmodern process is proving more favourable to women than did the heedless modernism of the earlier legislative approach of the early post-independence period. In the development of this argument Menski sets his face firmly against the feminist proponents of a uniform civil code; their approach is seen as imported western modernism without useful relevance to Hindu India.

I am not in a position to evaluate the evidence Menski provides for his argument, since I have not read a number of the cases he relies upon. But if this evidence stands up to analysis, it might be said that the contemporary Indian courts are now implementing an evolved version of what the Chief Court of Punjab tried to do in relation to customary law from 1866 until 1947. If Menski's reading of the case law is correct, then the new approach may well represent an appropriate response to the great variability of Indian practices in matters of 'personal law'. One can only speculate on what might have happened if one of the parties in the dhobis' dispute had taken their case to a court operating in the way Menski says Indian courts now do. Would the court have been prepared to come to the same decision as the dhobis' panchayat did, including acceptance of the dhobis' polygamy (contrary to the Hindu Marriage Act (1955))? I am attracted to the idea of courts looking patiently and sympathetically at social practices that may be different from modern westernized norms in India, provided that they are not oppressive to women. To that extent, Menski's account of the present judicial approach is consistent with the emphasis in this chapter on the great plurality of legal sources in India both historically and today. Of course, such a judicial approach gives rise to the not so small problem of reconciliation with 'the rule of law'. Which legislative principles is an activist judiciary permitted to enforce, and which to ignore?

The field of 'personal law' in India might be specially productive of such dilemmas.

Conclusion

The drift of my argument in this chapter should now be evident. In broad terms, it seems to me that India is unusual for the variety and strength of efforts to manage disputes in civil society without recourse to the institutions of the state. This vitality of processes within civil society is not primarily a function of the weakness of the Indian state either historically or today. Rather, patterns of Indian social organization, ideology, culture, and the historical conception of law have provided a foundation for communities taking more responsibility for their own ordering than in most other societies.

At the centre of this argument is the historical construction of Hindu law. We have seen that there is something of a consensus among contemporary students of Hindu law to the effect that there was no historical demand that the Dharmasastras be enforced by rulers responsible for maintaining order and distributing justice. In short, Hindu India did not develop a body of substantive law fit even presumptively to be enforced in problem cases. And yet the Dharmasastras seem to have retained their authority in the face of countervailing custom as the standard of governance. Conceivably, this pragmatic separation of Dharmic rules and practical governance encouraged the widespread taking of responsibility within diverse social formations in India.

As usual, it is critical to distinguish the problem of maintaining order from the task of administering law or justice. It is true that the Hindu scriptures charge the one body, the king, with both these functions. And there is evidence to suggest that Indian rulers did sometimes dispense justice even to distant villagers as well as to people closer at hand. But any judicial function of the king seems to have been far less prominent than military and other activities associated with the maintenance of order. Given the non-enforceability of the Dharmasastras, this might suggest that India was a society only lightly touched by law. It could more specifically be argued that for the most part order was successfully maintained in India without recourse to law. These last two propositions might be maintained even if it were conceded that Indian civil society is marked by a high degree of self-management by diverse communities formed on the basis of tribe, caste, religion and industrial situation. But while these propositions are plausible enough, they are not subscribed to here. India seems to me to be a society highly imbued with law, in the dual sense of embodying a deep respect for the principles and beliefs underlying the social order and also in a respect for properly constituted authority. That these deep principles and beliefs may be as much 'religious' as 'legal' does not seem to me to falsify this statement.

I am aware that I am being vague as to the conception of law I am employing here. Such vagueness seems to be an almost inescapable result of rejecting a view of law as only constituted by the state. But this rejection does not mean I have also abandoned the idea of distinguishing, at least in principle, processes that embody 'law' or 'legal authority' from those that do not. I have suggested above that the dhobis' dispute had the markings of a law case, despite the non-involvement of the state in that case. On the other hand, the interventions of the third party in the diamond industry seem to have been too tentative and lacking in authority to suggest they had some kind of legal quality. In many instances it may be too difficult or too artificial to bother trying to distinguish the legal from the non-legal, but it seems to me that the principle of the distinction remains of some importance. From a related perspective I need to distinguish my own position from that of someone like Menski, whom I have criticized early in this essay for suggesting that self-rule according to revealed truths in the Hindu tradition can itself constitute 'law'. I would want to say that there has to be some kind of external authority for a 'legal' situation to be formed. But in the end I have to concede that we will not be able to agree on a tightly formulated conception of 'law' so late in the day. We can all agree that the Supreme Court of India is engaged in matters of law, but there will be no unanimity when we consider processes within Indian civil society. Invoking a conception of 'customary law' will not help us resolve this problem.

To sum up, the Indian legal system seems highly distinctive or 'Indian' from a number of perspectives.[51] The most fundamental difference argued here is that India has a rich civil society that has been specially productive of activities that have to do with 'legal' or perhaps 'juridical' authority. In India, both historically and today, the state has asserted less complete a legal dominance over society than in other political formations with highly developed legal systems. I want to suggest that the difference is not primarily an artefact of a weak state in India but of the converse, that is, a particularly strong society, in the sense of a society unusually productive of legal authority asserted in the name of community (or, rather, plural communities). The British 'discovery' of customary law in Punjab is the leading example of the colonial state's encounter with this phenomenon. Of course, the underlying British ambition in Punjab was to dissolve the groups that gave rise to 'law' or 'custom' and to substitute a modern, western individualism in their stead. To a great extent many of the nationalist elite both before and after independence have sympathized with this ambition, though this sympathy may now be waning.

My reading of some of the recent English literature on Hindu law suggests that long before the European entry into India, the particular nature of Hindu law may have facilitated the profusion and assertiveness of legal authority within what can loosely be called 'civil society'. I have drawn attention to Lingat's elegant summary of this argument, viz., that the classical legal system of India did not embody a conception of *legality* to which actions had to conform but that the authority of the sacred truths always retained their *authority*. This is said to have freed the king, the designated legal authority, from enforcing any particular dogma derived from the books. Perhaps, by extension, this conception of law also encouraged the kind of legal pluralism discussed in this chapter. But admittedly, these are little more than speculations.

Successive waves of external influence have obviously shaped the Indian legal order quite profoundly—the Aryans, the Mughals and then the British conquerors have left their deep impress upon India. The impress of the British is the latest and in our time by far the most salient of these influences. But the argument of this essay is that there is an Indian legal pluralism that goes considerably beyond the pluralism represented by successive invasions and colonialisms. On the other hand, it might be objected that what I am pointing to could be said to mark a number of other nations in Asia, Africa and perhaps Latin America, too. A number of nations in these regions have had layer upon layer of external legal systems imposed upon indigenous foundations. In so far as the latter foundations have survived, the composite legal order might be said to resemble the pluralistic Indian order I have tried to sketch here. But my argument can be limited to this proposition—I know of no other nation-state that possesses an official legal system as sophisticated as that of India and which is also composed of a civil society so marked by patterns of authority and dispute settlement constituted without reference to the state. In terms of the sophistication of its legal order, India demands comparison with perhaps only one other Asian nation, Japan, and even more with the developed nations of the west. My current understanding is that those nations do not possess the kind and degree of pluralistic vigour within civil society that I have argued to exist in India. Perhaps I should add the value judgment that this seems to me to be one of India's greatest strengths as a society.

Notes

1. Henry Maine's most celebrated work is *Ancient Law*, first published in 1861.
2. The best statement of this argument is Marc Galanter, 'Justice in Many Rooms: Courts, Private Ordering and Indigenous Law', *Journal of Legal Pluralism* 19 (1981), pp. 1–47.
3. The most developed argument to this effect is Oliver Mendelsohn, 'The Pathology of the Indian Legal System', *Modern Asian Studies* 15(4) (1981), pp. 822–63.
4. See the *Indian Christian Marriage Act* (1872); *Special Marriage Act* (1872); *Parsi Marriage and Divorce Act* (1865).
5. My informant was the head of the sole dhobi family in the village (the sub-district headquarters) of Behror and, indeed, the head of the whole community council covering a large number of villages. As the principal *panch* or elder he took the leading role in addressing this matter, the precise date of which is unclear.
6. Polygamy is unlawful in India but this does not mean that it is not practised among some communities, some of them Hindu.
7. Outcasteing involves a total exclusion of the affected person and their closest relatives from all contact with any member of the community—the outcaste is completely shunned, such that he cannot speak or eat with his community, and his children cannot marry within the community and therefore effectively at all.
8. Curiously, this Act was repealed after independence by the Hindu Widows' Remarriage (Repeal) Act 1983. See Werner Menski, *Hindu Law: Beyond Tradition and Modernity* (Delhi: Oxford University Press, 2003), pp. 176–7.

9. Menski, *Hindu Law*, pp. 374–426.

10. '*Panch*' is the Sanskrit word for 'five', and panchayat is a council of five or, less literally, simply a council. The place of *caste* justice more generally is discussed below.

11. The dhobis are a 'scheduled caste', an official designation given to the old untouchable castes. This quite small community is widely dispersed throughout northern India, mostly in rural areas (K.S. Singh, *The Scheduled Castes* [Delhi: Oxford University Press, 1993], pp. 442–53). Seemingly there are few large concentrations of dhobis; typically, and presumably because of their occupation as washer folk, individual families are located in villages where their customary work is valued. In Behror, unlike the other untouchable communities, the sole dhobi family lived in the middle rather than the outskirts of the settlement. This suggests that their status was more ambiguous and higher than that of the other untouchable castes. For a discussion of the history and contemporary status of untouchables, see Oliver Mendelsohn and Marika Vicziany, *The Untouchables: Subordination, Poverty and the State in Modern India* (Cambridge: Cambridge University Press, 1998).

12. Galanter's 'Justice in Many Rooms: Courts, Private Ordering and Indigenous Law' was the first of three widely cited articles of the 1980s that played a major part in establishing an almost counter-orthodoxy to the hitherto prevailing conception of law in the west as solely a creature of the state. The other articles were by J. Griffiths ('What Is Legal Pluralism?', *Journal of Legal Pluralism* (24)(1) [1986]) and S.E. Merry ('Legal Pluralism', *Law and Society Review* (22)(869) [1988]). It was no accident that these authors had all worked on non-western societies, in many of which the state was not so developed as in the west. The phrase 'legal pluralism' came to be a common identifier of this approach to the study of law, and it became an underpinning of much of the 'law and society' approach to studies conducted in universities in the United States and Europe. Recently, Roberts has been highly critical of the 'law is everywhere' approach to law studies, insisting that law must have something to do with 'government'. See Simon Roberts, 'After Government?: On Representing Law without the State', *Modern Law Review* 68(1) (2005), pp. 1–24. Against this, Griffiths has found the approach applicable to new phenomena in a globalizing world. See Anne Griffiths, 'Customary Law in a Transnational World: Legal Pluralism Revisited', Conference on Customary Law in Polynesia (12 October 2004). Clearly the debate over 'legal pluralism' and older conceptions, often somewhat dismissively lumped into the category 'legal positivism', has a long way to run.

13. I am aware that this is a rather sweeping statement. I should make clear that my proposition is based on a judgment, perhaps contestable, that the official legal system of India is more highly developed than that of other nations in Asia and Africa, a number of which may well have judicial processes outside the state that are broadly analogous to that of the dhobis of Behror. So what I am drawing attention to is the conjunction of a highly developed and sophisticated state legal system and these other processes. I return to this issue at the end of this chapter.

14. Upendra Baxi's *The Crisis of the Indian Legal System* (Delhi: Vikas, 1982) remains the most serious attempt to comprehend the variety of legal phenomena within India as well as discuss their limitations. There is an urgent need to return to the themes that Professor Baxi laid out in that work.

15. This view has been most thoroughly developed by Professor Duncan M. Derrett. See J.D.M. Derrett, *Religion, Law and the State in India* (London: Faber & Faber, 1968).

16. Primarily for reasons of space, only Hindu and not Muslim law will be considered in what follows.

17. Menski, *Hindu Law*.

18. Robert Lingat, *The Classical Law of India* (Berkeley: University of California Press, 1973), p. 258.

19. Ibid.

20. Donald R. Davis Jr, 'A Realist View of Hindu Law', *Ratio Juris* 19(3) (September 2006), p. 290.

21. Ibid.

22. Ibid., p. 295.

23. Rocher; cited in Davis, 'A Realist View of Hindu Law', p. 302.

24. Menski cites with approval an observation of Dhavan to the effect that the Dharmasastra was really a part of civil society and not the state. See Rajeev Dhavan, 'Dharmasastra and Modern Indian Society: A Preliminary Exploration', *Journal of the Indian Law Institute*, 34(4) (1992), pp. 515–40.

25. Louis Dumont, *Homo Hierarchicus: The Caste System and Its Implications* (Delhi: Vikas, 1970), p. 181.

26. Ibid., p. 179.

27. M.N. Srinivas, 'The Social System of a Mysore Village', in McKim Marriott (ed.), *Village India* (Chicago: University of Chicago Press, 1955), p. 18.

28. Dumont, *Homo Hierarchicus*, p. 162.

29. Ibid.

30. Oliver Mendelsohn, 'The Transformation of Authority in Rural India', *Modern Asian Studies*, 27(4) (1993), pp. 805–42.

31. The classic account of the contending British administrative schools of the nineteenth century is Eric Stokes's, *The English Utilitarians and India* (Oxford: Oxford University Press, 1959).

32. Dumont's article remains a marvellously acute discussion of the career of this concept in the hands of the British and, later, nationalist Indians. See his 'The "Village Community" from Munro to Maine', *Contributions to Indian Sociology*, 9 (December 1966), pp. 67–89.

33. Report on the Codification of Customary Law Conference, Lahore, 1915, p. 11; quoted in Minoti Chakrabarty-Kaul, *Common Lands and Customary Law: Institutional Change in North India over the Past Two Centuries* (Delhi: Oxford University Press, 1996), p. 212. I am grateful to the Workshop in Political Theory and Policy Analysis, Indiana University, for providing me with a copy of C.L. Tupper's edited volume, *Punjab Customary Law*, Vols 1, 2, and 3 (Calcutta: Government of India, 1881), and to Dr Minoti Chakrabarty-Kaul for putting me in touch with the Workshop about this rarely available source.

34. Tupper (ed.), *Punjab Customary Law*, Vols 1, 2, and 3, pp. 2, 3.

35. The 'settlement' was the single largest administrative operation carried out by the British provincial administration. Its fundamental objective was to fix the amount of 'land revenue' or land tax payable from villages, and to assign liability for its payment. This entailed compilation of a minute record of 'ownership', since it was from the 'owners' that the revenue was collected. These basic objectives tended to ramify into the recording of a range of other matters (such as rights to share in common lands) relevant to the taxation and management of villages.

36. Tupper (ed.), *Punjab Customary Law*, Vols 1, 2, and 3, p. 38.

37. Ibid., pp. 221–2.

38. Chakrabarty-Kaul, *Common Lands and Customary Law*, pp. 187–219.

39. I am not suggesting that Punjab was fundamentally different in these matters from the rest of India; almost certainly there were historical, ideological and institutional developments more than the distinctiveness of Punjab that accounted for the recognition of 'customary law' in Punjab and not elsewhere.

40. Sir Charles Metclafe, *Report from the Select Committee in the House of Commons, Evidence*, III, Revenue, Appendices (App. 84, 328ff.), (1830).

41. Bernard Cohn, 'Anthropological Notes on Disputes and Law in India', *American Anthropologist*, 67(6)(2) (1965); reprinted in *An Anthropologist among the Historians and Other Essays* (Delhi: Oxford University Press, 1987).

42. Mendelsohn, 'The Transformation of Authority in Rural India'.

43. Chidanand Rajghatta, 'Antwerp Diary', 12 parts, *The Times of India* (17 November–4 December 2004), http://timesofindia.indiatimes.com/articlesshow/939105.

44. Interview with a leading diamond manufacturer in Bombay on 25 November 2004. Given their now geographical spread, this concept of the Palanpuri 'household' may be problematical.

45. The world's largest centre for the cutting and polishing of diamonds is Surat. Presumably most of the workers, as opposed to the proprietors and traders, in this industry are not Palanpuris.

46. Stewart Macaulay, 'Non-Contractual Relations in Business: A Preliminary Study', *American Sociological Review* 28(1) (1963), pp. 55–67.

47. Barak D. Richman, 'How Community Institutions Create Economic Advantage: Jewish Diamond Merchants in New York', *Law and Social Inquiry*, 31(2), (Spring 2006), p. 1.

48. Clifford Geertz, *The Religion of Java* (Glencoe: The Free Press, 1960).

49. Menski, *Hindu Law*, p. 244.

50. Ibid., p. 266.

51. I have noted above that the present work does not consider the way the official legal system of India actually works—that is, the organization of the legal profession, the characteristics of the courts and litigation, and so on. It is clear from a study of these factors alone that the Indian legal system is highly distinctive. This essay has sought to look at rather deeper factors to try to answer the question posed in the title of this chapter.

3

THE TRANSFORMATION OF AUTHORITY IN RURAL INDIA*

Who or what constitutes the dominant power and/or authority in village India today? This sort of question is hardly ever amenable to any generally agreed answer for any society, and the Indian case is no exception. But to say this is already to have made a comment on the main stream of post-independence scholarship on agrarian India. Very soon after independence an academic orthodoxy hardened as to the character of agrarian social structure and power. The argument of this paper is that this orthodoxy is no longer valid and that it obscures what is a profound transformation in the character of agrarian India.

For a period of roughly a generation dating from the early 1950s, scholars drawn from both India and abroad set about providing a new picture of social life in rural India. Like earlier accounts of the British period, these post-independence studies were preoccupied with the phenomenon of caste. But there were also important departures, on both methodological and substantive levels. The new methodology

* A number of bodies have supported the research on which this work is based. My major institutional debt is to La Trobe University for the requisite leave and some travel assistance. The people who have helped in village-level research are too many to mention. When I began this work I was helped greatly by P.C. Mathur of the University of Rajasthan. In Behror D.P. Sharma and Late Rang Bahadur Mathur, among many others, gave me invaluable assistance. This chapter was originally published in *Modern Asian Studies*, 27(4) (1993), pp. 805–42.

consisted simply in systematic field-work conducted by live-in professional anthropologists, as opposed to the less rigorously empirical style
of British, other European and Indian scholarship in earlier periods.
The fruit of this empiricism was what seemed to be a substantially
fresh account of the structure of rural society.

The image of village India to emerge from the new anthropology
was one of systematic domination and subordination that had little to
do with the great books of Hinduism. Agrarian society was now seen
to be organized according to a predominant formula whereby a single
caste was in effective control of a village or cluster of villages. This idea
of the *dominant caste* was first expressed by M.N. Srinivas in 1955 and
it seemed to epitomize agrarian structure to many of the new generation of field-workers and their readers. Srinivas defined the dominant
caste thus:

> A caste may be said to be 'dominant' when it preponderates numeri-
> cally over the other castes, and when it wields preponderant economic
> and political power. A large and powerful caste group can more easily
> be dominant if its position in the local caste hierarchy is not too low.[1]

Four years later he qualified the definition in several ways that are
not relevant here, stripping away some of its precision while increasing
the likelihood of its fit to diverse village situations.[2] But later Louis
Dumont more than restored the original sharpness by insisting that
dominance consists solely in economic power rather than in factors like
numerical preponderance, and that this power flows exclusively from
control of land.[3]

The concept of the dominant caste was subjected to vigorous
criticism in the years after it was propounded, and manifestly there
are problems with it. Just one difficulty is the assumption of a single
corporate interest in the dominant caste. The presence of factions,
let alone different class elements, within any caste grouping tends
in practice to falsify this assumption. At best dominance could be
expressed only through certain men (not women) drawn from but not
necessarily representing the landowning caste.[4] A more fundamental
limitation is the observation that some villages do not possess even
a presumptive dominant caste; power is seen to be shared.[5] Despite
these problems and the undeniable limitations of the concept, it has
proved remarkably resilient and perhaps still represents something of

an orthodoxy. This vitality owes much to the rise and fall of intellectual styles (chiefly Marxist inspired class analysis) in more recent years, and thus the absence of any simple analytical substitute. Inasmuch as caste is obviously still an important aspect of agrarian social structure, so the idea of 'the dominant caste' has continued to exert some influence on social analysis.

My own view is that despite major methodological and practical problems, the concept of the dominant caste did refer to a central reality of village life. Perhaps Srinivas was not saying very much more than that village life in India tended to revolve around a single strong caste in the village or wider locality. But this was a particularly important thing to say at the time, since he was showing that the *varna* system was not descriptive of contemporary life in the villages. At a behavioural as opposed to ideological level, caste was demonstrated to be a local and not an all-Indian form of organization. The hierarchy of the *varna* system was not necessarily the local hierarchy in practice— neither the Brahmin nor the Kshatriya necessarily reigned supreme at the level of the village or somewhat wider locality. At the same time but in a different intellectual direction, Srinivas' account undercut romantic nineteenth-century British views of the village as a kind of self-sufficient, yeoman republic.[6] The later nationalist Indian version of this myth took the form of nostalgia for a supposed village *panchayat* or deliberative body in which everybody (or at least all men) took part. In the hands of Srinivas and other anthropologists of the mid-fifties, the village took shape as a far more hierarchical world.

The argument here is that by now the concept of the dominant caste obscures more than it illuminates agrarian social structure in India. *The contrary argument of this paper is that land and authority have been de-linked in village India and that this amounts to an historic, if non-revolutionary, transformation.* I do not mean to say that land no longer delivers economic, social and political power in India—clearly it does. The proposition is that this power is not nearly so overwhelming as it once was and that it fails to provide a base for the kind of authority which the local dominants once tended to possess. This is particularly notable in the field of juridical authority or dispute settlement, which is the major empirical focus of this paper. The change has seemingly been working itself through over a period of many years, but the pace has greatly quickened since independence. *So the suggestion is not that*

Srinivas was wrong when he articulated the idea of the dominant caste in 1955, but rather that he was identifying something at the very historical moment when it was disappearing or at least becoming less significant.

The departure from the order depicted by Srinivas and Dumont has not entailed a radical redistribution of property and power—it has been too gradual and partial to amount to this. Precisely because of its non-revolutionary character, the transformation has tended to be downplayed or not even recognized. The changes are as much cultural and political as economic, and they are difficult to sum up in phrases drawn from a scholarship which inevitably reflects modern western experience. Indeed, it may be still too soon to be able to sum up the transformation at all. But it is at least possible to identify the past, and the argument here is that the dominant caste belongs to that past. Everyone in village India knows this instinctively, as it were, but social science has been painfully slow to recognize it. This is partly because we are programmed to see another kind of transformation on the basis of class, which has not taken place—at least not so as to erase 'traditional' Indian structures like caste. A second reason is that very few researchers are nowadays doing sustained village studies.

A simple but important example can identify the suggested trans-formation. It must strike any careful observer that low caste and even untouchable villagers are now less beholden to their economic and ritual superiors than is suggested in older accounts.[7] It is only the degree and therefore significance of the change that can be in question. For example, for many years now there have been suggestions that untouchable women are less at the sexual beck-and-call of local mag-nates than they used to be. Whatever the deeper origins of this change, its immediate cause has been the resolve of untouchable communities to end a degrading practice. They have felt sufficiently emboldened relative to the high castes to assert their will in this matter, whereas in an earlier era they would have been frightened to do so. Similarly, untouchable boys who leave the village to study at college report that they no longer accord high caste men the same deference they were taught to practise—they are unlikely to squat in the dust while a high caste man perches on a *charpai*. These sometimes subtle changes in the attitudes and behaviour of those at the very bottom of the hier-archy illustrate a developing cultural transformation. At the same time, of course, the fact there are still magnates and untouchables also exemplifies the awesome inequality that persists in India. Whether one stresses the persistence or the change is a matter of context.

If there has been a significant stiffening of resistance on the part of untouchables as a general phenomenon throughout India, then this can only reflect a major change in the structure of authority. This is because the untouchables have been almost by definition the most subordinated group in the Indian countryside. In pointing to this change I am not making the mistake of assuming that untouchables were ever totally compliant and never resisted their masters with the aid of what James Scott has called 'the weapons of the weak'.[8] But what is at issue is a resistance which is both more resolute and more open than can generally have been the case before the suggested change.

The Structure of Juridical Authority in Village India

1. The Scheme According to Srinivas and Dumont

Srinivas, Dumont and a number of other anthropologists have tended to identify dominance chiefly by reference to a capacity to exercise *juridical authority*, do *justice* or bring about *dispute settlement*—the terms vary with the author. In his initial article on the subject, Srinivas notes in passing that 'members of the non-dominant castes may be abused, beaten, grossly underpaid, or their women required to gratify the sexual desires of the powerful men in the dominant caste'.[9] But for the rest, he concentrates almost exclusively on the matter of the dominant caste's role in dispute settlement.

Just why is there so much attention paid to a matter which is undeniably important but at the same time seemingly not a primary constitutive force in agrarian society? Certainly the focus must appear unsound to a Marxist trained to look first to the mode of production. The answer may be partly evidentiary or methodological in nature and partly more substantial. As to the first, moments of conflict and stress might be thought to reveal an underlying structure of control/order/power which is ordinarily not so visible. On this view, the disposition of problem cases provides the otherwise elusive evidence of patterns of dominance.

The more substantial reason for concentrating on disputes, formal processes like *panchayats*, and 'juridical authority', is that the capacity to impose one's will in situations of conflict is taken to represent the pinnacle of social dominance. Probably both these evidentiary and more substantial propositions are accepted by the writers examined here. What Dumont and the others seem to be identifying in the dominants is a capacity to make *law*, though they shrink from using this term. And presumably they regard this capacity as a property of only the most highly developed social authority. But while they seem to have an unspoken model of law in mind, they also seem to be identifying the source of *order* in the countryside. Now, *law* and *order* are not the same conceptual thing—it is possible to have law without order, and vice versa—though empirically it may sometimes be difficult to distinguish them.[10] But in the case of Srinivas, Dumont, Cohn and others, the implicit suggestion seems to be that there was/is a moral economy in which the source of order is a caste whose authority is ultimately legal or 'juridical' in its depth of dominance. In short, the two concepts are not adequately distinguished in this writing.

Srinivas claims that the dominant caste (1) characteristically settles disputes where both parties are from non-dominant castes; and (2) even frequently settles disputes where both parties are from one (non-dominant) caste, despite the seemingly orthodox procedure whereby a caste *panchayat* has authority to settle disputes internal to its own caste. Only the untouchables can be seen to make an effort to settle their disputes among themselves.[11] A similar view is painted by Cohn at about the same time.[12]

Dumont sets about creating a larger analytical scheme into which the authority of the dominant caste can be fitted: 'contemporary observation shows that there are three main organs of justice: the caste panchayat, the panchayat of the dominant caste, and the official courts'.[13] So Dumont is suggesting that 'justice' is dispensed by two kinds of caste organization and also the courts of the state. He wants to argue further that the same three sources supplied justice in the pre-British era too: 'the continuity between former royal justice and today's official justice should be pointed out. Whatever novelties were introduced by British justice, it was no novelty in so far as being official justice....'[14]

The dominant caste may not be, and usually will not be, the Brahmin or ritually highest caste. It is only where the Brahmins happen to control the land that this occurs. Land delivers economic and political power. And power yields authority too: 'just as the Brahmans have authority in religious matters, so the dominants have authority in judicial matters'.[15] Dumont does not elaborate on the translation of 'power' into 'authority', being content to note that the dominated recognize the authority of the dominants 'to the extent of having recourse to them to settle internal disputes'.[16]

The link between the village and the wider world in the pre-British era is through the dominant caste: 'the dominant caste to a greater or lesser extent reproduces the royal function on a smaller territorial scale...'[17] So the court of the king becomes, at the village level, the 'panchayat of the dominant caste'—there is often an institutional connexion between the two. Royal justice is thus organically linked to the justice of the dominant caste.

The third source of justice is the *panchayat* of individual castes, a body which has jurisdiction only over the members of the particular caste. The most notable penalty imposed by such *panchayats* is outcasteing or excommunication for wrongdoing which damages the reputation of the caste. But apart from this penal justice which looks outwards to the reputation of the caste as a whole, the caste *panchayat* will also dispense another kind of inward looking justice by conciliation and arbitration. The *panchayat* does this in order to 'reestablish harmony within the group and to maintain the authority of the panchayat'.[18]

Thus in Dumont's scheme caste authority operates both vertically or hierarchically and also horizontally among equals. Within any one village all but the dominant caste will be subject to two-fold authority—that of the dominants and that of their caste fellows. The dominants will be subject to only one authority, that of their caste fellows. Both groups will be subject to a third authority outside the village, that of the king and now the law of the state. And beyond this authority structure lies a parallel scheme of religious authority in which the Brahmin is supreme but does not necessarily hold sway in the world of affairs. The principal difference that the British arrival made to this structure was to substitute their official courts for the juridical authority of the king.

From what has already been said it will be apparent that these accounts of juridical authority are not accepted here. The basis of my position is fieldwork extending over almost 20 years in Behror, a village (now township) in Alwar District of Rajasthan, together with less intensive inquiries in various parts of India. These sources suggest quite a different picture of the structure of authority than the one presented by Srinivas, Dumont or a number of other anthropologists of the same generation. But first, it will be helpful to look at a couple of earlier case studies of a less theoretical nature than Dumont's work.

2. Two Village Studies—Devisar and Madhopur

(a) Devisar. The first of these studies is Chakravarti's account of a village in Jaipur District, published in 1975 and based on fieldwork done a decade earlier in 1964/65; this may be one of the very last whole village studies undertaken by an anthropologist.[19] Chakravarti's study is somewhat different from earlier village studies in its single-minded interest in the matter of changing authority relations within the village of Devisar. His effort is to show that the Rajput *phase* of Devisar is now in the past, replaced by more competitive political relations within the village. The watershed was the year 1954, when *jagirdari abolition* deprived the Rajputs of much of their land. Prior to this event, the concept of dominant caste was an 'adequate frame of reference' for understanding relations between dominant and non-dominant castes in the village, though it did not comprehend the totality of relations of power in Devisar. But after 1954 the concept is no longer a sufficient guide to the constitution of the village.

Jagirdari abolition in 1954 accomplished two things in Devisar. First, it redistributed landholding in the village. Prior to the redistribution the Rajputs owned over 84% of the village land but they now own only slightly more than 29%—they had lost over half the village, mainly to the cultivating castes of Jats, Kumavats and Ahirs.[20] Secondly, and increasingly over time, jagirdari abolition combined with the new statutory *panchayat* scheme to de-legitimate the *traditional* authority of the Rajputs and pave the way for acceptance of the legal authority of the Administration.[21] The greatest engine of change was the new, anti-traditional (and therefore anti-Rajput) political environment in Rajasthan which in effect forced itself upon the village of Devisar. This change in the external environment was amplified by certain local factors of leadership, thereby hastening the demise of Rajput power in the village.

Chakravarti does not seem to regard the actual loss of land by the Rajputs of Devisar as the primary condition for the destruction of their dominant status. What is emphasized far more than questions of local land structure is the ideological and general political environment outside the village and also leadership factors internal to the village.

Chakravarti is able to give a number of examples of Rajput authority during the period of their dominance prior to 1954; indeed, this work is richer in case studies of disputes or conflict than any of the other field studies. A number of the examples are of the Rajput landholders or *bhomias* 'upholding the traditional social order'.[22] In about 1928, for example, the Rajputs were successfully able to intervene in a dispute arising from the sexual liaison between a Brahmin widow and a Mahajan man.[23] Both had been excommunicated by their caste but the assistance of the *bhomias* was enlisted to bring about a resolution of the matter. In consultation with elders of both castes, the two paid a fine of Rs 151 and were readmitted to their caste. What was novel about this—though Chakravarti does not take it up—is that one might expect this problem to have been handled exclusively by the Brahmin and Mahajan caste *panchayats* sitting separately. After all, it was their members involved in a breach of caste rules. But apparently the authority of the Rajput *bhomias* was such that their help could be enlisted in what was conceivably a delicate set of negotiations involving two twice-born castes. Both Srinivas and Dumont had previously noted the occurrence of this sort of involvement of the dominants.

Chakravarti gives several other examples of this maintenance of 'the traditional order' by the Rajputs. In about 1924 an altercation arose out of a calf straying into fields where it did not belong, and it culminated in a blow to a Rajput struck by a fourteen year old Ahir. All of the *bhomias* met soon afterwards and some suggested that a fine of Rs 101 be levied on the miscreant for having dared to raise a hand against a *bhomia*. But in response to pleas about the youth of the offender, the matter was dropped. But the case shows that 'the beating of a *bhomia* by a non-Rajput was a serious enough issue to merit the consideration of all the *bhomias*'.[24] The second case in about 1954 was similar, except that it involved an untouchable. The dispute arose over the illicit milking of a couple of goats that belonged to a Raegar.[25] During the altercation a Rajput man lost his temper and struck one of the Raegars with a rake, whereupon the Raegar responded with a blow of his own. All the Raegars of the village were required to bow down in symbolic submission and apology before the father of the Rajput who had been slapped, and the father of the offending youth was fined eleven rupees. In a third case, in 1952 a Raegar was beaten and ultimately forced to remove the carcass of an animal belonging to a Brahmin for whom the Raegar traditionally performed this task. The Raegar was following a resolution of his community in refusing to perform the task but it was not for some years that the Raegars were able to make their resolution stick.

At this point we can interpolate a case collected by Kathleen Gough and reproduced by Cohn.[26] Cohn cites as an example of what he *calls juridical authority* this case wherein Brahmins castrated, beat to death and then hung a cowherd who had been for some time cohabiting with the young wife of an old and bedridden Brahmin. The violence was apparently precipitated by the cowherd having compounded his sin by using the front door of the Brahmin's house, contrary to caste rules. The killers were father and son neighbours of the wronged husband and there was further Brahmin involvement in the successful cover-up. Cohn is not explicit as to why he chooses to call this action *juridical* but the use seems to arise from the ritual aspect of the violence. The affair was a right-minded punishment for wrongs done to the whole dominant Brahmin community. What makes the term *juridical* stand out is that it would not ordinarily be applied to an angry and violent act entered into without deliberation of any formal kind and where the juridical authority is a party to the dispute rather than a third party. But clearly Cohn is trying to find language appropriate to describe the awful and self-righteous execution of their inferior by the dominant Brahmins.

If we return to Chakravarti's cases, we can see a similar problem of categorization. It may be true that the four cases are examples of the Rajput bhomias 'upholding the traditional social order'. But they can also be categorized in a different way. Thus cases two and three (the beatings) are of the same type if not the same seriousness as Kathleen Gough's case, *viz.*, members of the dominant and ritually purer caste angrily handing out punishment to a subordinate who has defied and hence defiled them. The far stronger reaction to the untouchable presumably reflects the greater insult in being beaten by such a person—

bad enough from an Ahir, far worse from an untouchable. In the fourth case the dominants may be less immediately interested in the outcome, since they are protecting the interest of a Brahmin rather than one of their own number. At the same time, the Rajputs must have been able to see that their own interests would be immediately infringed if the Raegars were allowed to stop their polluting work of removing dead animals. So arguably this case also concerns the interest—albeit the economic interest rather than the status—of the dominant Rajputs. And all three cases are analytically distinct from the first case, where the Rajputs are an invited third party authority in a dispute between two other castes.

Chakravarti is concentrating in these examples on the immense power of the Rajputs in old Devisar. This concentration has led him to ignore an obvious distinction between an authority voluntarily accepted and one that is imposed by physical force or other compulsion. Perhaps Chakravarty is assuming that in the old order in Devisar there was no meaningful distinction between direct force on the part of the Rajputs and seeming acceptance of their superior role by the subordinates. The argument might be that concepts of willingness or acceptance have no real meaning in an order built on local force, which is in turn buttressed by a shared Hindu ideology of hierarchy. Such an approach is essentially Weberian in its conception of the nature of *traditional* authority. It is also the general line taken by Dumont. While the view has considerable plausibility, its weakness is that it tends to pass over the outlook of the subordinates as opposed to the dominants. The Ahir and the Raegars were punished precisely because they returned blows or, in the carcass case, refused to do a polluting job which traditionally fell to them. In short, they were *resisting, rebelling,* or *challenging the authority* of the Rajputs.

Similarly in relation to the case described by Gough, we can agree with Cohn that through their gruesome violence the Brahmins were trying to affirm a traditional order in which they were supreme in a moral as well as political sense. But it is precisely this moral claim that the cowherd adulterer was denying when he came in by the front door of his Brahmin lover's house. He may not have been part of any organized resistance but he was clearly asserting a claim to some kind of social equality. *Authority* is a relational concept which seems to entail some underlying acceptance. It therefore seems one-sided to call the castration and murder an act of juridical authority. At the other extreme, Chakravarti's example of the Rajputs being invited to resolve the dispute between the Mahajans and Brahmins is a case where the term *juridical authority* appears appropriate. The middle position may be seen as those cases perhaps typical of the jajmani relationship, where the subordinate is obliged to attend to his/her patron's wants but where the compulsions fall short of, or are at least not invariably, gross physical force.

The foregoing discussion may seem artificial in its attempt to slice up and assign to different pigeon-holes the various relationships typical of agrarian life. But I am not trying to make some neat linguistic point. Today, throughout India, there are still cases of the kind cited by Gough and Chakravarti, whereby ritually inferior, most frequently untouchable, persons, are violently or humiliatingly subdued for daring to stand up to their superiors. What is now extremely difficult to find, however, is an example like Chakravarti's case of the Brahmin and Mahajan freely tolerating and perhaps inviting the authoritative intervention of their Rajput masters. Nor would one easily find an example such as that of the whole Raegar community agreeing without the production of naked force to bow down in symbolic submission and expiation for the (retaliatory) blow of an individual Raegar youth. These events depended on a pool of tradition which is no longer available to the dominants.

The *ancien régime* has died without a revolution because there was always rather less acceptance and more resistance than accounts like that of Dumont and Srinivas depicted. On the surface the principal change sometimes seems to lie in the psychology of the subordinates, the untouchables above all, and undoubtedly there have been important changes. But it is easy to exaggerate the degree of psychological subordination before the transformation. It is certain external changes which have intruded themselves and enabled significant breaks with the past.

The passage from dominance to post-dominance has been a gradual process, and this is the major difficulty with Chakravarti's work. It is simply implausible that Rajput dominance was perfectly intact until 1954, when it was suddenly destroyed by land reform and the injection of competitive politics. Chakravarti seems too wedded to a Weberian approach in which he is looking for a change from *traditional* authority to the authority of *the state*. In his telling, this transition did not take place until the integration of Jaipur State with the rest of independent India. He concedes that

> by the time of the abolition of *jagirs* in 1954 the village had already become in some degree integrated into the wider political society. But this did not result in any major change in the authority wielded by the *bhomias because both their authority and that of the princely state were traditional* (emphasis added).[27]

This argument is implausible for two reasons. First, it is artificial to distinguish the character of Jaipur State from that of British India on the ground that the former was *traditional* (because it was run by Rajput princes, presumably). Jaipur State was deeply penetrated by the British *raj*, to the extent that the basic nature of the bureaucratic apparatus was the same. And second, the incursion into the power of the dominant Rajputs is unlikely to have been simply and neatly a matter of power being taken up by *the state*.

(b) Madhopur. Among a number of Bernard Cohn's articles derived from his 1952/53 field work in Madhopur, a village near Banaras, is a work on the changing status of Chamars.[28] Cohn's contention is that these untouchable labourers were no longer quite so beholden to their Thakur masters as they once had been. The relationship between the two castes is an important test case, since the Rajputs' authority over the lowly untouchables exceeded their authority over any other caste. If that authority was slipping here, then *a fortiori* it was slipping in relation to all other castes.

Cohn fails to sum up the change in any simple way but I understand its essence to consist in a decline in the moral authority of the Thakurs, such that the Chamars are now increasingly concerned to govern themselves and raise their own status. So the relationship between the two groups is now weaker than it was previously. The change has been subtle rather than dramatic and the causes far from clear—factors of identification and cause are run together. What does stand out is that the Chamars have come to depend somewhat less on the Thakurs, particularly in an economic sense, while Thakur solidarity has simultaneously declined. Through moving out of the village for work, the Chamars have increasingly (though still only to a limited extent) been integrated into the wider economy. This temporary migration is not new—it has been going on for 100 and even 200 years—but during and after World War II the numbers have grown more rapidly. Their participation in various local and national elections since the 1920s has fed their political consciousness and made them more intolerant of their subordinate status. Ritually, they have been concerned to rid themselves of polluting and demeaning tasks and emulate the religious customs of higher castes. And they have been anxious to settle disputes among their number internally, without resort to the Thakurs.

On the side of the Thakurs, their capacity to impose their will on the non-dominants, including the Chamars, can be seen to have declined over a long period. The elaborate and formal Thakur *panchayat* for the *taluka* has disintegrated. Up to the nineteenth century this structure was crucial in dispensing authority in problem cases but thereafter it appears to have crumbled under the impact of competitive and otherwise destructive forces. One of the competing structures was the administrative hierarchy established by the British revenue administration and an overlapping police hierarchy. There was also an abortive early twentieth-century attempt to set up a statutory village *panchayat* system. And, of course, there were the courts established by the British; the first 'plague of lawsuits' began only in 1906: 'When people learned that there were outside legal agencies to which they could turn and which could enforce decisions through the official revenue and police administration, the traditional panchayats of the village and of the taluka began to wither'.[29] But Cohn is able to note that despite all of the signs of a weakening of Thakur control, 'most (Chamars) continue to identify their own interests closely with those of their Lords and of the *Thakurs* of Madhopur in general'.[30]

There is obviously considerable convergence between the observations of Cohn and Chakravarti. Both of them are writing about a decline in power of the Rajputs, traditionally the most powerful caste of North India. Where the accounts differ most clearly is in the relevant time-frame. Cohn studied Madhopur before *zamindari abolition* had made a substantial difference to Rajput landholding in Madhopur and amidst an early collapse in low caste solidarity in the new statutory *panchayats*. But he was already able to discern a substantial diminution in Rajput power which had been working itself through since at least the nineteenth century. It was in the earlier period that the Rajputs' solidarity started breaking down and rather later that the low castes began to take steps to increase their own power.

Cohn's approach is convincing despite his sketchy evidence for long-term Rajput decline in Madhopur. But while Chakravarti appears to have posited too sudden a collapse of the *ancien régime* of Devisar, he is no doubt right to have discerned a very sharp difference in social life after *jagirdari abolition* and the introduction of *panchayat raj*. Even where land reform did not entail the radical redistribution that it did in Devisar, post-independence social developments have generally been dramatic relative to change in the nineteenth or first half of the twentieth centuries. A number of institutions and facilities have played their part in this—the spread of schools, for example—but surely the single most important factor has been the rapid penetration of electoral politics. The moral economy of the old order was nothing less than delegitimated by the individualist ideology of representative democracy. Just how this has worked itself through has obviously varied but the direction of change has been the same.

3. The Ahirs of Behror as a Non-Dominant Caste

In the village of Behror and over much of the whole *block*, the dominant landholding caste are the Ahirs. M.F. O'Dwyer's Settlement of 1901 makes clear that this pattern has prevailed for at least the last 150 years, and conceivably it could be many centuries older.[31] The Ahirs are now the proprietary tenants, in effect owners, of the great majority of lands under the village, though redistributive measures since independence have invested people from various other communities with small plots. But to know the land structure of Behror is not simultaneously to discover its political nature or its pattern of authority. The Ahirs do not *control* the village of Behror—it is comparatively easy to show this. What is far more difficult to develop is an alternative framework that makes sense of the social structure and process of Behror today. The reason is that Behror does not have any simple essence, just as a small contemporary township in America or England is unlikely to have such an essence. Behror has become too complex to be crystallized with a simple analytical formula.

Behror is not an ideal example in an argument about the demise of old-style dominance, since there is no evidence to show that the

Ahirs ever possessed the degree of dominance identified by Srinivas or Dumont.[32] While this may limit the utility of this village study in an argument about change, my own understanding from many visits to other villages in the area (see below for one example) is that the present condition of Behror broadly conforms to the situation of those villages which did once approximate to the Srinivas/Dumont model. Behror can thus be used as an example to make some broader remarks about the structure of authority in village India today, and just how it differs from earlier periods. Moreover, the study of Behror was undertaken in terms not merely of its internal processes but also of the relation of those internal processes to the institutions of the state—chiefly, the courts and statutory *panchayats*. I will take up this perspective later in the paper.

It may be helpful to begin by specifying as a counter-factual, the kind of power that could be expected if the Ahirs of Behror were in fact dominant. First, individual Ahirs would presumably have power over the lives of their immediate retainers. This could be predicted to arise through patron–client ties, whereby the patron is entitled to goods and services in return for allowing the subordinate a designated share of the produce of his land. Secondly, there could be agreed policies among the Ahirs as to how to treat the other castes in particular matters. This could take the form of agreements or customs as to the entitlements of their dependent clients, and general policies calculated to entrench and ramify their superior status in relation to all the other castes of the village. And thirdly, the Ahirs might conceivably be the authority for subordinate castes when the latter are unable to resolve problems either within a single caste or between two or more castes. This situation is the distinctive form of triadic authority which Srinivas, Dumont, Cohn and the other anthropologists take to represent a particularly advanced dominant status.

Today, and as early as 1971, when I first encountered the village, the Ahirs of Behror do not possess any of this hypothetical power. Two interconnected explanations are offered here for the comparative weakness of the Ahirs relative to the model of the dominant caste. First, they lack the coherence and will to pretend to such status. Secondly, and more important, the social structure of the village has developed to a point where it would be impossible for the Ahirs to embody

old-style authority even if they had a mind to. This second aspect will
be examined first.

The most basic constraint on the Ahirs is their lack of sufficient
economic power to make the rest of the village inescapably dependent
on them. There are two aspects to the economic question. First, the
apparently traditional system of patron–client relations, usually called
jajmani, cannot be seen at work in contemporary Behror. This system
was first identified in the literature of social science by the Wisers' book
in 1930,[33] and has very widely been seen to have been the basis of
the non-monetary economy of the village whereby goods and services
were exchanged between different castes. Although a *jajman* or patron
was not necessarily a landholder—the Brahmin priest might serve the
lowly barber in return for services provided by the barber—it was the
dominant landholders who are said to have commanded the widest
and most intense array of services within the village.[34] In Behror today,
the landed Ahirs still receive goods and services from other castes
in return for an annual share of the crop from their land. But such
arrangements are no more than marginal to the overall economy of
the village. Most economic relationships between the Ahirs and other
villagers are strictly monetary in nature.

Secondly, and parallel to this, the villagers of Behror are now so
extensively engaged in economic activity outside the village that there
is no longer a discrete village economy remaining. A great many of the
workers of Behror are not now dependent on the Ahirs who control
the land because they find employment outside the village or even
within the village but not from the Ahirs. And without solid economic
domination built on the basis of land control, possession of authority
sufficient to resolve the disputes of subordinate castes is scarcely
conceivable.

Again, it has to be conceded that Behror is not typical in the degree
of its economic integration with the larger regional economy. The
settlement stands adjacent to the national highway linking Delhi and
Jaipur and, subsequent to my initial stay there, has developed a tourist
stop and major regional bus interchange. Even before this, it was a trading centre with a *kasbah*. Moreover, the reason I chose to study Behror
was its position as the subdivision centre and seat of magistrates' courts.
All of this brought a flow of outsiders and economic opportunities to

the people of Behror; it was never a backwater village. At the same time, Behror is not so much exceptional as more developed along a continuum that is characteristic of the whole surrounding region of northeastern Rajasthan and Haryana. The region is a 'green revolution' area whivh has seen the expansion of grain output, establishment of stone quarries, brick kilns, and small workshops of various kinds.

Every community has been affected by the rapid economic growth over the last quarter-century but this has no more than built on a foundation that was already well advanced. Take the Bhangis, for example, who are ritually the lowest community in Behror. In 1985 all but five of the 60 houses in the Bhangi colony were *pukka*—made out of brick and stone—whereas 20 years previously there was only one such house. This first brick house was built by a tailor, then the one Bhangi to have made a break with the traditional occupation of sweeping. By now the Bhangis have a long tradition of working outside the village. In 1985, 32 men were working outside the village—20 in Pune, 5 in Ambala, 3 in Delhi, 2 in Bombay, and 2 in Darjeeling. Some of the men had been working in Pune for more than 30 years. With the development of the bus stand the Bhangis have become local rickshaw pullers too; in 1985 15 men were carting goods and people to and from the stand.

Another untouchable community, the Dhanaks, had become so progressive by 1985 that all their men and most of their women had resolved to perform no more agricultural work, not even the financially rewarding task of harvesting. The reason is simply that such work is regarded as menial and beneath the dignity of a community bent on progress through education and the acquisition of 'service' positions. Only a small proportion of the community is currently employed in these desirable positions—in 1985 there were two teachers, two police-men, an office orderly and a *patwari*. Most of the Dhanak men are either skilled or unskilled construction workers. This manual employ-ment is not necessarily more lucrative than field labouring; indeed, at harvest the returns can be higher in the field. But there are perceived status distinctions which make construction a better option in lieu of the most preferred service positions.

A lessening of dependence on agricultural labour among many communities in Behror has gone hand-in-hand with a reduced need for such labour among the landholding castes. Nowadays non-family labour is sometimes needed only for the harvest. Ploughing tends to be done by tractor and is likely to be performed from within even a prosperous landholding family. So the retention of field-servants is now very rare among the Ahirs of Behror. If they need a labourer they will usually hire him or her on a daily basis.

At the higher end of the social scale in Behror, employment outside the village is even more marked and has a longer history. For example, the Brahmins have long ago moved out in large numbers into accountancy, clerical and teaching positions and into other 'respectable' occupations such as that of medical orderly in the army. The Brahmins of Behror have not on the whole been a wealthy community and their livelihood depends absolutely on achieving 'service' positions in the wider economy. They have tended to lose most of the usually quite small parcels of land they formerly controlled and therefore have nothing to fall back on.

The Ahirs too have long since raised their sights outside the village. As individuals and as a community, the Ahirs are becoming more ambitious all the time. Their sons and to a lesser extent their daughters too are expected to study, many of them at tertiary level. Professional, government, military or business occupations are almost a universal ambition and have already been taken up by many of the sons of the village. The community is fast erasing the gap between its own sophistication and that of the Brahmins, Banias and Kayasthas. There are now a number of Ahir commercial entrepreneurs operating trucking and bus lines, brick kilns, stone quarries and even a synthetic yarn mill. Most of these enterprises are centred on Behror and the area nearby but one family, for example, operates a trucking business in and out of Kathmandu. Poorer Ahirs have worked for at least a generation in the grain *mandis* of Punjab. The rate of pay for this work has always been relatively good but, just as important, the venue is far away from the village; for reasons of status, none but the most desperate Ahir will work in a paid labouring situation in the vicinity of Behror.

The connexion between Behror and the District town of Alwar has become increasingly close over the years. Daily bus, truck and even private vehicle traffic between the two settlements is intense. Many of the leading figures of Behror and the surrounding villages have established households in Alwar as a support for their increasingly urban ambitions. One step down from this urbanization, Behror itself has attracted a number of the Ahirs from smaller villages in the block. This is particularly true for Ahir lawyers practising in Behror; they have found it convenient and politically useful—they often have political ambitions—to establish a household in the sub-district head-quarters. All of this functional migration and urbanization is typical of many areas of India today, and again serves to blur the boundaries of 'the village'.

Nonetheless, it is still possible to find persisting examples of what looks like the 'traditional' economic life of Behror. There are still some more-or-less permanent relationships between individuals from service castes in Behror and their 'patrons'. Barbers will cut the hair and shave the beards of men in particular Ahir families and they will tend to be paid in kind for these services. Potters, too, tend to supply pots on a regular basis to particular families and this is sometimes done on an annual exchange basis rather than by monetary charge for individual transactions. On the other hand, the carpenters of Behror seem to operate in an ordinary contractual way. And in the case of the barbers and potters, their arrangements are not always limited to the Ahirs. The barbers in particular seem prepared to enter into permanent arrange-ments with any comparatively well-to-do family in Behror—Brahmins and Banias, for example. So the persistence of such arrangements is not really evidence of the continuing hold of *jajmani* relationships so much as the persistence of a mutually convenient alternative to charging and paying for individual services. Moreover, the two styles of doing busi-ness in fact coexist—the potters of Behror supply pots to individuals within Behror and also a number of surrounding villages on the basis of a charge per item too.

Even where something like the old *jajmani* relationship seems to persist, it has now diminished in intensity and is increasingly strained. Thus the barbers of Behror do not enjoy an easy relationship with their Ahir employers —they complain that the Ahirs are active in prevent-ing them getting ahead. There is probably nothing new in this but the difference is that the barbers are now prepared to talk freely about it and even to act against their employers' interests. Thus the barbers have drawn back by refusing to perform the ritually polluting task of removing the dirty plates at their employers' banquets. This ban is not special to the barbers of Behror but was enacted more than a quarter of a century ago at what was said to be an all-India meeting of barbers.

The penalty for breaching the ban or for having contact with someone who has breached it, is outcasteing. And some years prior to my stay in Behror one of the barbers of the village had in fact been outcasted by his fellows for having had contact with a man in the nearby town of Rewari, Haryana, who had himself been outcasted for performing the polluting task of cleaning up plates. What all of this tends to show is that the old relationship between the barbers and their patrons is increasingly fragile. Manifestly the Ahirs are not able to dominate their barbers in any thoroughgoing way.

All of the activity directed outside the village has had the effect of stripping away much of the old significance of village affairs to the more enterprising people in Behror. Among the Ahirs, their leading figures now display little interest in village issues. But the less than whole-hearted concern to dominate the village arises not merely from a lack of interest but also from a lack of coherence in the community. While the caste in Behror and more generally throughout North India has been highly ambitious and successful in the post-independence period, success has brought with it the atomization that now affects all the high caste communities of Behror and indeed India in general. On an everyday level there now seems very little point to caste solidarity. Factionalism was once believed to be the principal impediment to achievement of one-caste village dominance, but it now seems that a pragmatic individualism or at least family-centredness may be a still more fundamental barrier.

This lack of coherence can be seen partly in the fact that the Ahirs never meet as a community and no-one I spoke to was able to recall any such meeting in the past. Of course many of them gather for weddings and funerals but unlike some other castes, these occasions are not routinely used to hammer out agreements in disputes internal to the community. The only meetings attended by the Ahirs of Behror were whole District affairs held many years ago in the town of Alwar for the purpose of encouraging social advancement through ritual emulation of the high castes (Sanskritzation) and education. On a day-to-day basis, the Ahirs do not behave as a community and, even more, do not have any obvious community of interest. They behave as large, medium or small peasants, as small-to-medium commercial entrepreneurs, as teachers or army officers. It is too early to talk of *class* among the Ahirs of Behror but there is already considerable inequality based on occupational differentiation. Of course, it would be foolish to understate the importance of their personal identity as Ahirs. This caste identity remains fundamental to their being and is sustained by rules of endogamy and a myriad of cultural traditions. At the same time, it now appears unwarranted to treat this culture and psychology as dictating all the important associations and life choices of the Ahirs of Behror. Certainly, there is a decreasing willingness to accept authority in the person of elders of their caste community. A young man who has been educated to tertiary standard, for example, is now going to care little for the so-called authority of an elder who may be illiterate.

In these characteristics the Ahirs of Behror are scarcely unique, since all the high castes of the village are also similarly fragmented. The Brahmins, for example, never meet as a community. The last time they did meet was more than 40 years ago, to consider the affront of one of their men cohabiting with a Chamar woman. The man was duly outcasted and it was decreed that no Brahmin sit with him, that he not be invited to community functions, and that his children be denied marriage within the community. This state lasted some ten years, after which time the man finally made an apology and was readmitted to the community. Nowadays, a similar transgression could not be confronted in this same resolute way. The energies of the Brahmins have been directed away from the world of the village and also away from orthodoxy.

Another way of calling attention to the erosion of authority in the high caste, Ahir and some low caste communities is to talk in terms of a decline and subsequent disappearance of the *caste panchayat*. This second of Dumont's three sources of justice now fails to exist in any recognizable form for these communities. By contrast, they continue to play a role of some significance in a number of the low and particularly untouchable castes of Behror. By far the tightest and most active caste *panchayat* is that of the Bhangis. But the Bhangi tailor who is his community's most respected figure, can foresee that increased prosperity will soon erode the community's solidarity.

To return to the Ahirs, it can be seen that they lack solidarity sufficient to want or be able to resolve conflicts within their own community through any formal mechanism. Clearly this says something about the coherence of the community, though not sufficient to conclude that they totally lack the will to dominate others. But it has also been established that the capacity to dominate is now reduced by the development of a progressively more open and outward-looking economy, rather than the prevalence of patron–client, non-market relations. It is now quite beyond possibility that the Ahirs could act as arbitral authority in a dispute internal to or between members of other castes. All the time people are busy intervening in other people's disputes in Behror—sometimes even by invitation—but the Ahirs have no special status in such matters. Someone from a prosperous group who is at the same time generally regarded as a fair person, may possess unusual influence and may sometimes be approached as a third party in other people's disputes. In the nature of things, such a person might well be an Ahir—I came across one case where the Ahir MLA for Behror was drafted into such a role. But the third party in such a case is clearly something of a mediator rather than the judge of anthropological literature. And he will not necessarily be an Ahir.

It might be thought that the Ahirs would always have been a weak candidate for dominance by virtue of their relatively low ritual status. Most of the examples of dominant castes in the literature are twice-born—Rajputs are the favourite example for North India. But Kessinger has demonstrated a high degree of control in the hands of a Jat community in Punjab, and it is doubtful that the Ahirs are 'too low', in Srinivas' language, to acquire dominance.[35] Moreover, in the immediate vicinity of Behror, those villages that did once conform to the Srinivas model can be seen to have moved in the same direction as has Behror.

The village of Tasing, some 7 miles from Behror, is a good example. Tasing was the seat of four small *jagirs* covering some 12 villages prior to independence. The *jagirdars* were Rajputs of a different clan from that of the ruling clan of the State but the four families appear to have acquired effectively permanent tenure of the *jagirs*. The *jagirdars* are generally conceded to have exercised very considerable personal power over the villagers within their small *jagir* prior to independence, seemingly greater power than that of any Ahir in Behror. As usual, their power appears to have been greatest in relation to the invariably landless untouchables.

Jagirdari abolition stripped the Tasing Rajputs of much of their land and delivered it to Ahirs and other cultivating castes of the area. Loss of power in village affairs followed. In 1972 Rajput power in Tasing

was very far from the model of the *ancien régime*, though still closer to
that model than Ahir power in Behror. It was still possible to find some
residual Rajput involvement in the disputes of subordinates. Thus, like
their caste fellows in Behror, the Bhangis of Tasing tried to contain
internal disputes within their community. But if this proved impossible
or if one of the parties to the dispute was from another caste, they
were apparently still prepared in 1972 to seek the intervention of their
old *jagirdar*. It so happened, however, that the figure they sought out
was by then Sarpanch of the *gram panchayat*—he was thus part of the
modern as well as the old order. And his personal power was far greater
than that of the other ex-*jagirdars*—one of these complained loudly
and openly that nowadays he possessed no power: 'Not only do people
not consult me about disputes. They even call me a fool!' In the case
of the Sarpanch, his traditional status was clearly an additional source
of power. But without his statutory position, it seemed doubtful that
much of his old power would remain. I have not visited Tasing since
1972 but there can be no doubt that the vestiges of the old order have
further eroded in the intervening years. The reason is simple: there is
no longer any structural basis for Rajput dominance in Tasing.

　　If the landowning Ahirs of Behror lack the quality of power suggested by the literature of 'the dominant caste', just what is their position relative to the other castes of the village/township? To answer this
question one needs evidence of common action and, except during
elections, such evidence is difficult to find. I came across the odd assertion that Ahirs sought to impose their corporate will over others in
the village; for example, claims about suppression of the barbers are
reported above. And there is some evidence that the Ahirs as a group
of landholders have been active in seeking to prevent the redistribution
of government owned lands to landless persons, usually untouchables.
But these examples are not really central.

　　What is of central importance to the village is the common interest that many of the Ahirs have as farmers and employers. But these
interests look more like class than caste interests. Clearly the category
of employer is far wider than the boundaries of the Ahir caste in the
context of an outward-looking economy. And conversely, the Ahirs
are far from homogeneous—there are both employers and employed
persons among them. Even if it is appropriate to see the Ahirs as
having a largely common interest in keeping wages as low as possible,

the Ahir employers of Behror are only a fragment of a much larger labour market. The wage rates in Behror reflect rates prevailing in the larger region.

Beyond the common pursuit of cultural norms, caste consciousness and collective action are least ambiguously seen among the Ahirs during elections. Statutory *panchayat*, State Assembly and Lok Sabha elections bring caste tensions and even violence to Behror. In the words of a Brahmin 'social worker' (i.e., politician) of the village, the Ahirs want to win every seat that is open to them and this causes ill-feeling. The apparent contradiction of this ambition coexisting with an increasingly westernized, secular, even individualistic outlook demands explanation. What must be avoided is the assumption that there is a simple material interest of the caste at stake in elections. Often the only interest is in the sheer victory of their caste fellow. Whereas daily life makes no claim on caste solidarity because there are seldom any corporate caste interests, an election provides a competitive format which readily lends itself to caste rivalry of an almost atavistic kind. Every Ahir can feel personally gratified by the success of a caste fellow against an outsider—an election reproduces the competition that is part of the overall caste order.

The major political groupings have long since realized the advantages of fielding an Ahir candidate in the Rajasthan Assembly seat of Behror. Congress has been represented by an Ahir candidate in every Assembly election since their inception after independence. With the exception of 1985, they have won the seat every time. Since the early 1970s a grouping with some roots in the Lohia socialists of the 1950s has developed into a credible opposition force in the area, and its most successful representative has been an Ahir resident (though not native of) Behror. When Ramjilal Yadav stands in an election and Congress is represented by another Ahir, the caste factor is effectively neutralized. But he is powerless to deliver the Ahir votes which he can command for himself to a non-Ahir candidate he is supporting. Thus in the Assembly election of 1985 Ramjilal acted as a loyal Janata Party member and threw his support behind the Brahmin candidate of the Party. His Ahir followers refused to follow him. It was too much to vote for a Brahmin against a fellow Ahir turning out for Congress. Questions of ideology or personal faction gave way to straightforward caste feeling.

During its existence (ended by the advent of the municipality), the Ahirs did not dominate Behror's *gram panchayat*. In 1974 the caste composition of *panchs* elected from the 14 wards of the panchayat was Ahir 6, Brahmin 4, Bania 2 and Chamar 2. So the Ahirs just failed to constitute a majority, an outcome which closely parallels their share in the population of Behror. More important, the directly elected Sarpanch or head of the Behror panchayat was never an Ahir. The man who made this position almost a career was a Bania. He was able to take advantage of the fact that whatever the differences among them, the non-Ahirs are almost united in their opposition to the Ahirs in local elections.

The basis of this opposition varies to some extent with the different communities. The high caste Brahmins, Banias and Kayasthas tend to look down on the Ahirs as peasants who have pretensions above their true status and deserts. The attitude of low caste and untouchable people is more complicated. Basically, they have nothing to gain from the ascendancy of the Ahirs and possibly something to lose. Their general perception is that the Ahirs are happy to block improvements in their own position. And some of them look back to an earlier era of unpleasant domination by the Ahirs, though this is never well documented. The Ahirs of Behror are unlike many of their caste fellows across North India, in that they were not the subordinate tenants of high-caste proprietors. But they still have much in common with Ahirs elsewhere. They represent a predominantly middle-to-poor peasantry—in Bihar, for example, there are a great many poor Ahirs—who have been rising fast in the post-independence period. Their ambitions have tended to engender tensions among both those above and those beneath them in the rural hierarchy. Some of the political alignments hostile to the Ahirs of Behror reflect these same tensions.

This lengthy discussion of the character of Behror will scarcely be novel to those who are familiar with contemporary village India. Some of the tendencies which are now more mature in Behror were described as early as the mid-fifties in the works of Cohn,[36] F.G. Bailey[37] and, somewhat later, André Béteille,[38] to name several. But since more recent village accounts are rare, I have thought it useful to describe a village at a later stage of this process of change. What emerges from this discussion is a village where the landowning and most numerous caste is the principal political power without being dominant as this is understood in the literature of the dominant caste. It is my understanding that this is a very common situation throughout India, whatever the past character of the village. The particular focus of this paper has been on what Dumont calls the system of 'justice', and clearly there is nothing like the 'panchayat of the dominant caste' to be discerned in Behror today. Nor is it possible to sustain the more general proposition implicit in Dumont, Srinivas and others that the landowning caste is the source of *order* in the village: the political power of the Ahirs falls far short of this. The more limited justice dispensed by individual caste panchayats can still be found in Behror and sometimes it retains substantial importance for particular castes. But caste panchayats are confined to untouchables and a few other low castes, and they make little overall impact on village life.

4. Dominance in the Wider Context

If authority arising from sources outside the state has declined in Behror and elsewhere, then logically it would seem to follow that the void will have been filled by the state. There is indeed a good deal of evidence that this is the case. Certainly the state is a much larger presence in Behror than it was during the British period, and the same can be said generally throughout India. The welfare and development activities of the post-independence state have connected government officials and villagers in a far closer way than occurred during the British era. Statutory panchayats have been established to promote local development activities and to act as a form of local government in the physical settlement of the village. Other specifically judicial panchayats, often called *nyaya panchayats*, were established in order to provide the accessible and affordable justice which the regular courts were believed not to provide. And the intense world of electoral politics is obviously part of the apparatus of the state. Moreover, the police, as principal enforcement agency of the state, have been greatly strengthened following independence. All these developments have been part of the closer integration of village life into a larger political and administrative construct.

But we also need to be cautious about conceiving of the change as a transfer of authority from social formations outside the state to the institutions of the state. Despite the erosion of local authority, the state still exerts a relatively light presence in Behror. The courts, in particular, have declined rather than grown more formidable as a presence in Behror and generally throughout India. Put simply, there is a declining case-load. So there is no question of Dumont's third source of 'justice' picking up the slack created by the decline of village dominance.

This is not the place for any extended analysis of the sociology of the Indian court system, but a little needs to be said about the perhaps counter-intuitive decline of lawyer's law in village India. From their inception the courts were dominated by disputes over land, and a larger proportion of these were an artefact of the distinctive British interventions in land administration. Post-independence changes including *zamindari abolition* have served to reduce the number of disputes arising directly from land administration. To give only one example, rent suits in Bengal fell from an annual figure of over half-a-million in the 1940s to zero with *zamindari abolition* after independence. These rent suits were simply part of the zamindars' tactics to extract rent from their tenants, a portion of which was then passed on to the state as land revenue. When the state abolished the structure of revenue intermediaries, it took away the whole rationale of the rent suit: now the state collects the revenue directly from every landholder.[39]

In Behror there has not been the same decline in court usage, since there was never as high a resort to litigation in the first place: the region was settled on the more direct lines of Punjab rather than on the eastern *zamindari* model. But in Behror too, the structure of land-holding is now more settled than it has been since the intrusion of the British in the latter part of the nineteenth century, indeed probably more than it has ever been. So litigation and also criminal prosecution arising from disputes over land have declined. And there is no major new source of litigation in the countryside, in contradistinction to the cities. The ever growing bar of lawyers in Behror has to share a steadily declining quantum of litigation. Nor has judicial business been transferred to the statutory *nyaya panchayats*: in Behror and more widely, these have tended to fall into desuetude.[40] The courts and quasi-judicial institutions of the state can thus be said to represent a diminished rather than an enhanced presence at the very same time that the authority of the dominants has been declining.

Further, it is easy to exaggerate the separation between state and society. Locally powerful communities and persons can shape, sometimes dictate, the performance of institutions of the state. So the Ahirs of Behror and their counterparts throughout India have scarcely been displaced in any systematic way by the expansion of state institutions in the post-independence period. To give a simple example, the size and power of the police establishment have greatly increased over the last half-century; logically, this must have worked to increase state power at the expense of village autonomy. But notoriously in regions like Bihar and universally throughout India (indeed virtually anywhere in the world), the behaviour of the police proceeds in an intensely political context. Often the caste composition of the police force will reflect regional patterns of caste power, and this composition is bound to have some effect on police behaviour. So powerful caste communities have been able to adapt to the loss of local autonomy by influencing institutional behaviour at local or higher levels.

Beyond these questions of the nature and impact of the state apparatus, it is clearly a major distortion to think of the changes to agrarian structure only in narrowly institutional or even political terms. A major fault of much of the anthropological literature—this applies strongly to Dumont, for example—is that it fails to attend sufficiently to the structural impact of new economic forces. The discussion of employment in Behror together with a wealth of other writing shows that the force pushing/pulling people out of the village has frequently been the developing capitalist market. This force has proceeded under the umbrella of the modern state but it would be absurd to reduce it to the status of some kind of element of the state. Again, the precise impact of developing capitalist relations on agrarian structure is an empirical question. But clearly one effect has been to create a wider field of vision for both dominants and subordinates. In the case of Behror I have tried to show that the Ahirs have a dwindling interest in the affairs of the village, since their ambitions are now directed to advancement in the modern, urban sector and to political representation at levels higher than the councils of the village. On the other side, the subordinates have escaped some of the rigours of the old order by taking advantage of new economic opportunities outside the village.

If dominance at the village level has clearly waned in India, the leading castes have not so clearly lost their power at State and even national levels. In many of the States of Indian it is possible to locate one or sometimes several castes which tend to dominate politics and administration. The Lingayats and Vokkaligas of Karnataka fall into this category; so do the Nayars and, to some extent, the Ezhavas of Kerala; the Rajputs, Brahmins, Bhumihars and Kayasthas of Bihar; the Jats of Rajasthan and also Haryana; the Reddys and the Kammas of Andhra; and so on.[41] The nature of this new-style dominance and its relation to older forms needs to be clarified. Clearly there is a connexion between the two, since many of the castes which are now most prominent in State politics are the same castes which earlier exercised dominant power in many of the particular region's villages and which still own a high proportion of lands. But not all the castes named above were in this category: the Ezhavas, for example, can lay claim to have once been ritually untouchable, and certainly they were a poor community at the turn of the twentieth century. The Ezhavas prospered socially and later politically by virtue of their large numbers and an early attachment to advancement through modern education rather than from a base in landholding.

The Jats of Rajasthan, Punjab, Haryana and Uttar Pradesh represent a different case. In Rajasthan, Jats were very often the subordinate culti-vators of Rajputs during the princely period but after *jagirdari abolition* their economic position has improved greatly and they have become the State's most successful caste in terms of political representation. In Punjab, Haryana and in western U.P., the Jats' post-independence success has been built on what was already a stronger base than was prevalent in Rajasthan. In these regions Jat cultivators tend to have been recognized by the colonial authorities as proprietors rather than subordinate tenants under the intermediary system. In some instances their power was sufficient to qualify them as a 'dominant caste' within Srinivas' or Dumont's specifications.[42] Overall, their position can be seen as broadly comparable with that of the Ahirs of Behror.

In the small State of Haryana, Jats have come to dominate recent politics. But the more interesting case is that of the largest State of Uttar Pradesh. The greatest population of this State is located in the east-ern regions, where the two traditionally most powerful castes are the Thakurs (Rajputs) and the Brahmins. These castes dominated Congress Governments from 1952 to 1967.[43] But since 1967, a grouping of so-called backward castes, led for many years by Charan Singh, has been an alternative and sometimes governing political coalition. This grouping is more socially heterogeneous than its mixture of Gandhian and socialist ideology would sometimes suggest. The most powerful group within-what became the Janata coalition in 1977 was Charan Singh's own Jat community, which is neither high caste nor backward. Their occasional position as the principal political power of the State has by no means converted the Jats to the status of the dominant caste of Uttar Pradesh. The Thakurs and Brahmins are still far more powerful by virtue of their landholding—there are still very large individual parcels of land—and increasingly because of their position in the bureaucracy, the professions and business. Especially during the early days of independence but persisting to the present, they have won political representation disproportionate to their numbers. But equally, their position is now far less dominant than it was during the *zamindari* period, since they have had to make a good deal of room for the Jats and some of the backward castes.

The great variety of caste relations in the various States makes generalization difficult. But the U.P. example is more generally instructive in suggesting that once caste dominance has been lost at the village level, it cannot functionally be replaced at a higher political level. The Thakurs of U.P. turned in the fifties to the new electoral politics of India at the very time that they were losing control of village affairs. For a time the Thakurs and the Brahmins were able to exert a high level of dominance of the ruling Congress Party. But the period since 1967 has seen intense electoral competition among different parties drawing on different caste communities. The neighbouring State of Bihar has undergone a similar political transformation over a slightly later time frame, with an increasingly powerful opposition based on the so-called backward classes in continuous competition with the high caste dominated Congress Party. So while the once dominant local fragments of castes have adapted to the world of electoral politics through a process of aggregation on a whole State or even multi-State basis, their opposition has been doing the same thing.

This competition between parties drawing on different castes is not the only State pattern of politics—it does not adequately sum up the contemporary politics of Tamil Nadu, for example. What it also masks is the increasing power of commercial, industrial and administrative elites based in the cities of India and indeed internationally. These have social connections with caste groupings in the various regions but analytically they are increasingly distinct from them. The development of these urban elites has the effect of making the intense competition for resources between caste-based groupings at the State level seem of less central importance. Given the economic power, wealth and desired life-styles being built in the large centres, regional and village power tends to lose its attraction to those who can aspire to these. Attitudinal shifts of this kind have taken place first among the traditionally best educated and most mobile high caste communities but have quickly spread to the others communities. There can be no doubt that Indian life decreasingly revolves around the concerns of the agrarian scene, despite the continuing concentration of population there. And one of the effects of this development is to make the categories of class rather than caste increasingly relevant in social analysis.

To sum up, the decline of the dominant caste at the village level has been part of an economic, social and political integration of villages into larger units under the aegis of the modern state. This has not yet resulted in any tidy pattern of power or authority throughout India as a whole—the institutions of the state have not simply succeeded to functions previously discharged by the dominant caste. Nor can it be said that the apparatus of the state has been perfectly captured by the castes which were once dominant in the villages. It is true that these castes have often successfully organized at territorially more inclusive levels over the period since independence, but their success in the face of stiff competition has been far from invariable. They have had to compete with other caste coalitions while the competition itself has been downgraded by the increasing significance of the commercial, industrial and bureaucratic establishments. The once dominant castes supply many of the personnel for these modern organizations but the latter have taken on a life of their own in the context of world economic developments.

5. Juridical Authority in Historical Perspective

This essay is essentially about change and it therefore rests on the identification of states before and after the change. Earlier the idea of the dominant caste was endorsed as a general guide to the structure of power and/or authority in village India before the historical change, but no substantial evidence was offered in support of this endorsement. This was not an oversight but rather a postponement of what is a difficult exercise. Conclusive evidence of the decline of local and regional authority would need to include field observations across time and region. Even for the post-independence period such material is scanty, and there are only fragments available for earlier periods. Instead, for the pre-British period we have to make inferences from documentary and epigraphical material. If we read this material in the light of observations of the recent past made by Srinivas and others, it tends very broadly to confirm the dominant caste thesis.

Some of the most significant confirmation for the pre-British period comes from writing on the Mughal regime. The literature on Mughal administration suggests by way of negative inference that imperial reach into the villages was largely indirect. Moreland is probably correct in his claim that the Mughal administration was overwhelmingly directed to the production of revenue and the maintenance of military security.[44] A study of administrative and judicial officials—particularly the *amil, qazi, faujdar* and *kotwal*—leads to the conclusion that there was no systematic judicial presence in the countryside as opposed to the towns of Mughal India.[45] The *qazi*, in particular, fails to emerge as the free-ranging judge he is sometimes supposed to have been. Certainly, there was no regular bureaucratic hierarchy of courts during Mughal times. There was considerable judicial activity in the cities and at least occasional such action in serious criminal matters throughout the rural areas controlled by the Mughals. Disputes surrounding revenue collection seem to have frequently been addressed by revenue officials of the central authorities, but these interventions were never inflated into a great judicial enterprise. Unlike the British, the Mughals did not conflate the administrative problem of maximizing revenue with conceptual enquiries into the true and/or proper basis of land ownership in India.

The administrative picture of Mughal India needs to be set beside the view of agrarian life to be gained from accounts like those of Irfan Habib[46] and Nurul Hasan.[47] These establish quite convincingly that local and regional power was concentrated in what Habib calls *primary zamindars* (the *village zamindars* of the early British administration), who were marked by two characteristics: first, they tended to be drawn from particular castes or clans, such that there was often a monopoly of that caste/clan in a particular region. And secondly, they often possessed great military strength, which arose independent of the Mughal regime. So in the context of a minimalist central Mughal power, the idea of village control in the hands of the dominant caste becomes plausible. At the same time, this concept lacks the detail to be a model of a working system.

Cohn developed a somewhat parallel idea in his argument that the Banaras region was organized in the eighteenth century on the basis of 'the little kingdom' and that the operative unit for governance in the kingdom was generally the *taluka*. These *talukas* were constituted as revenue units of the larger administration of the Raja of Banaras but they were built on the basis of a unit of sociological significance: the *taluka* was in the control of a particular, usually Rajput, lineage, which had absolute control of land revenue assessment, taxation, police and judicial functions. Cohn's account is emphatic about the high degree of autonomy of the *taluka*.

While this formulation has greater specificity than a blanket claim about control by the dominant caste, it, too, lacks empirical detail. One of its problems is an assumption that there is a single corporate body within the *taluka*, whereas in practice there are likely to have been serious and endemic structural tensions between different levels of the controlling clan.[48] The clan members resident in a particular village may have had different histories and different interests than non-residents at structurally higher levels. Just who controlled the village and dispensed 'justice'—the resident Thakurs or the more powerful clansmen resident at sometimes distant centres? Questions like this demonstrate the deep imprecision of accounts such as that of Cohn. And even if Cohn's account is accurate in a schematic sense for Banaras, generalization from the Banaras model is hazardous.

Despite these various limitations of the material on agrarian authority in the Mughal and inter-regnum periods, the accounts are convincing as to the primarily local or regional character of this authority. Certainly it is no refutation to point to the many instances of intervention in village affairs, particularly about revenue matters, by officers of the imperial authorities. The argument about localism is one about broad tendencies, not invariability.

Some of the most illuminating recent writing on the pre-British period has concentrated on South India.[49] This work suggests that earlier historical accounts may be flawed. Thus Dirks conceives of his work as an engagement with Dumont, whose work is seen to be flawed by a profound Orientalism. Specifically Dirks objects to Dumont's emphasis on Brahmanism, and hence 'religion', within the caste order, at the expense of the political power of the king. Dirks wants to substitute a view of India which is less sacred and Oriental, more down to earth:

> It is my contention ... that until the emergence of British colonial rule in southern India the crown was not so hollow as it has generally been made out to be. Kings were not inferior to Brahmans; the political domain was not encompassed by a religious domain. State forms, while not fully assailable to western categories of the state, were powerful components in Indian Civilization. Indian society, indeed caste itself, was shaped by political struggles and processes.[50]

This debate is no doubt an important one but it exists alongside, rather than cuts across, the concerns of the present paper. Both Dirks and Ludden provide a wealth of material to illustrate the fundamental importance of caste in general and the dominant caste in particular, in the ordering of pre-British South India.[51] Thus Ludden talks about 'dominant caste domains' based on 'status, power and interests in land'.[52] The conception of 'dominant caste' employed by these writers is by-and-large the standard one that has so preoccupied thinking about India for almost 40 years now. Moreover, both these accounts are consciously built on the foundation of Cohn's concept of 'the little kingdom', a concept we have seen to be enmeshed with the idea of the dominant caste. So whatever challenge to orthodoxies the new history of the South represents, it builds on rather than challenges the idea of *dominant caste* as a crucial part of the Indian past.

If one follows Srinivas and Dumont, nothing much seems to have changed in the basic constitution of authority since Mughal times or the periods and regions discussed by Dirks and Ludden. Of the anthropologists who have concerned themselves with agrarian authority, only Cohn has sought to develop an historical perspective which points to a long-term erosion of local authority. But Cohn's field-work was done immediately after independence, at a time when he was no more than tentative about the decline of the local dominants. His remarks about the agents of change are only impressionistic and conjectural. Over the succeeding decades the surprising tenacity of the idea of *the dominant caste* and also the persistence of an opposition view that the concept never referred to a solid phenomenon have inhibited work on historical change in patterns of agrarian authority.

Two historical dividing lines can be seen to stand out in the decline of dominance: the arrival of the British and then the coming of independence in 1947. As to the first, the British eventually built a state apparatus that was both more extensive in its geographical reach and more intensive in its bureaucratic form than its predecessor regimes. In the context of the wider economic and social impact which gathered force from late in the nineteenth century, this state apparatus represented a threat to entrenched village power. Thus the establishment by the Anglo-Indian state of a much used judicial apparatus must have worked against the authority of local dominants. This is not as self-evident as it may seem, since the new courts of the *raj* did not compete directly with village dominants in most matters that came to their attention. The courts were overwhelmingly preoccupied with land matters, which had sometimes occupied the central authorities even during the Mughal period. But the institutional presence of the Collector in his administrative and judicial roles and the progressive expansion of the court system from the late nineteenth century can only have represented a challenge to local authority. The pacification of the countryside through the superiority of British arms and, mainly in the twentieth century, the development of a police force, were a more straightforward downgrading of local authority.

The indirect impact of the *raj* may have been scarcely less important in destabilizing local authority than the institutions of the state. The gradual blurring of the boundaries of the village economy; the nationalist movement against British rule; the campaigns for social reform, including the abolition of untouchability; the tentative steps towards electoral participation; the building of railways, roads and cities; these were some of the developments during the colonial period which helped break down local isolation. Indeed, it is less the decline than the persistence of local autonomy and dominance that demands explanation. So-called traditional life carried on largely because of limited British ambitions: the *raj* may not have been so minimalist as the Mughals, but its aims and institutional apparatus were far more modest than those of a modern European state or of post-independence India. Mass education, for example, was never an accomplishment or even an aim of the Anglo-Indian state. For many villages, contact with *sarkar* must have been minimal even at the end of the *raj*; this was particularly true in the *zamindari* areas, where land revenue collection was not a direct function of the state. The chief government presence in the Districts was the Collector, a combined revenue, general administrative and judicial figure. The legendary power and status of the Collector no doubt reflected the authoritarian nature of the *raj*, but it also said something about his institutional isolation out there in the District.

The pace of change has speeded up enormously since independence, the second of our two dividing lines. If the argument of this paper is accepted, then Srinivas identified the phenomenon of *the dominant caste* on the eve of its disintegration. That disintegration has been proceeding with remarkable speed when measured against the weight of history and tradition that kept the old order in place. Among the engines of change, central place must go to the competitive electoral process which has reached maturity in the post-independence period. The phenomenon of the dominant caste can scarcely coexist with serious elections premised on the concept of individualism. But there has also been the profoundly important impingement of capitalist relations onto the agrarian scene; the phenomenon of temporary migration to employment centres; the liberating force of education; the impact of radical ideology; and so on. Whatever the continuing force of purely ritual hierarchy, the old secular hierarchy of village power has not been able to withstand such erosion of its ground.

Conclusion

This paper has sought to identify some important changes in the structure of agrarian life which have been too little recognised in the literature of social science. In a word, the power of landholders has fallen quite dramatically relative to historical models and even relative to life in the early 1950s. Villages are now more closely integrated into larger economic and political units, and the quality of domination that was possible in an isolated village is not replicable in the wider world. This change has tended to strip power from groupings which are portrayed in influential anthropological literature as examples of a special category called *the dominant caste*. No such special category is now useful in agrarian analysis. The change has many of the outward characteristics of the European transition from feudalism to capitalism, though the difficulties with this analogy are such that it is not defended here. But even mention of the European parallel helps make the crucial observation that the collapse of the *ancien régime* of village India has not ushered in an era of equality. The reduction of local tyrannies does not necessarily entail the emergence of a whole social and political order significantly more attuned to the interests of the most subordinated Indians.

Notes

1. M.N. Srinivas, 'The Social System of a Mysore Village', in McKim Marriott (ed.), *Village India* (Chicago: University of Chicago Press, 1955), p. 8.
2. M.N. Srinivas, 'The Dominant Caste in Rampura', *American Anthropologist*, 61 (1959).
3. Louis Dumont, *Homo Hierarchicus* (Delhi: Vikas, 1970), pp. 161–2.
4. S.C. Dube, 'Caste Dominance and Factionalism', *Contributions to Indian Sociology (New Series)* No. 2 (December 1968), p. 59.
5. Bernard S. Cohn, 'Anthropological Notes on Disputes and Law in India', *American Anthropologist*, 67(6), Pt II (December), reprinted in Cohn, *An Anthropologist among the Historians and Other Essays* (Delhi: Oxford University Press, 1987).
6. C. Metcalfe, 'Minute', in *Report from Select Committee*, Evidence, III, Revenue, App. No. 84, 328ff (1832).
7. It scarcely seems necessary to document this observation. The theme comes through in innumerable conversations and interviews I have had over the years with untouchables and other persons in many different regions. See, for example, Oliver Mendelsohn, 'Life and Struggles in the Stone Quarries of India', *The Journal of Commonwealth and Comparative Politics*, 29(1) (1991), *passim*.
8. James C. Scott, *Weapons of the Weak. Everyday Forms of Peasant Resistance* (New Haven: Yale University Press, 1985).
9. M.N. Srinivas, 'The Social System of a Mysore Village', in McKim Marriott (ed.), *Village India* (Chicago: University of Chicago Press, 1955), p. 15.
10. Bronislaw Malinowski was the first anthropologist to argue a rigorous case for the existence of law in stateless societies, and his *Crime and Custom in Savage Society* (London: Routledge and Kegan Paul, 1926) was a crucial work in the development of a conception of legal pluralism. But it has long been objected that Malinowski was really trying to find the source of *order* in Trobriand society and that he assumed that whatever produced order must be called *law*. The argument is that despite his seeming lack

of ethno-centrism and his rejection of Maine's evolutionary legal history, Malinowski had not freed himself from a nineteenth-century positivist jurisprudence which assumed that order always arises from law.

11. M.N. Srinivas, 'The Dominant Caste in Rampura', *American Anthropologist*, 61 (1959), p. 8.

12. Bernard S. Cohn, 'The Changing Status of a Depressed Caste', in McKim Marriott (ed.), *Village India* (Chicago: University of Chicago Press, 1955), pp. 269–73.

13. Dumont, *Homo Hierarchicus*, p. 181.

14. Ibid., p. 169.

15. Ibid., p. 167.

16. Ibid., p. 182.

17. Ibid., p. 287.

18. Ibid., p. 180.

19. Anand Chakravarti, *Contradiction and Change—Emerging Patterns of Authority in a Rajasthan Village* (Delhi: Oxford University Press, 1975).

20. Ibid., p. 95.

21. Ibid., p. 191.

22. Ibid., p. 58.

23. Ibid., p. 61.

24. Ibid., pp. 58–9.

25. Ibid., p. 59.

26. Bernard S. Cohn, (1965/1987), 'Anthropological Notes on Disputes and Law in India', p. 87.

27. Chakravarti, *Contradiction and Change*, p. 67.

28. Bernard S. Cohn, 'The Changing Status of a Depressed Caste'.

29. Ibid., p. 66.

30. Ibid., p. 66.

31. From late in the nineteenth century the land administration of Alwar State was reorganized by British officials along the lines pursued in Punjab. So the object was to make peasants the primary landholders of the State, rather than to pursue the *zamindari* model of eastern India.

32. The only serious effort to write the history of a village is in Tom G. Kessinger, *Vilayatpur 1848–68* (New Delhi: Young Asia, 1979). Valuable though this study is, it is highly sketchy on the matter of juridical authority or dispute settlement. The basic problem in developing historical accounts of this is the absence of documentary materials.

33. W. Wiser and C.V. Wiser (1930/1963), *Behind Mud Walls* (Berkeley: University of California Press).

34. The first systematic account of the system is in W.H. Wiser, *The Hindu Jajmani System* (Lucknow: Lucknow Publishing House, 1936). Wiser is

concerned only with the reciprocity of the arrangements, not with questions of domination and subordination. Srinivas, on the other hand, talks
of *patrons* as members of the dominant caste. See Srinivas, 'The Dominant
Caste in Rampura'.

35. Kessinger, *Vilayatpur 1848–68*.
36. Cohn, 'The Changing Status of a Depressed Caste'; 'Anthropological
    Notes on Disputes and Law in India'.
37. F.G. Bailey, *Caste and the Economic Frontier* (Manchester: Manchester
    University Press, 1957).
38. André Béteille, *Caste, Class and Power* (Bombay: Oxford University Press,
    1965).
39. Oliver Mendelsohn, 'The Pathology of the Indian Legal System', *Modern
    Asian Studies*, Pt 4 (October 1981); reproduced in chapter 1 of this volume.
40. Ibid.
41. A recent two-volume set of studies edited by Frankel and Rao is devoted
    to consideration of the theme of dominance and its decline in the post-
    independence period. The evidence of decline is seen, of course, to be far
    from uniform across India. One of the weaknesses of the volumes is that
    they generally fail to take much notice of what has been happening in
    villages. The argument of the present paper suggests that evidence of the
    decline of dominance is far stronger at this level and that this perspective
    is crucial to an overall assessment of the problem. We are rightly past the
    era when village studies are seen to be *the* way of penetrating to the *real*
    India. But there is a danger that we are falling into the opposite trap of
    thinking that village studies tell us very little about the developing char-
    acter of India. See Francine R. Frankel and M.S.A. Rao (eds) (1989/1990),
    Dominance and State Power in Modern India. Vols I and II (Delhi: Oxford
    University Press).
42. Kessinger, *Vilayatpur 1848–68*.
43. Zoya Hasan, 'Patterns of Resilience and Change in Uttar Pradesh Politics',
    in Francine R. Frankel and M.S.A. Rao (eds), *Dominance and State Power
    in Modern India*. Vols I and II (Delhi: Oxford University Press, 1989),
    pp. 170–85.
44. W.H. Moreland, *India at the Death of Akbar* (London: Macmillan, 1920).
45. P. Saran, *The Provincial Government of the Mughals 1526–1658*, 2nd
    edition (London: Asia Publishing House, 1973).
46. Irfan Habib, *The Agrarian System of Moghul India* (New York: Asia
    Publishing House, 1963).
47. S. Nurul Hasan, 'Zamindars under the Mughals', in R.E. Frykenberg (ed.),
    Land Control and Social Structure in Indian History (Madison: University
    of Wisconsin Press, 1969).

48. Richard G. Fox, *Kin, Clan, Raja and Rule; State-Hinterland Relations in Preindustrial India* (Bombay: Oxford University Press, 1971), 1136ff.

49. See, for example, Nicholas B. Dirks, *The Hollow Crown: Ethnohistory of an Indian Kingdom* (Cambridge: Cambridge University Press, 1987); David Ludden, *Peasant History in South India* (Princeton: Princeton University Press, 1985); and Burton Stein, *Peasant State and Society in Medieval South India* (Delhi: Oxford University Press, 1980).

50. Dirks, *The Hollow Crown*, pp. 4–5.

51. Ludden, *Peasant History in South India*.

52. Ibid., p. 66.

4

THE QUESTION OF
THE 'HARIJAN ATROCITY'*

For thirty years after Independence the Untouchables were no more than a marginal issue in India. Then, almost immediately after the cessation of Indira Gandhi's Emergency in 1977, the matter of their connection with violence suddenly became the stuff of front-page news. A series of particularly gruesome 'Harijan atrocities' genuinely shocked national opinion makers. In the present context we need to ask whether these incidents, and the routinely high level of violence apparently suffered by Untouchables, is the summation of age-old subordination or whether it arises from a new consciousness and resistance on their part. In trying to answer these questions we are setting out to present just one more image, albeit an important one, of the contemporary condition of Untouchables. We should resist the temptation to see this violence as the distilled essence of the whole historical system of Untouchability. But at the same time, violence may be able to point us towards powerful currents moving beneath the surface of Indian life.

Reportage of violence done to Untouchables is a recent affair, as can be seen from the *Reports of the Commissioner for Scheduled Castes and Scheduled Tribes* (RCSCST). As the Constitutional authority

* This chapter is wholly the work of the author, and was originally published in Oliver Mendelsohn and Marika Vicziany, *The Untouchables: Subordination, Poverty and the State in Modern India* (Cambridge: Cambridge University Press, 1998), pp. 44–76.

charged with measuring the progress of the Scheduled Castes (Article 338), the Commissioner has been reporting on 'complaints' since the Sixth Report of 1956-7. In that Report the Commissioner provided six examples of what he considered to be justified complaints in the scant two pages he devoted to the topic. But he also included five cases where the facts were 'exaggerated and distorted', and with studied concern for impartiality he reported more generally on the difficulty of judging 'whether the complaints of harassment, etc., made to me are genuine or false'.[1] By the time of the twenty-first Report of 1971-3, perceptions had changed. The much larger complaints section was restyled 'Cases of Atrocities and Harassment', a nomenclature which seemed to fit mounting concern about violence done to Untouchables. In the variant form 'Harijan atrocity', this was a term that quickly slipped into the vernacular of Indian newspaper reportage and official documents as an omnibus identifier of the frequent violence suffered by Untouchables. Over the following two decades the term 'Harijan atrocity' became scarcely more emotive in impact than the language it replaced. The term was routinised and bureaucratised at a time when wider political developments suggested that India as a whole was an increasingly violent society and therefore that the Untouchables were not such exceptional victims. So despite occasional thunderings from politicians or bureaucrats, India, if not the Untouchables themselves, had learnt to live with 'Harijan atrocities'.

It is not easy to say just how prevalent such violence is, or what the trends are. The best run of figures is the annual survey published in the Commissioner's Report, and this shows a major increase in acts of violence over the years: typically there are now thousands of cases registered each year. But periodically the Reports also say that their own figures are not to be believed because of variable administrative and hence reporting regimes at the provincial level[2] and changing definitions of what is to be recorded as a 'Harijan atrocity'.[3] Another Report notes major deviations in the incidence of violence from year to year, 'if statistics relating to atrocities on Scheduled Castes and Scheduled Tribes are any indication'.[4] In short, it would be unwise to make any precise claims about incidence and trends.

This said, it is highly likely that the incidence of violence involving Untouchables has indeed increased significantly over the post-Independence period. Beyond the evidence represented by figures and the far greater reportage of such matters over the last two decades, this trend is suggested by the actual nature of the violence. This can be divided into two broad categories: first, 'traditional' violence; and secondly, that which flows from modern forms of resistance on the part of Untouchables or is a caste Hindu response to the changing situation of Untouchables. The second category is now dominant, and it tends to revolve around a new and still emerging social and political identity constructed over the period of the present century. Nowadays violence is by and large not being visited upon Dalits as totally passive victims, but rather comes about as a reaction to demands they are making or their uptake of benefits provided by the state.

'Traditional' Violence against Untouchables

Clearly violence against Untouchables is not a new phenomenon, despite the silence of the historical record. Their vulnerability arose partly from their utter dependence on their masters: it defies belief to think that a slave, for example, was always free from the physical wrath of a brutish master. The position of women must have been particularly weak, say, 200 years ago. Women were easy sexual prey, either in return for some inducement or through sheer force.[5] Continuing cases of abuse of Untouchable women have fuelled the campaigns for 'social respectability' waged by radical groups in regions like Bihar. Nowadays it is more likely that a 'traditional' act of violence like rape of an Untouchable woman will at least be reported to the authorities, though not necessarily pursued with any seriousness. Still, there are a disturbing number of references to exploitative liaisons and prostitution of Untouchable women in our own period. Very clearly, this will become a major focus of inquiry, debate and resistance in the years to come.[6]

It is possible to find other recent examples of 'traditional' violence against Untouchables. Thus there are reports of violence or at least force being applied to Untouchables on the basis of their association in the caste Hindu mind with the dark forces of life: they are taken to embody and have power over evil spirits. So in a village in the Saurashtra region of Gujarat State the people (presumably caste Hindus) believed that the Untouchables were the cause of disease being suffered by cattle of the village. They went in a mob to an Untouchable house and forced a woman and her daughter to go to the cattle and remove the curse upon them by stretching their hands over the beasts and eating an offering of coconut.[7]

Similarly, in a village in Saharsa District of Bihar a boy from a lower-caste family died of snake bite in August 1973. After the body was brought back from the hospital his family was persuaded that the tragedy had come about from the witchcraft of an aged Untouchable woman. Four women and the male head of an Untouchable family physically isolated from the other Untouchables of the village were dragged from their house to the home of the dead boy, and the women were ordered to chant *mantras* to bring the boy back to life. The women pleaded their ignorance of witchcraft and the furious caste Hindus stripped, kicked and beat them. When this produced no results, 'iron sickles were heated in front of the women and their feet, arms and other delicate parts were branded'.[8]

Whether or not there were contributing circumstances to these events, there is no doubt that a belief in the dark powers of Untouchables is an important aspect of folk culture throughout India. For example, in Maharashtra the Mahars are typically the guardians of Mariai, the goddess of cholera, and her shrine is located in their colony.[9] At times such Untouchable potency may work to offset customary oppression. For example, a survey of the practice of Untouchability conducted by the Commissioner for Scheduled Castes and Scheduled Tribes during the year 1958–9 (unsurprisingly) found that Untouchability was practised in the Siva temple of a suburban village of Azamgarh District, Uttar Pradesh: the Untouchables had to gain *darshan* from outside, and could offer money but not flowers or edible items. But this discrimination was relieved at certain times of the year: 'During the Dashahara and Bhagwati Puja, when the goddess is propitiated to ward off an epidemic like small-pox, no caste discrimination is observed'.[10] So the potency of Untouchables in warding off evil spirits gains them some temporary favour from custodians of the temple.

The importance of the above examples should not be minimised, not least because they provide a glimpse of an important dimension of caste Hindu attitudes towards the Untouchables. At the same time, and with the crucial exception of sexual assaults/coercion of women, we can say that most contemporary acts of violence against Untouchables should not be classified as 'traditional'. Rather, to repeat, they arise in the context of the new and still emerging identity of the Dalits. Sometimes violence is directly provoked by their claims, whereas at other times there is caste Hindu backlash against new government benefits or rising economic and status levels enjoyed by Untouchables. Perhaps most disturbing of all, there is abundant evidence of severe mistreatment and often violence visited upon Untouchables by the very government agencies supposed to protect them—notably the police. No doubt the poor have always been mistreated by the state—in this sense violence from this source could also be regarded as 'traditional'. But clearly the problem has been getting far worse as battle lines have been drawn by both rising and falling elements in civil society. The behaviour of state officials is directly linked to power relations in society at large.

If we concentrate on the demands of the Untouchables themselves, these can be discussed under two major headings: first, objections to discrimination arising from the practice of ritual Untouchability, together with more general claims to social respect, and secondly, claims to agricultural land, housing sites, and payment of statutory minimum wages. The second of these categories encompasses far more of the violent confrontations that have broken out in recent years. But the two categories have in common an attitude which can usefully be termed *resistance*. Sometimes the particular claims are made by individuals or groups acting outside any organised political context. At other times they are encouraged by political parties or even revolutionary organisations (the so-called Naxalites). The nature and context of the claims will become apparent through discussion of a number of concrete examples.

Violence Arising from Resistance to Ritual Untouchability

Removal of Dead Cattle

On the first occasion the Commissioner of Scheduled Castes and Scheduled Tribes discussed 'complaints', he reported that a 'Harijan' family was harassed and beaten because of 'their refusal to lift the dead cattle'.[11] We are not told anything more about the nature of the conflicts save that the people doing the harassment were Gujars and that local authorities took the case to court and that the accused 'were brought to book'. It is possible to flesh out this story from what we know about similar disputes, many of which have been detailed in official reports and press accounts over the years.

The Harijans referred to in the Report were probably Chamars, who represent the largest Untouchable caste in India (and the second largest caste overall, behind the Brahmins). The occupation of the Chamars, or their equivalents in other parts of India, includes the removal of carcasses of dead cattle and all dealing in hides, including skinning and tanning, and the fabrication of leather articles, such as shoes, saddles and leather buckets for wells. Some Chamars perform only particular elements of this broad occupational connection with leather: for example, particular Chamar sub-castes or at least occupational communities will work with finished leather but not engage in the lower-status activity of tanning. Some will remove the carcasses of camels and horses but not cattle, whereas other communities will do the reverse. But despite the overall identification of Chamars with hides and leather, this involvement represents a strictly minority occupation for them. Overwhelmingly the Chamars are agricultural labourers, often working for high-caste landholders for whom ploughing is a sin.[12]

Particular sub-castes or religious communities among the Chamars have foresworn all contact with hides or leather in order to try to increase the status of the group by ridding it of low-status activities which are the presumptive basis of Untouchability. But, of course, this leaves caste Hindus with a problem. Contact with dead cows is unthinkable to a high-caste person, and involvement with any other dead animals is scarcely much better. The animal is valuable for its meat and skin, but only if someone processes it. In the meantime, fallen animals will foul the air. So the violent incident mentioned by the Commissioner in his sixth Report begins to be more comprehensible. The Gujars are a peasant rather than high caste, but clearly they would not welcome the dilemma into which the local Chamars had thrust them.

Admittedly the above is not a simple case of the practice of ritual Untouchability. What is at issue is the cessation of a task which is the suggested basis of a particular community's ritual Untouchability. It could be argued that the Gujars are only seeking to enforce the traditional industrial order of the village. Who could easily be recruited to perform the task vacated by the Chamars? On the other hand, the case makes no sense outside the context of Untouchability: if the task did not involve ritual pollution, the Gujars would no doubt have been willing to do it themselves. While putting hand to plough is a sin for Brahmins, here we are dealing with a task that is rejected by all Hindus within the varna order. So it seems appropriate to regard the attempt to force the Chamars back to their job of carcass disposal as an effort to enforce the order of Untouchability.

Again and again, in different locations across India, the same issue has been fought throughout the present century. Chakravarti reports a case from his field-work village in Rajasthan.[13] A Raegar (closely related to the Chamars) refused to remove a fallen buffalo in 1952 in conformity with a decision of his caste fellows in the village and in the wider Jaipur region. This provoked a major crisis for the Rajput landholders of the village, and they delivered a heavy beating to the dissenting Raegar. He was forced to resume his traditional duty, and it was not until a couple of years later that the Raegars of the village managed to make their ban stick. In a village near Lucknow a case with the same essential ingredients resulted in a mass attack by some forty armed Ahirs; thirteen Untouchables were hospitalised.[14] The severity of this incident seemed to arise from a considerable history of tension over the issue. Even in West Bengal—supposedly free from ritual Untouchability today—it is possible to find reports of the very same conflicts.[15]

Access to Water

The question of access to water by Untouchables continues to be a source of discord and sometimes violent conflict. The Commissioner reported on a case from Gujarat in 1974 which involved the murder of two Untouchables and the injury of a number of others.[16] Water had dried up in the wells used by the Untouchables, so they had to take recourse to the common wells of the village. The Patels, presumably the dominant landholders of the villager, objected to this. The Dalits approached the authorities for assistance, and the police duly registered a case under the Untouchability Offences Act 1955. Two low-level policemen were also assigned to the village to keep the peace. But several weeks later the conflict broke out in earnest again, this time between women from the two communities. The Patel men were summoned and they obliged by beating up the police and then ransacking houses of the Dalits and severely beating a number of them, in two cases leading to death.

This case is by no means singular as an example of discrimination against Untouchables in the matter of access to common water sources. I.P. Desai's survey of villages in South Gujarat some twenty-five years ago found such discrimination to be the norm. But to a large extent it was masked by the widespread government policy (no doubt correct) of providing wells and taps within Untouchable settlements. The problem in the above case, of course, was that the Dalits' own wells had run dry. In the past they would have had to hang around waiting for caste Hindus to draw water and pour it into their buckets—no doubt the caste Hindus saw the extra work as a small price to pay (by women!) for perpetuating dominance—but clearly they were no longer prepared to do this. Given such a generational development of resistance on the part of Dalits, it is only massive efforts in sinking wells dedicated to Untouchables that have limited the violence.

Teashops

There are widespread reports of Untouchability continuing to be practised in teashops in various parts of India; clearly this problem is more likely to occur in villages or small towns where the identity of customers will be known.[17] One such case exploded into a major incident at the town of Hathras, Aligarh District of Uttar Pradesh, in May 1980. Five young men from the Valmiki (Bhangi or Sweeper) community 'who happened to be under the influence of drinks' asked for *lassi* (buttermilk) at a tea stall in the town. As was apparently the custom in the shop, they were served the drink in *kullarhs* or disposable earthenware pots. The men became angry at being served in this way and demanded that the drink be served in glasses. The issue quickly ignited into a major confrontation involving supporters of the Valmikis and the caste Hindu shopkeeper. Before the issue died down three days later, there had been vigorous stone throwing with attendant injuries, the burning of tens of houses of the Untouchables, strikes by Valmiki municipal sweepers and reciprocal *hartals* or closure of shops by caste Hindus. In the view of the investigating team sent out by the

Commissioner, the context of the incident was an Assembly election which inflamed a preexisting political conflict. The incident arose as 'a result of pre-planned political manoeuvrings and to some extent infightings between two groups of a political party'. Once the Assembly elections were over, the caste tension started receding.[18]

Assuming that the above judgment is correct, clearly the Valmikis had pressed the right button to provoke a conflict with their caste Hindu opponents. What they had done was nothing more than set aside the avoidance strategy that we have referred to as ubiquitous in contemporary India. The issue of Untouchability in the teashops of Hathras had been side-stepped by usually, though apparently not invariably, serving tea in disposable containers rather than reusable glasses (which it also had). By a simple device the shopkeepers had shrouded the question of Untouchability in a fog of ambiguity, apparently satisfying both Untouchables and caste Hindus. Clearly this was an advance over the past, when Untouchables would have been refused service altogether. But for once it did not suit the Untouchables to put up with the ambiguity, since they believed that it did in fact mask the persistence of discrimination on the basis of the ideology of Untouchability.

Marriage Processions

The reports are dotted with cases that seem peculiarly rooted in another era. Thus there are a number of violent incidents that arise from wedding processions. Violence has broken put in response to the assumption by Untouchables of traditions previously monopolised by caste Hindus, including the groom's riding of a white horse or being borne in a palanquin during wedding processions. The most serious report of this kind comes from the mountainous Almora District of Uttar Pradesh, an incident in which fourteen Untouchables were killed in May 1980.[19] It began when caste Hindus demanded that the groom dismount from the palanquin at the entrance to a village which lay on the path to the marriage party's destination. This was required, the caste Hindus said, to show reverence to the deity located in a temple at the other end of the village. A week earlier the very same situation had arisen, and the Untouchables had given in. But apparently this time the 'youths' were determined to press ahead. A scuffle broke out and one of the caste Hindus was stabbed to death. The infuriated caste Hindus regrouped and chased some of their opponents into a house, which was torched with the loss of six lives. Another eight Untouchables were stoned and clubbed to death.

The Commissioner's investigation was unable to make a conclusive determination between the rival accounts of village tradition. It was asserted by the Untouchables that they were being discriminated against *qua* Untouchables, and that there was no general policy that required the groom to dismount outside the village as opposed to in the immediate vicinity of the temple. They said they had every intention to dismount and offer prayer to the deity at the appropriate point in the procession. The alternative view from the caste Hindu side was that everyone, and not merely Untouchables, was obliged to dismount from a palanquin at the entrance to the village.[20] Whatever the truth of the matter, the Commissioner had no doubt that the affair was the outcome of 'caste animosities and hatred'. 'Some of the Scheduled Castes persons educated and living outside in places like Delhi have imbibed an urge to do away with all social discrimination'.[21]

This incident is revealing for several reasons. First, the incapacity of the Commissioner's investigators, albeit on a very short visit, to discern the 'truth' about conventional behaviour relative to the village deity is not surprising. This question would presumably have been overlaid with multiple and inconsistent perceptions among the different communities. We can assume that there was indeed discrimination in the village on the basis of Untouchability, though we have no knowledge of its form or its severity. Certainly we know as a general matter that where Untouchables stand, squat or ride relative to caste Hindus has always been a major point of division. Untouchables were by tradition obliged to be physically lower than caste Hindus if the two were in some proximity, and they can never have been allowed to ride in ceremonial style through a caste Hindu quarter.[22] As to the Untouchables' state of mind, it is quite plausible that their consciousness had been progressively transformed. Many of the Untouchables are said to have had experience in the world outside their remote region, particularly in the city of Delhi. In short, the Untouchables may have been becoming more militant. This may have predisposed them to believe that in the matter of wedding processions they were being subjected to discriminations that did not apply to the high-caste population. So even if it could be sustained that there was something of a convention among high-caste people that they did in fact dismount from a horse or palanquin well before coming to the temple, any Untouchable failure to observe this convention might not have been wilful.

Secondly, the sheer brutality of this incident is striking. How is the murder of so many Untouchables to be explained? Undoubtedly it has something to do with the event that a high-caste man had been killed before any Untouchables had been so dealt with. The thread of extravagant revenge runs through a number of the cases of multiple murders of Untouchables: it runs through the *Pipra* incident discussed below, for example. Revenge is not a difficult emotion to understand, but extravagant revenge has another element in its constitution. In the present case we need to explain the massing together of large numbers of high-caste men and their *premeditated* orgy of violence—the burning and the beating.

Mass violence in the Indian sub-continent is scarcely limited to attacks on Untouchables. The greatest recent scenes of uncontrolled carnage have been enacted in conflicts between Hindus and Muslims at the time of partition and even in post-partition India. Hindu–Muslim communalism and mass mobilisation against Untouchables spring from different sources, but what the two have in common is belief in the *otherness* of the object of their violence. This same sense is present in exacerbated racism, in whatever national or international context this presents itself. In India, such a sense goes some distance towards explaining the sheer passion that enables mobilisation of numbers of people and the willingness to exceed ordinary social bounds.

What is special to incidents like the Almora palanquin case or Belchi or Pipra is the outrage that is felt when those most lowly raise their heads—in the palanquin case, literally. It is bad enough when the Untouchables assert rights to equal treatment. But when they go so far as to spill the first blood, the sense of outraged hierarchy bursts its bounds. So the worst Harijan atrocity cases consist in large numbers of caste Hindus—sometimes many hundreds—pursuing Untouchables in vengeful retribution for a wrong, perhaps a death, done to one of them. Invariably in such cases, there is a great asymmetry between the organised caste Hindu mob—this is no spontaneous passion—and the terrified Untouchable rabble who flee before *force majeure*.

Land, Wages and Social Oppression

The most severe conflict of a routine kind that now involves Untouchables is over land. This phenomenon is a comparatively new development, predominantly confined to the last two decades. Sometimes the dispute is over ownership of land; more often it is over the level of wages paid to Untouchables for working the land. This issue in a sense brings the Untouchables into conformity with the rest of the agrarian population. For rural India as a whole, land has been the predominant issue in dispute for the whole of the modern period. Throughout both the British and post-Independence periods, for example, the criminal jurisdiction has been dominated by incidents that arise from underlying disputes over land between individual farmers. Thus land disputes are the most common cause of assaults (including murder) and allegations of theft (deriving from disputed ownership of crops).[23] But such disputes almost never involved Untouchables, who were bystanders to conflicts between caste Hindus or other landholders in the countryside. Untouchables, after all, were generally landless.

The change has taken place in the post-Independence period, indeed over the last two decades. The most telling failure of post-Independence policy affecting the Untouchables has been the failure of so-called land reform to deliver land to the tiller. This failure of policy has entailed an absence of any large-scale transfer of land ownership across the country from landed to landless people, and by far the most numerous single grouping of the landless is the Untouchables. At the same time, the Government of India has been consistently committed at the rhetorical and to some extent behavioural level to redistributive policies (most notably, the scheme of compensatory discrimination for Scheduled Castes and Tribes). And there has continued to be some emphasis on redistribution of land. This reached its most recent peak in Indira Gandhi's Emergency of 1975–7, during which there was some little redistribution of land accomplished even in States where none had been done previously—Bihar, for one. The continual rhetorical and occasionally behavioural commitment to land reform has had a marked effect on the consciousness of landless people—they have come to believe that they are entitled to land which is surplus to 'ceiling' levels fixed by the State governments. Similarly, they are now ready to claim plots of land which have for one reason or another reverted to the ownership of the state.

As part of a whole regime of progressive labour regulation, the Union and State governments have also enacted minimum wages legislation. This legislation is conspicuous for its non-implementation, but it too has brought about changes in consciousness and is the focus of widespread agitation for enforcement. In the agrarian sphere, the call for enforcement of statutory minimum wages legislation is properly conceived as an aspect of the wider campaign for land reform. If the fruits of land are spread more evenly among those who are conceded to have a legitimate interest in it, then a measure of (admittedly non-radical) reform has been accomplished. Together, the claims for land and higher wages have provoked major agrarian confrontations in many parts of India. Some of the most severe conflicts have been in Bihar, and we will concentrate on this State for a more detailed discussion of the matter.

The Case of Bihar

Bihar is the second largest State in India, with a population of over 86 million in the 1991 Census. It is also one of the poorest and least developed States despite the fertility of its land and its concentration of mineral resources. In the 1991 Census Bihar's literacy level of under 39 per cent was the lowest of all the States of India. The contemporary political character of Bihar has taken shape in the context of rapidly changing social relations and an economy that is barely growing. Nowadays Bihar gives the impression of being racked by social warfare which is variously characterised as caste conflict, class conflict or violence fomented by Naxalites (revolutionary communists). We need to try to sort out the character of the conflict in order to understand the contemporary condition of Untouchables in Bihar.

With some simplification, it is possible to think of Bihari society as composed of three strata defined according to both caste and class criteria. The top stratum is composed of Brahmins, Rajputs and Bhumihars—all 'twice-born' (high) castes which have historically controlled the land and been by far the wealthiest communities in the region. A fourth caste, the Kayasthas, also became part of this upper stratum during the British period, though they may not be strictly 'twice-born' and certainly did not acquire the same degree of landed property as the other castes. This upper stratum supplied the overwhelming preponderance of *zamindars* (revenue intermediaries) under the Permanent Settlement, which so shaped the economic life of the province for a century-and-a-half. Most of these people have never worked the land by their own hand: indeed for Brahmins, to put hand to plough is a positive sin. Rather, they managed the farming of 'their' land through a variety of arrangements. Sometimes they had tenants, some of whom (the so-called occupancy tenants) had legally protected tenure under the Permanent Settlement. Often, particularly in North Bihar, land was given out to *bataidars* or sharecroppers. In other instances, these high-caste zamindars operated the land with paid labour of a continuing or daily nature. The size of holdings varied greatly among this upper stratum of Bihari society, and there was a general divide between the regions north and south of the Ganges: the northern Districts contained zamindaris of far greater size than the holdings south of the river in central Bihar. (There is a further region to the south which is the so-called tribal belt; this region is not discussed here.)

The middle stratum of Bihari society is mainly composed of 'backward' or peasant castes, the most numerous of which are Yadavs (or Ahirs), Kurmis and Koiris. Characteristically but far from universally, these people are now peasant proprietors with holdings which in Indian terms are classifiable as small-to-medium. During the British period these farmers were usually the tenants of high-caste zamindars. In terms of population, this is the largest grouping within Bihari society.

At the bottom are the landless people, the largest component of which is some 14 million Untouchables. Not all Untouchables are landless, and not all the landless are Untouchables. Many among the 'backward' castes of Bihar are also landless, particularly among what are known as the 'backward backwards': the boating and fishing community of Mallahas, for example, is desperately poor and probably quite as landless as the Untouchables.[24] Perhaps the least homogenous caste is the Yadavs, apparently the largest caste of the State. The Yadavs are usually and quite reasonably characterised as a core element of the rising middle castes of Bihari society, but many Yadavs are in fact poor and landless labourers.

In very broad terms, the great agrarian winner of the post-Independence era has been the middle stratum. The abolition of the zamindari system whereby relations between tenants and the state were mediated by a landlord class, served to convert a great many of this stratum into a newly independent peasantry. They have not merely contrived to hold onto their land but have greatly expanded their total holdings through purchases from the upper stratum. There are no figures available on the extent of this redistribution through the marketplace, but it has clearly been a major phenomenon over the last several decades. The corollary is that the upper castes' grip on the countryside has been slipping. They have been forced to sell agricultural land for family expenses such as dowry, the higher education of their sons and even daughters, and the construction of urban houses as they progressively realign their ambitions in an urban direction. Relations between the upper and middle strata have become increasingly tense as the peasant castes grow in self-confidence and are concerned to challenge their hereditary masters in every area of economic, social and political life. The Yadavs have been at the very centre of this conflict; their relations with the Bhumihars, who are the predominant upper caste south of the Ganges, have been particularly embittered. A measure of the progress made by the Yadavs since Independence is Lalloo Prasad Yadav's occupancy of the Chief Minister's position from 1991 to 1997.

For the first thirty years after Independence it was not possible to think of the bottom stratum of Bihari society as a political actor in any sense comparable with the other two broad groupings. Over the last twenty years this situation has changed. There is still no question of treating the bottom stratum as a serious pretender to power in the State. But to the surprise of almost all observers, this stratum—and the Untouchables in particular—have begun to assert themselves with considerable political force. The violence they have both suffered and dealt out since the late seventies can now be seen as predominantly political violence.

A table produced by the Commissioner for Scheduled Castes and Scheduled Tribes in the Report for 1979–81 shows that Bihar was not among the twelve States with the highest number of 'Harijan atrocities' between 1967 and 1974. Suddenly in that year Bihar made its first appearance as the sixth worst case; in 1974 it was ranked fourth, and then third for the four years from 1976 to 1979. In subsequent years Bihar has remained near the top of the table. But by the Commissioner's own admissions such figures are unreliable. Conceivably, the reporting regime in Bihar improved suddenly in the mid-seventies to reveal the dimensions of a problem that had existed previously. But it is also likely that as the political situation in Bihar became more embattled and particularly as Untouchables began to resist as never before, their new situation began to be reflected in the statistics on violence.

On one reading of what has been happening to the Untouchables, they have been sucked into the vortex of violent and utterly primordial casteism that is seen to have overtaken Bihar. In this account, each of the major Untouchable castes—the three largest are the Chamars, the Dusadhs and the Musahars—is taken to be acting in a corporate manner that imitates the behaviour of the other castes in the State. Evidence for this perspective is quite easy to find. There can be no doubt that there is a high degree of group political consciousness among individual castes in Bihar, including Untouchable castes, and that if possible they tend to act in ways calculated to advance their common good. Thus one of the more sinister developments of recent years is the mushrooming of *Senas* or armies as the enforcers of caste interest in the increasingly bloody Bihari countryside. So there is the *Bhoomi Sena* as the armed force of the Kurmis, the *Lorik Sena* as an arm of the Yadavs, the *Brahmarshi Sena* of the Bhumihars, and so on. Although there is no Dusadh or Chamar *Sena*, there is the *Lal Sena* (Red Army) organised by Naxalite revolutionaries and dedicated to and partly composed of Untouchables. So the proposition is sometimes put that radical political activity of Untouchables is really only Bihari caste politics in a different guise.

Clearly there is some truth in the account of Bihar as an atavistic war between the castes, but in the end this image distorts more than it illuminates. There is a great deal of irrationality in Bihar, and some-times a frightening lack of ordinary social cooperativeness between the castes. But there is also more rational calculation than may sometimes appear, and a powerful class as well as caste logic in Bihari behaviour. This is our basis for dividing Bihari society into the three broad strata described above. So the primary political struggle since Independence has been between those castes which have dominated Bihar for centuries and the castes which have been immediately inferior to them in economic and social terms. This is a class struggle as much as it is a struggle between castes. Although there is great traditional rivalry between the upper castes of Bihar, and an early post-Independence history of intense competition between them within Congress, there is not the edge of bitterness or violence that often characterises relations between, say, the Bhumihars of the upper stratum and the Yadavs of the middle. The latter struggle is a complex of status, class and cultural antagonisms fed by the weight of history.

In the case of the castes which lie in the bottom stratum of Bihari society, particularly the Untouchables, they too are acting out of a class as well as a caste logic. So their enemies are far from constant in terms of caste identity: Untouchables have violently clashed with Kurmis and Yadavs from the middle stratum, and Bhumihars, Rajputs and Brahmins from the upper stratum. The key characteristic of their opponents has not been caste identity but rather land control: in the particular region where violent conflict has become endemic, Untouchables have tended to come into conflict with those castes which happen to control the land. Nor is this a merely Bihari phenomenon: throughout India there have been reports of Untouchables coming into conflict with newly rising peasant communities, rather than simply their traditional exploiters from upper castes. The focus on land control rather than caste identity helps explain how it is possible that (landowning and exploitative) Yadavs can be the bitter enemies of Untouchables in one situation, whereas (poor and landless) Yadavs can fight beside Untouchables elsewhere. Sometimes caste feeling works to weld together Yadavs of different class positions, but often it does not.

There is at least one other general explanation which competes with the idea of Bihari casteism to account for the aggressive grassroots political action in Bihar south of the Ganges. In this account the violent activity around the particular issues of land and social respect is part of a broader insurrectionary movement systematically organised by professional revolutionaries and calculated to appeal to Untouchables and various backward class elements. This is a view that gained much credence in official and police circles in both Patna and New Delhi, particularly during the 1970s and early 1980s. But in a variant form it is sometimes the view of the revolutionaries themselves.[25] Again, the view has considerable plausibility. The most striking piece of evidence in its favour is that political action taken by Untouchables and other radical backward caste groups against harsh landlords is heavily concentrated in those Districts south of the Ganges where revolutionary parties have invested their major organisational efforts. Although arguments of a cultural, structural and historical nature are frequently advanced to account for the disparity in radical action and overall violence between north and south Bihar, the most plausible explanation is that there has simply been more Naxalite organisation south of the Ganges than to the north.

In order to understand more fully what has been happening in south Bihar, something of the wider context needs to be sketched in. First, the appearance of the so-called Naxalites should be explained. The name comes from an insurrectionary movement beginning in 1967 around the small town of Naxalbari in West Bengal. Inspired by the strategies of Mao Tse-tung as interpreted by veteran communist Charu Mazumadar, a band of mostly upper-caste young Bengalis sought to create a revolutionary base in the countryside of West Bengal. The movement in Naxalbari was brutally suppressed within several months and Charu Mazumdar died in custody in 1972.[26] Thereafter the revolutionary mantle was monopolised in Bengal by the two mainstream communist parties. But Mazumdar's Communist Party of India (Marxist–Leninist) or CPI(M–L) was not altogether killed in Naxalbari. Its spirit and perhaps a little of its organisation too was resurrected in Bihar. The first site of Naxalite organisation in Bihar was in Bhojpur District.[27] From the beginning Naxalism in Bihar was marked by the participation of leaders from a number of backward and Untouchable castes, and was closely centred on the situation of Untouchables. The height of the insurrectionary activities in Bhojpur was reached in 1975, when Indira Gandhi imposed her State of Emergency. 'Operation Thunder', a police operation of the State government during the Emergency, appears to have struck a decisive blow against Naxalite activities in Bhojpur.[28] But even before then the movement had spilled over into adjoining Districts.

But to concede the crucial role played by Naxalite revolutionaries in the continuing struggle over economic and social issues in south Bihar is not to suggest that there is anything like a revolutionary situation in that area. A better characterisation is that a small band of revolutionary activists has been able to organise a still relatively small number of active supporters in south Bihar. But to an extent that was not generally predicted, the Naxalites have also contrived over a period now of many years to influence—or, at the very least, not to alienate—mainstream opinion among Untouchables and other landless people. The Naxalites began with direct and sometimes violent action—an early Naxalite slogan was that the appropriate response to oppressive landlords was *che inch chote kardenge* (literally translated, to lower them by six inches—by beheading). But already in 1982 the Indian People's Front (IPF) had been set up as an above-ground organisation designed to attract mass support, and in the late eighties and early nineties this organisation contested State and national elections[29] and even published a quite sophisticated book in 1986 setting their movement in context (*Report from the Flaming Fields of Bihar*). The IPF went so far as to win a seat in the Parliamentary election of 1989, as well as a number of State seats. In short, the Naxalites have proceeded from the politics of insurrection to a predominantly, though not exclusively, lawful approach to political action.

The State of Emergency was a major factor in the emergence of the violent politics of contemporary Bihar. This period was notable not merely for right-wing authoritarianism exemplified by Operation Thunder, but also a left authoritarianism in the form of efforts to bring about land reform. (There were other anti-poverty and social reform measures that were part of the '20 Point Programme' of the Emergency, including the ending of bonded labour—a matter which mostly affected Untouchables and tribals.) Prior to the Emergency in Bihar, not a single acre of land had been resumed and redistributed to the landless under the existing land ceiling legislation. Under strict instructions from New Delhi, some 225,000 acres were redistributed during the Emergency. Of course, this figure was pitiful relative to the overall need for redistribution 'to the tiller'. Even worse, in the ensuing years most of this land was clawed back by the owners through court action. Nonetheless, for the first time land was changing hands at the behest of the state, and it was mainly Untouchables who were the beneficiaries. Such action contributed to a long-term heightening of consciousness among Untouchables that their lot in life was not merely to accept their own landlessness.

Another precipitating factor in the new violence involving Untouchables was the outcome of the election at the end of the

Emergency in 1977. Karpoori Thakur's Janata Government was the first non-Congress government elected in Bihar, and also the first to be led by a person from the 'backward' castes (though the Untouchable Bhole Paswan Shastri had had short periods as Chief Minister in Congress governments). Thakur was from the small and ritually low barber caste, and he was a long-time socialist by conviction and career. His most decisive act as Chief Minister was to extend the system of reservation of government jobs so as to include not merely the Scheduled Castes and Tribes but also 'backwards'. This policy was explosive in the already strained relations between the upper and middle strata of Bihari society. Suddenly in 1978 it seemed that Bihar was utterly split between 'backwards' and 'forwards'—with the Untouchables standing uneasily beside this divide, since they were already beneficiaries of reservation and therefore had nothing to gain from the policy change. The conflicts in Bihar in the late seventies were a perfect foretaste of the reaction engendered by the V.P. Singh Government when it sought to enact the same policy at the Centre in 1990.

The period of Karpoori Thakur's Chief Ministership from 1977 to 1980 marked the beginning of a major upsurge in the number of 'Harijan atrocities' reported from Bihar. There remains doubt as to the extent to which Thakur's own actions precipitated the upsurge. Thus part of the explanation for the increased violence at this time was that the legacy of the Emergency was being contested in relation to land that had been at least notionally reassigned by the State to Untouchables and other landless people. Sometimes the land so assigned was 'wasteland' used as a common grazing resource for the village as a whole. On other occasions the land had been resumed from individual landlords as being surplus to the enacted ceiling on land ownership. In both situations, typically the new assignment of land was bitterly resented and was the direct cause of many violent clashes between dominant landholding communities and Untouchables. The first notorious 'Harijan atrocity' of this kind was Belchi, which occurred in May 1977—after the ending of the Emergency but before the election which delivered power to Karpoori Thakur.

Karpoori Thakur could become indignant at suggestions that he himself should bear any responsibility for violence against Untouchables—indeed, he denied the factual premise of such increase. He was able to point to a long record of support for Harijans, as they continue to be called in Bihar, and to his particular and highly controversial articulation of the desirability that Harijans arm themselves in order to fight their oppressors in the countryside.[30] But this very call was one of the factors that raised the temperature of politics in Bihar, and so may have further contributed to the phenomenon he was seeking to curb. Above all, Karpoori Thakur's regime provided the opportunity for radical groups to organise the countryside in a way that had been impossible during the Emergency. It was during his time that the Naxalites first made their strong presence felt outside their original Bihari base in Bhojpur District.

Although we have characterised the rising level of violence surrounding Untouchables in Bihar as a consequence of increased assertiveness of the Untouchables themselves, far more often than not it is they who have been the major victims of the violence. True, in the early period there were 'executions' of oppressive landlords undertaken by the Naxalites–and on some occasions the 'executioners' may have been Untouchable members of the underground organisation that ordered the killing. And more generally, Bihari Untouchables have learnt to dispense as well as suffer violence—country guns made from bicycle pumps have become almost a motif of Untouchable resistance. But inevitably Untouchables have literally and figuratively been outgunned. They have had to contend not merely with the forces of the village but also with the might of the state, particularly in the form of the police. This can be seen in a number of major Harijan atrocities since the late 1970s.

Pipra

The Pipra event was the third large-scale massacre of Untouchables in Bihar carried out by Kurmis in a period of two-and-a-half years: the earlier ones were in Belchi in 1977, and Bishrampur in 1978.[31] We have singled out this rather than any of the other events simply because there is a credible published account of the background to the event. Pipra is a village in Punpun Division of Patna District, and on the night of 25/26 February 1980 four men, four women, three boys and three girls from two families of the Chamar community were shot dead by a mob of some five hundred people apparently organised by a couple of Kurmi landlords. The bodies were set on fire, along with houses and cattle in the Chamar hamlet some 100 metres from the main village occupied by the caste Hindus; the pall of smoke could be seen for many miles. When the police van arrived on the scene at about 4 am, the mob vanished.

There was a considerable history of conflict which led to this massacre. The fundamental dispute was over land, but these bad relations were ramified by other serious differences. Conflict over land goes back to partition, at which time much of the land of Pipra was owned by Muslims. It seems that during the communal clashes of 1947 the Chamars had given protection to some Muslims, and their story is that they were rewarded with the gift of 4 bighas of land when the Muslims left the village. This land has been the subject of dispute ever since. In the subsequent period and through mechanisms that are not clear, the Kurmis have succeeded to virtually all other lands under the village: the Chamars have tiny plots of land other than the land in dispute. The Kurmis' status has changed from being predominantly labourers on lands owned by the Muslim landlords to employers of labour on their own land.[32] As to the disputed land, particular Kurmis have continuously asserted that they bought it from the departing Muslims. The dispute has been promoted in the courts, including the High Court of Bihar, for many years. Allegedly unlawfully, the disputed land had been occupied by Bhola Singh (since murdered) with the help of other Kurmis of the village.

Meanwhile, there was a long-standing sexual scandal. Taramani, a divorced Chamar woman, had entered into a long-term liaison with Radhika Singh, one of the Kurmi landowners of Pipra. The Chamars were very angry about this affair, which they took to be a slur on their honour. Some three months before the massacre, Taramani had finally been forced out of Pipra—apparently to the fury of Radhika Singh.[33]

The village disputes were fed by the surrounding political conflict general to Punpun Division, a centre of Naxalite activities in Bihar both before and after the Pipra massacre. This conflict had included land grab movements, campaigns for social respect and, above all, the push for payment of statutory minimum wages. There had been a strike over the wages issue in Pipra followed by permanent withdrawal of labour by many of the Chamars: at the time of the massacre there were only a few labourers left working for the Kurmis of the village.

The Chamars of Pipra are said to have had contact and considerable sympathy with the Naxalite movement.

The most potent factor which precipitated the massacre was the murder of two prominent Kurmi landlords of nearby villages in December 1979 and January 1980. Bhola Singh was Chairman and Deonandan Singh Treasurer of the Kisan Suraksha Sangh, an organisation of peasant caste landholders established to promote their common interest in the conflictual politics of Punpun Division. Given this history of conflict, the Kurmis of Pipra suspected that it was the Chamars of their village who had committed the murder of at least Bhola Singh; he had been an employer of Untouchable labour in Pipra. Indeed the police account was that the massacre was revenge for the death of the landlords. Between the time of the murder of the Kurmis and the mass murder of the Chamars there was continuing conflict in the form of theft of standing crops in fields owned by die Kurmis.

It is possible but by no means certain on the public evidence that the Chamars of Pipra killed the two Kurmi landlords. But the question of just who performed the murders is not strictly pertinent here. It is perceptions that matter, and clearly the Kurmis of Pipra believed that the deaths and all the other aggravation they were suffering were the responsibility of the Chamars of Pipra. Assuming that revenge and a political show of strength were the dominant motives of the Kurmis, what again impresses an observer is the planning of the affair and its scale. The event was clearly premeditated and carefully organised so as to mass together 500 Kurmis from a number of villages.[34] Given such organisation, it is difficult to conceive that the killing of women and children was simply the action of a mob that ran out of control. There may not have been a concrete ambition to kill, say, children, but it must have been the case that ordinary feelings of restraint had been set aside before the attack began. The killing of obviously innocent parties then follows as a matter of course. Perhaps it is instructive to note that the shoe is almost never on the other foot—we have come across no comparable instance of heedless massacre done by, rather than to, Untouchables.

Arwal

The massacre at Arwal in Jehanabad District, 19 April 1986, was an affair of a different character. Twenty-one Untouchables were shot dead by armed police. The venue was a confined space next to a library, and the savagery and one-sidedness of the affair have given rise to comparisons with the Jallianwallabagh massacre—one of the most potent symbols of the oppressiveness of British rule in India. In this case the underlying issue was a dispute between two Untouchable parties over proprietorship of certain land in a village close to the township of Arwal. This land is said to have originally been waste land but proprietorship had been assigned by officials to one Rameshwar Rajak; he is apparently a relatively prosperous person from an unnamed Untouchable caste.[35] The land had been simultaneously claimed by nine poorer Untouchable families whose houses adjoined the area. In ways that are far from clear, this dispute had been transformed into a major local issue. The Mazdoor Kisan Sangram Sarniti (MKSS)—one of several Naxalite groups operating in the region—had become involved, and on 19 April it organised a rally variously estimated in size at between 500 and 800 persons. It seems that the crowd was very largely composed of Untouchables, some of them women and children.

The procession of protesters first demolished the mud wall built by Rameshwar to enclose the disputed land, and then they made their way to a field in front of the local library. This field borders the police station, and there are only two paths out of the field if one is not to trespass into the police precinct.[36] A large contingent of police and armed constabulary, including Gurkhas, had been assembled to confront the gathering organised by the MKSS. Naturally, the police and the protesters' versions of what happened differ. The police allege provocation, but the investigating team from the People's Union for Civil Liberties (PUCL)—a voluntary civil liberties organisation—found no evidence of this. These investigators could find no documentation of any injuries suffered by the police. The police confiscated several country-made firearms, but there was said to be no evidence that they were used in the affair. The meeting was judged to have been peaceful, 'though strong worded speeches might have been delivered'.[37] The PUCL team concluded that 'it is not believable that the crowd holding a few country made pistols and a riketty (sic) rifle will indulge in the sheer madness and open fire on police armed with rifles and stenguns'.[38]

Despite the peacenik, if angry, nature of the assembly, the police are said to have fired fifty-three rounds of bullets, killing twenty-one persons. The PUCL team found that:

> the general hostility of the police towards the so called Naxalites or Extremists and their hurt ego in their failure to protect the compound wall of Rameshwar Rajak were the main inspiring factors for the police to engage in inhuman and barbaric killing of the people.[39]

A subsequent and more authoritative Report of the Indian People's Human Rights Tribunal (including two former State Chief Justices) said:

> This brutal and indiscriminate firing was mainly the result of state guidelines issued on April 6, 1986 for the police to treat the agitations arising out of the unbalanced economical structure of society as a purely 'law and order' problem and to ensure more positive and forward policing.[40]

The Arwal tragedy is a specially dramatic case of violent repression of protesters organised under the banner of a proscribed Naxalite organisation. But as the two Reports cited above make clear, it is really a story of the repression of poor people, mainly Untouchables, by the forces of the state. It is only the somewhat hysterical identification of ordinary villagers as Naxalite extremists that allows such a massacre to take place. The Untouchables at Arwal were flocking to the banner of one of the radical organisations which have gained the confidence of poor people, in the face of the manifest failure of mainstream parties to further their interests or protect them. Like the above Reports, we too find incredible the idea that the assembly that day was of Naxalite extremists. The assembly had been organised by the MKSS, which can, not unreasonably, be called 'Naxalite'. But clearly most of the participants were ordinary poor people trying to protest what they saw to be an injustice. Perhaps it might be argued that they were being used to stage-manage a political event, but they were clearly far from a dangerous revolutionary rabble that needed to be brutally fired upon.

The Arwal massacre is scarcely a typical event even for Bihar, but nor is it to be cast aside as an aberration. It is a particularly dramatic example of the way in which the state is routinely, if not universally, arraigned against those at the bottom of Indian society. The police, in particular, are very often the oppressors rather than protectors of poor people. What is different about this particular case is that the police were closely following government orders to confront with severity the forces of 'extremism' in the region. Ordinarily police oppression of the poor arises not so directly from official and public policy but from the interaction of local power and public administration at the local and regional levels. Clearly Arwal is not a case of Untouchables being persecuted *qua* Untouchables—after all, the land dispute that provoked the assembly was between two parties of Untouchables. But the poverty of Untouchables is an integral part of their makeup as a people, so it matters little whether they are being oppressed by police as Untouchables or merely as poor people trying to find a political path denied them by the regular parties. As Karpoori Thakur said in what turned out to be the last interview of his life, what shocked him most about contemporary Bihar was the extent to which the state had become the positive enemy of the people.[41]

Pipra and Arwal are, then, two sides of the one coin. They represent both civil power and the power of the state arraigned against Untouchables asserting their rights. It is impossible to judge the merits of the land disputes that figured in these two particular conflicts, but we can say that Untouchables have generally been fighting for what is theirs by clear moral and legal right. This is clearly true of their pursuit of 'social respect' and the receipt of wage levels prescribed in the minimum wages legislation. But in the present condition of society in Bihar, such demands provoke violent resistance. Pipra may be one of the worst examples of such violence, but it remains an accurate pointer to what is happening on almost a daily basis in south Bihar.

Any assessment of the gains to have been made by Untouchable resistance in Bihar is problematic. In the matter of wage rates in Bihar, Government of India figures suggest that these have risen over the last two decades; indeed, they have risen considerably more than productivity.[42] But even if these figures are reliable, there is currently too little evidence to attribute the rise to the political activity we have been describing. Wage rates for agricultural labour are highly variable as between the various States of India.[43] There is some correlation between labour productivity and wages, such that the highest wage rates are in the most productive States of Punjab and Haryana. But the less productive State of Kerala enjoys wage rates (as opposed to income) not much inferior to those of Punjab and Haryana, and the usual explanation is couched in terms of more effective labour organisation and the intervention of Governments sympathetic to rural labour.[44] It is possible that in Bihar too, and despite a hostile government, wage rates for labourers have been rising in response to pressure exerted by the labourers. But Bihar is not the only State in which official figures show wage rises to have considerably outstripped productivity gains, so any such conclusion would need to be sustained by a great deal of empirical work.

In any case, there is real doubt as to the accuracy of available figures on wage rates. One prominent observer of Bihar reported the results of an emprical study of a number of villages thus:

> There are large variations in wage rates (wage received per person-day) from village to village, from one season to another and even from person to person. The mode of payment involves cash, grains, land, meals, breakfast and any combination of these. In 12 villages there were as many as 71 types of such wages per person-day. When these were converted to money values using prices of grains prevailing in different villages of the sample, there were 210 wage rates.[45]

Our own observations bear out this view. We were able to get a detailed account of wages in one particular village of what is now Jehanabad District, one of the regions most convulsed by political conflict. The visit was in May 1984 and there had been a strike (lasting a mere one day) by labourers of the village earlier that year. Because this action followed many strikes in surrounding villages, employers quickly conceded some ground to the labourers. But the concrete outcome of the strike was equivocal. Apparently the major gain was that the going rate for casual daily labour rose from 1 kg of grain plus the supply of breakfast of 250 grams weight and a main meal of 500 grams (a total of 1.75 kg) to a figure of 1.5 kg of grain plus the two meals (a total of 2.25 kg). At the same time the amount of land given for cultivation to tied labourers (as opposed to 'free' labourers who are not attached to a particular family for a fixed period) was reduced: this was to offset a reduction in the number of days of unpaid labour extracted from tied labourers, and was connected to technological change surrounding the introduction of a winter crop. At the time of our visit to the village very few of the employers were actually paying the new rate. No employer was paying enhanced wages to tied as opposed to free labour—a large proportion of the workforce. And even in the case of free labourers, apparently few of them were benefiting from the enhanced rate. One of our informants (an academic from the dominant Bhumihar community) even doubted whether payment of the new rates would actually represent an advance for the labourers, given the complexity of the whole employment package.

This short discussion on wage rates is designed simply to impart a sense of how difficult it is to measure payment to agricultural labourers, and therefore to plot improvements in wages and overall income. Only after this is achieved with some accuracy will it be possible to address seriously the question of causes for any increases.

But even without evidence of significant redistribution of the fruits of agriculture, the new political movements of south Bihar clearly represent a major social turning point. What stands out again and again is the surprising boldness of the Untouchables. The tribals have long had a reputation for physical resistance to their *diku* or outsider oppressors,[46] but the Untouchables had seemingly been more downtrodden and fearful in their landlessness. This has now changed once-and-for all, at least in 'the Naxalite affected belt'. The intensity and longevity of the struggle has surprised everyone; it has now been proceeding for some two decades, and has assumed the status of a constantly simmering local insurrection. This phenomenon does not seem to fit perceptions about the quiescence and sheer backwardness of Untouchables in this abjectly poor region. To some the symbol of the insurrection has become the Musahars, the most downtrodden of all Untouchables castes in Bihar: their previous identity in the Bihari mind was an association with the field rats they catch and eat as a delicacy during the rainy season. The Musahars have been at the very centre of Untouchable resistance.

Of course, it is far from true that all Untouchables even in the half-dozen 'disturbed' Districts are militant. Old patterns of deference persist: the Chamar leader of the strike in the Jehanabad village described above recounted his story while squatting on the ground in front of a charpai on which one of us and a high-caste person sat. If the Chamar had asserted a right to sit next to us on the charpai, no doubt it would have been bitterly resented by high-caste people. But it is also significant that the Chamar leader was a middle-aged man—young men find such enforced deference increasingly irksome. Nor should traditional patterns of outward deference deflect an appreciation of the sea-change in outlook even among older Untouchables throughout India. What was clearly more significant in this particular situation was the militancy of the Chamar strike leader—his history of action and his declarations about future action—rather than his adherence to old forms of physical deference.

In short, the positive side to the unrest and violence in Bihar is its rootedness in the more assertive stance of Untouchables. Since Untouchable assertiveness is bound to provoke resentment and opposition on the part of the privileged classes, tension and even some violence is no doubt to be expected. But equally, it has to be recognised that the Untouchables continue to be predominantly the victims of the violence in which they are parties. Any glorification of the violence—suggested, for example, in the revolutionary romanticism of the Indian People's Front's book title, *Report from the Flaming Fields of Bihar*—is shallow. And always the painful modesty of the claims advanced by and on behalf of Untouchables needs to be recalled, half a century after Indian Independence.

Karnataka

There is sometimes a tendency to see Bihar—or perhaps Bihar plus eastern Uttar Pradesh—as a case by itself. The work of scholars like Pradhan Prasad has fed this tendency, with his insistence that Bihar is mired in a state of 'semi-feudalism' as against the capitalist relations that mark many other regions of rural India.[47] Although the cumulative situation in Bihar and nearby districts is uniquely conflictual many aspects of the embattled circumstances of Bihari Untouchables are present throughout India. A couple of examples taken from Karnataka are instructive on this issue. Karnataka is perhaps the best example of a 'moderate' Indian State. It is on the poorer end of the scale of States, though it has a significant high-tech industrial establishment in the city of Bangalore. The abjectness of poverty in Bihar or West Bengal or Uttar Pradesh is said not to be characteristic of Karnataka. It has had relatively progressive Congress and non-Congress governments which have had credible, if far from wholly successful, anti-poverty strategies. Karnataka does not have a national reputation for violence. But the following incidents show that there is serious violence involving Untouchables in Karnataka.

The two cases described here came to our attention during field-work in Karnataka. Only one of them can be said to have involved a 'Harijan atrocity', and even this was not a major case such as that of Pipra. The second case is one of avoidance of violence, but much can be learnt from the unfolding of this conflict too. In the first case the act of violence consisted in a group of Dalits (and a caste Hindu who was caught up in the affair) being forced to consume human faeces. The event took place in a village in Belgaum District during August 1987, and we examined it in January 1988 on the basis of reports and interviews with some of the participants in the village.[48]

There were a number of factors in the chain that led to this 'Harijan atrocity'. The first factor was an election in 1987 for the statutory *panchayats* or local government bodies, which at the time were being clothed with much greater power to disburse development funds. The electoral system had also been recently changed to provide for reserva-tion of seats for Scheduled Castes and Tribes and for women. In the village in question the three seats on the panchayat were all won by the Janata Party against fierce opposition from a locally based peasant party. The position of pradhan or head of the panchayat was taken by a Lingayat, the most powerful caste in Karnataka, and the Scheduled Caste seat went to an Holeya (a large Untouchable caste). The unsuc-cessful candidate for pradhan was also from the dominant Lingayat caste, and this man was said to be the main organiser of the atroc-ity. One of the victims was the son of the successful Dalit candidate. Apparently the defeated Lingayat blamed the Holeyas for his defeat, and there had been many bitter words after the election.

A second destabilising factor was the Integrated Rural Development Program (IRDP). In the present case the successful Dalit in the election had received IRDP assistance to buy a milch buffalo. But the advent of the buffalo increased as well as reduced the Dalit's dependence on high-caste farmers. The new owners did not have sufficient agricultural land to feed the buffalo, so they were dependent on caste Hindus and the Lingayats in particular to allow them to cut green fodder from their fields. Presumably there were reciprocal arrangements whereby the fodder was paid for in labour.

On the day in question Subhash, son of the newly elected Dalit, had gone to the fields with three other Dalits and a Maratha (caste Hindu) friend to cut some fodder for the buffalo. Night was beginning to fall and it had started to rain. Out of prior agreement, mischief making or simple laziness—the version varies with the witness—they began to cut fodder from a field belonging to someone in the unsuccessful Lingayat candidate's family. The latter were furious and managed to capture the five young men and herd them to the chief accused's house. Along the way the Lingayats forced Subhash to pick up some human faeces that lay by the roadside and carry it in a piece of paper. When they got to the accused's house, Subhash and his friends were forced to eat the faeces. They had to comply for fear of death at the point of a scythe.

The victims told us that they wanted to commit suicide out of a sense of shame for what they had been forced to do. Feelings were greatly inflamed in the village—particularly among the Marathas, since one of their number had by chance been caught up in the affair—but no general violence had broken out. The incident had become a major issue throughout Karnataka, and the Dalit Sangharsh Samiti (the principal Dalit organisation in Karnataka) organised a number of rallies demanding government action against the culprits.[49] In late January the latter were officially expelled from the village pending charges being heard in a court.

This incident is instructive on a number of counts. Of course, the grotesque action was quite out of proportion to any provocation caused by the fodder cutting. Even when the aggravated feelings following the election are taken into accounts there is a gap in reconstructing causation. That gap cannot be filled, we believe, by more empirical material on the incident itself—there would always remain an empirical gap. The degrading incident can only be understood by reference to the outraged feelings of people such as these particular Lingayats at the rise of Untouchables in the village. How dare they own buffalo, contest and win elections and act against the interests of their moral superiors! Who do these people think they are?

There is a great deal of powerful anecdotal evidence to the effect that any rising prosperity of Untouchables is usually greeted with hostility from caste Hindus. Of course, social envy is scarcely an unusual emotion. What is significant about such feeling relative to Untouchables is that they remain a peculiarly vulnerable people and as such are more easily damaged and deterred from activities that promote their own welfare. We came across another situation in Belgaum District of Karnataka which exemplifies this. This is not a case of 'Harijan atrocity' but rather of the avoidance of any serious violence. But the sheer arduousness of such avoidance suggests the dimensions of the problem.

The conflict in this instance was between the dominant Jain land-holders in a particular village and Holeya Untouchables: there were said to be 400–500 Jain families and 82 Holeya households, together with a number of other castes in smaller numbers. The problem presented itself to the outside world in October 1985, when the Holeyas staged a *dharna* or sit-in outside the office of the local *tehsildar* (a minor official). They said they were being oppressed in their village and wished to be relocated to a safer environment. When they declined to return to their village, the District Commissioner, the head official, had to be called in. In his own telling the Commissioner had a reluctance to intervene. He thought it could be the beginning of a movement which would present a major problem of public order; he did not wish to encourage this. If the situation did get out of hand because of his own sympathy with the Untouchables, a black mark would be placed against his name and his career might be permanently ruined. It would be far easier to get them to go home.

But despite these forebodings, the Commissioner felt he had to take seriously the Holeyas' claim that they could not be protected in the village. So he inspected the village and found the situation to be much as they had painted it. The Holeyas were living in miserable houses on a flood plain of the Krishna river—when it burst its banks, many of their houses were flooded. Their predominant occupation was that of labourers for the Jain landholders, whose major crop was sugar cane. Very slowly, the Holeyas were bettering their condition. Some of them had acquired a cow or two, and they were managing to sell a bit of milk to a nearby dairy. Five of the Holeyas were employed in the dairy, two of them as permanent employees earning 900 rupees a month. So their utter dependence on the Jains had slightly waned.

At the same time the Holeyas' acquisition of a few cows had set up a new dependence on the landholders for fodder. They had been permitted to crop some of the waste leaves of the sugar cane, but there had been minor skirmishes over this—the allegation was that they were cutting new leaves and therefore damaging the crop. One day a Holeya boy was driven off when he sought to cut fodder. Out of their new spirit of boldness, the Holeyas forced the Jains into a dialogue on the matter—after all, the Jains needed the Holeyas as much as the Holeyas needed the work. The rich Jains are said to have been greatly displeased at having to talk to the lowly Holeyas as if they were equals, and the result of the dialogue was not a happy one for the Holeyas. They were authorised to cut fodder for their animals but their daily wages were reduced from 10 to 8 rupees. This was the last straw for the Holeyas and led to their dharna before the authorities.

Since the Commissioner judged that the village situation was oppressive and intractable, he agreed to help the Holeyas relocate if they could find a suitable place. They were duly transported to a likely village, but within a short period of time were driven off as unwelcome. The Commissioner was finally able to settle them on part of a tract of some 450 acres which had been resumed under land reform legislation from the control of a temple. The land had been earmarked for a sugar factory but it was now judged that both uses could be accommodated. Our visit in 1988 showed the Holeyas to have been successfully settled with decent housing, clean water and sufficient land to till.

Already the Holeyas' story has become something of a fable among Dalit activists in Karnataka. But as a fable it has no capacity to provide guidance in comparable struggles: the conjunction of a large tract of vacant land and an unusually dedicated District Officer will be rare indeed. The case is more instructive on the question of contemporary strains arising from the most modest of improvements in the condition of Untouchables, and on the particular nature of the stress points that are developing. In comparable cases of endemic conflict over wages, social exploitation and land use, there are more likely to be 'Harijan atrocities' than magnificent resolutions.

The Riots over Renaming Marathwada University

Despite the overall failure of the Mahar movement in the era following Ambedkar's death, from time to time a particular issue excites sufficient passion to mobilise large numbers of Mahars and to provoke violent backlash from caste Hindus. The event that provoked the greatest violence in recent times was the seemingly innocuous effort to change the name of 'Marathwada University' in the city of Aurangabad to 'Dr Babasaheb Ambedkar Marathwada University'. As the great figure of Untouchable history in the modern period, Ambedkar's inspirational status has been steadily growing throughout the period of Indian Independence. So on 26 July 1978 Sharad Pawar, Chief Minister of Maharashtra, responded to pressure from the Mahars in Ambedkar's own region and moved a resolution in the State Assembly renaming Marathwada University after the great man.[50] Although the demand was longstanding and controversial, perhaps the Chief Minister thought that he was engaging in little more than parish pump politics. The announcement immediately provoked widespread uproar.

On the very day of the proclamation about 2,000 students from the University marched in protest. They demanded that shops in Aurangabad be closed. The next day violence increased, including the throwing of stones at various targets. On 28 July government cars and rail carriages were burnt, and huge mobs went on the rampage in a number of locations in the state. Despite signs at various times that the mobs were beginning to lose momentum, what happened was only a change of direction. For the first six days the violence was mainly directed against government institutions and property. From 1 August until about 6 August the Untouchables and particularly the Mahars became a major focus of the protesters. Only two Dalits are said to have been killed, but as many as 900 of their households were directly affected by the riots in their villages. For example, in one particular village fifty-five Dalit houses were burnt down; in another, it was forty-three houses; and in a third, forty houses. There was a dreadful orgy of burning and beating by caste Hindu villagers in five Districts of Maharashtra.[51]

Punalekar's study is directed to just why such an outpouring of violence occurred in rural Maharashtra, as opposed to the intrinsically more understandable rioting of students directly affected by the symbolic name change. He pursued this object by asking questions in a number of villages affected by the riots. Punalekar reports a deep resentment fuelled by the growing independence, resoluteness and modest improvement in the economic and social circumstances of the Mahars. He quotes one Mahar to this effect: 'It is a common tendency among Savarnas [upper castes], rich or poor, to pull back the Mahars from any advancement. They will constantly wish to keep them backward and behind them'.[52]

There have been strains caused by disputes over access to water, elections, the withdrawal of external social deference, the celebration of Ambedkar Jayanti (birthday), the practice of Buddhist rather than Hindu rituals, the relative prosperity of Mahars who have studied and entered professions such as medicine through the reservation system, and so on. The Mahars are compared unfavourably with the other large Untouchable caste of Maharashtra, the Mangs. A caste Hindu is quoted as saying: 'Look at the Mangs. How obedient and submissive they are to the villagers. They follow the traditions of our village society better. Their behaviour is also restrained. They are not defiant like the Mahars'.[53]

Punalekar's explanation for the Marathwada riots, then, is that the tinder of resentment built up in the caste Hindu (predominantly middle-caste landowners') mind was ignited by the symbolic change of name to 'Dr Babasaheb Ambedkar Marathwada University'. All the resentment that had been building up for many years exploded in the Districts surrounding the University.

This explanation is consistent with the material commented on throughout this chapter. The theme of resentment at what we have called Untouchable *resistance* emerges strongly throughout India. Much of the violence suffered by Untouchables represents a bitter outpouring of cumulative resentment which is triggered by an event of relative significance. The violence of the reaction is usually incomprehensible without the larger context of anger at the changing outlook and behaviour of Untouchables. Significantly, all the cases we have discussed involve the reactions of caste Hindus, middle and high caste, rather than those of other communities. There is far less violence between Untouchables and Muslims.[54] This is partly a result of less involvement between the two groupings: for example, there appear to be comparatively few Muslim landholders who employ Untouchable labourers. But this is not the whole of the story. There is a ritual dimension to the caste Hindu objection to the changing status of Untouchables.

Conclusion

Our aim in this chapter has not been to encourage an inference that the life of Untouchables is overwhelmingly disfigured by violence in contemporary India. This cannot be said about any region in India, and in some regions there is very little violence. Moreover, while violence is ugly and destructive, it can also be a measure of potentially progressive change in the circumstances or at least the outlook of Untouchables. But again, there can be no simple conclusion that the presence of violence is an indicator of either greater amenity or greater hope for Dalits. Thus there are few complaints of violence in Punjab and West Bengal, yet these are certainly not among the most oppressive social regimes. On a broader geographical basis, south India is far less productive of violence than the north; perhaps the generally more peaceable character of life in the south has something to do with this. But there are also differences within the south: Karnataka reports far more cases than do Tamil Nadu or Andhra Pradesh, possibly because of the influence of Maharashtra culture from the north. Kerala has few cases other than in two of its Districts, Palghat and Kasargod; these border Karnataka, and report a large number of violent incidents. The largest number of cases, both in absolute and per capita terms, is reported from Uttar Pradesh, Madhya Pradesh, Bihar, Gujarat, Maharashtra and Rajasthan.[55] In at least the first three States, land relations are at the heart of a large proportion of these clashes. But in all six States, dominant interests have fiercely defended the social and economic hierarchy in the face of demands put by an increasingly assertive Untouchable population. Why have West Bengal and Punjab escaped this violence? In the case of West Bengal, the comparatively relaxed attitude towards ritual pollution may have inhibited the development of violent resistance to (the highly moderate) land reforms which benefited many Untouchables in the 1970s and 1980s. The low incidence of violence in Punjab is not so easily accounted for, and probably owes little to the greater prosperity of that State in the recent past. It may be that explanations are to be found in the historical character of agrarian relations in Punjab, where there were few large estates and perhaps less capacity for Untouchables to claim land as legitimately theirs.

This brief consideration of regional variations must warn us against any easy conclusions about the larger causes of violence. But equally, it is utterly transparent that violence done to Untouchables is a serious dimension of social life in India today. From the analysis in this chapter it will be apparent that Untouchables are not suffering the violence as the eternal victims of caste Hindu society. The phenomenon is more complex than this. We have suggested that it is precisely the changing character of Untouchable consciousness that lies behind the increased incidence of violence that broke out from the late 1970s.

Notes

1. RCSCST 1956–7, p. 21.
2. RCSCST 1971–3, p. 162.
3. RCSCST 1983–4, p. 52.
4. RCSCST 1979–81, p. 340.
5. George W. Briggs, *The Chamars* (Delhi: B.R. Publishing, 1920/1975), p. 43.
6. If official figures are to be believed, the incidence of sexual assaults against Untouchable women is not disproportionate to that for the population as a whole (see RCSCST 1979–81, p. 353). Unfortunately, official figures must always be taken with extreme caution and it is quite possible that sexual assault on such women is specially under-reported.
7. RCSCST 1957–8, p. 23.
8. RCSCST 1971–3, pp. 165–6.
9. Alexander Robertson, *The Mahar Folk* (Calcutta: YMCA Publishing House, 1938), p. 23.
10. RCSCST 1958–9, p. 35.
11. RCSCST 1956–7, p. 20.
12. Briggs, *The Chamars*, pp. 22, 24, 56–57; Pauline Kolenda, *Caste in Contemporary India: Beyond Organic Solidarity* (Menlo Park: Benjamin/ Cummings, 1978), p. 54.
13. Anand Chakravarti, *Contradiction and Change: Emerging Patterns of Authority in a Rajasthan Village* (Delhi: Oxford University Press, 1975), pp. 59–61.
14. RCSCST 1973–4, p. 190.
15. RCSCST 1975–7, p. 45.
16. RCSCST 1973–4, pp. 186–8.
17. See, for example, I.P. Desai, *Untouchability in Rural Gujarat* (Bombay: Popular Prakashan, 1976), pp. 255–6.
18. RCSCST 1979–81, p. 367.
19. Ibid., pp. 361–4.

20. Ibid., p. 362.

21. Ibid., p. 363.

22. In the near past this was readily apparent to everyone, including the present writer during fieldwork in Alwar District of Rajasthan in the early 1970s. An old Chamar man resolutely declined to sit on the *charpai* while telling his story in the presence of Brahmins of the village. It was more trouble than it was worth for him to do this, though during the conversation he provoked some derisory laughter by contrasting the politeness of the foreigner's language with the roughness of the Brahmins' address.

23. Oliver Mendelsohn, 'The Pathology of the Indian Legal System', *Modern Asian Studies*, 15(4) (1981), pp. 837–8 (also Chapter 1 of this book).

24. This became apparent to us during a field trip to East Champaran District in 1980. The Mallahas of this District were demonstrably among the poorest of Indians. We visited households in which there were simply no possessions at all, no items of a personal or a domestic nature.

25. Anonymous, *Report from the Flaming Fields of Bihar* (Calcutta: Prabodh Bhattacharya, 1986).

26. S. Banerjee, *In the Wake of Naxalbari: A History of the Naxalite Movement in India* (Calcutta: Subarnarekha, 1980), p. 422.

27. Kalyan Mukherjee and Rajendra Singh Yadav, *Bhojpur: Naxalism in the Plains of Bihar* (New Delhi: Radha Krishna, 1980), p. 7; Arvind N. Das, *Agrarian Unrest and Socio-Economic Change in Bihar 1900–1980* (New Delhi: Manohar, 1983), pp. 245–54.

28. Francine R. Frankel, 'Caste, Land and Dominance in Bihar: Breakdown of the Brahmanical Social Order', in Francine R. Frankel and M.S.A. Rao (eds), *Dominance and State Power in Modern India: Decline of a Social Order*, Vol. 1 (1989), p. 120.

29. Walter Hauser, 'Violence, Agrarian Radicalism, and the Audibility of Dissent: Electoral Politics and the Indian People's Front', in Harold Gould and Sumit Ganguly (eds), *India Votes: Alliance Politics and Minority Governments in the Ninth and Tenth General Elections* (Boulder: Westview, 1993), p. 351.

30. Interview, 10 May 1985.

31. A.N. Sinha Institute of Social Studies, Harijan Cell, 'The Pipra Carnage: An Interim Report', Patna (unpublished paper), p. 9.

32. Ibid., pp. 8–9.

33. Ibid., p. 26.

34. Ibid., p. 29.

35. People's Union for Civil Liberties (PUCL), 'Report of the Bihar PUCL Fact Finding Team on Arwal Massacre', Patna (unpublished paper, nd), p. 2.

36. Ibid., p. 3.

37. Ibid., p. 14.

38. Ibid., p. 13.

39. Ibid., p. 14.

40. Quoted in Hauser, 'Violence, Agrarian Radicalism, and the Audibility of Dissent', p. 345.

41. Oliver Mendelsohn, 'Last Interview with Karpoori Thakur', *Times of India* (18 February 1988).

42. A.V. Jose, 'Agricultural Wages in India', *Economic and Political Weekly*, Review of Agriculture, 23(26) (1988), Table 13.

43. Ibid., p. A-49.

44. Ibid., p. Table 6B.

45. Pradhan Prasad, 'Agrarian Violence in India', *Economic and Political Weekly*, 22(22) (1988), p. 849.

46. Ranajit Guha, Elementary Aspects of Peasant Insurgency in Colonial India (Delhi: Oxford University Press, 1983), pp. 64–5.

47. Prasad, 'Agrarian Violence in India', p. 852.

48. Interviews with Holeyas and the Lingayat *pradhan* in Bendegeri Village, Belgaum District, 14 January 1988.

49. Press handout by the State Convener of the Karnataka Dalitha Sangharsha Samithi, Bangalore, n.d. (*c.* 18 January 1988).

50. S.P. Punalekar, *Aspects of Class and Caste in Social Tensions: A Study of Marathwada Riots* (Surat: Centre for Social Studies, 1981), p. 62.

51. Ibid., pp. 72–81, 95, 124; RCST 1977–8, II, pp. 129–32.

52. Ibid., p. 129.

53. Ibid., p. 152.

54. There have been a number of serious incidents between Untouchables and Muslims in urban locations of Uttar Pradesh. The trigger for some of these incidents has been the keeping of pigs by particular Untouchable communities. And in other situations Untouchables may have been used by high-caste interests to engage in anti-Muslim action. But tensions between these two large populations in Uttar Pradesh have not been a central dynamic of social life there.

55. RSCST 1986–7, p. 229.

5

FROM COLONIAL TO POST-COLONIAL LAW IN INDIA*

Introduction

India can lay claim to having the oldest and most developed of the modern legal systems of Asia.[1] The doctrinal content of the system is elaborate and complex; the number of its judicial institutions and legal professionals is large; and what we can call 'legal culture' is highly entrenched and widely ramified in the general population of both rural and urban areas. But while India has to be taken seriously as a modern legal order, this is not to say that the system is currently in sound health. To use an overworked but apposite term, the situation of Indian law today is one of intense crisis. This crisis is symptomatic of the same general disorder that afflicts many other public institutions in contemporary India, but it presents itself in particular ways. Liberalisation of the Indian economy has now directed new attention to the legal order, which is seen as both potential aid and significant impediment to rapid and appropriate economic growth. The object of this chapter is to set this contemporary character of Indian law in the context of the earlier development of the system during the British and post-Independence periods. Without some attention to historical context, it is not possible to develop a clear view of the present nature and direction of change of the Indian legal order.

* This chapter was originally published in Veronica Taylor (ed.), *Asian Law through Australian Eyes* (Sydney: LBC Information Services, 1997), pp. 297–315.

The Making of the Anglo-Indian Legal System

Law had a place at the very centre of the British *raj*, and it made its appearance almost at the beginning of the British encounter with India. The legal task first presented itself as nothing more than the administration of justice to the English servants of the East India Company. But when the island of Bombay was ceded to the Company by Portugal in 1668, the Company was authorised by Britain to establish a Court of Judicature and to make laws for the island 'consonant to reason, and not repugnant to, but as near as may be agreeable to the laws of England'.[2] This formula became a general standard for British colonies in a number of regions of the world.

Despite these early beginnings, a durable form of what can be called 'Anglo-Indian' law did not take shape until well into the 19th century. In the intervening years, opinion had divided over a number of fundamental questions. Where were courts to be established, and who was to be given access to them—Indians or only Europeans, and just what kinds of people? Were the judges to be Company servants discharging a variety of administrative tasks or was the principle of the separation of powers to be recognised, such that judges were to be professionally trained and independent of the administration? Was there to be a place for Indians on the bench, at least in the subordinate judiciary? Which body of law was to be administered by the courts: British law or pre-existing Indian law, and if the latter, in what did this consist and who was to expound it? Thus in Bengal, Warren Hastings' Regulation of 1772 laid down the rule that in matters of 'personal' law—marriage, inheritance, religious duty—the laws of Hindus and of Muslims were to be administered to the respective communities. Bengal also led the way some years later by framing a major distinction between the judicial approach to be taken in the city of Calcutta and that to be adopted in the *mofussil* or country areas. By the turn of the 19th century, the residual law in all three 'Presidency' towns—Calcutta, Bombay and Madras—was the law of England. In the countryside, by contrast, gaps or ambiguities in the law were to be resolved in more free-wheeling style by consulting 'justice, equity and good conscience'. But both these formulas, and even the intention to administer Hindu and Muslim law in the so-called personal sphere, produced a great transfer of European legal principles to India.[3]

The most rapid development of institutions and principles of state in India was during the second half of the 19th century, in the years following the Mutiny and assumption of direct power by the Crown. By far the most famous symbol of this 19th century legal creativity was the *Indian Penal Code*, drafted by Lord Macaulay as early as 1837 but adopted only in 1860.[4] This Code still constitutes the basis of Indian crime legislation, and it has been no more than lightly amended in a life of almost 150 years. Macaulay's Benthamite plan to codify and simultaneously reform all British law relevant to Indian conditions was thwarted, but *Codes of Civil and Criminal Procedure* and other basic legislation were eventually passed between 1859 and the early 1880s. This expansion of the body of substantive law was broadcast throughout British India, since from the early 1860s the dual system of *mofussil* and Presidency town law was abolished in favour of a single standard incorporating the doctrinal and procedural complexities of the urban model.

But formal accounts of the jurisdiction and institutional apparatus of Anglo-Indian law yield little insight into the functioning character of the system. Such exercises fail to account for the most salient characteristic of the system, *viz.*, its apparent popularity. In the collective wisdom of the *raj*, law was the greatest of British gifts to India. But at the coalface, District officials were alarmed at what they saw to be an over-indulgence in litigation. Such concerns grew rapidly in the years after assumption of power by the Crown in 1858, when opportunities for litigation multiplied in rural areas. As officials cast around for explanations of what they took to be an irrational indulgence in litigation, they often fixed on a psychology of 'litigiousness' comparable with perceived extravagance in the celebration of marriage. Weddings and litigation could be pronounced to be the ruin of many a community.[5]

Land and Litigation in British India

Far and away the greatest subject of litigation in British India was agricultural land. There was nothing 'natural' to such an outcome, even granted the importance of land in a peasant society such as India. In central Africa, by contrast, the most fertile subject of litigation in courts established by the British was the incidents of marriage—brideprice, for example.[6] Why, then, did agricultural land become so intense a judicial subject in India? The short answer is that the Anglo-Indian state intervened to a unique degree in the administration of land, and that litigation over land was an aspect of this intervention. At the same time, no substantial body of land litigation could have developed unless land had been a valuable and scarce resource.[7]

The early British ambition in land matters was best represented in the Permanent Settlement of Bengal in 1793. This was a once-and-for-all fixing of the identity of those who were liable to pay the land revenue demands of the Company, and the amount they were to pay. The settlement was framed with the object of extracting for the state a large share of agricultural production, while adhering to Whiggish principles of limited government. Together, these two pillars of public policy would promote optimal levels of industry in the population. Law was to be a crucial support for the regime:

> The law defined and protected the private rights of subjects against all-comers, including the encroachments of the executive itself. Among these private rights was that to property: the legal subject was guaranteed enjoyment of all his possessions free from external interference. Second, to facilitate economic relationships between propertied subjects, the public law developed a number of conventions. The sale of property was held always to be valid. A vendor could not subsequently claim it back. Contracts for debt and services were held to be binding and enforceable at law on the property of the party who failed to meet his obligations.... The Permanent Settlement envisioned a society whose prosperity was underpinned by a free market in all commodities, including and especially land.[8]

In fact, this individualist world never came about in British India. Even today, the undoubtedly capitalist Indian agriculture does not conform to the rigorous individualism of the eighteenth century framers of the Permanent Settlement. Washbrook notes that from the beginning there was a countervailing, more conservative, philosophy espoused by the *raj*:

> If the public side of the law sought to subordinate the rule of 'Indian status' to that of 'British contract' and to free the individual in a world of amoral market relations, the personal side entrenched ascriptive (caste, religions and familial) status as the basis of individual right.[9]

This ideological contradiction had important implications for property relations and therefore for litigation. In a word, this second 'private' side of the law sought to limit the free operation of an impersonal and radical market in favour of the preservation of 'tradition'. This was one of the factors that limited the wholesale displacement of landholders in British India.

This question of displacement is tricky. In formal legal terms, there was indeed massive transfer of ownership at different periods and different locations in British India. In the region around Benaras, for example, more than half the land changed hands in the period.[10] Most of this transfer of legal right took place at compulsory auctions held upon the landholder's default in relation to the government's annual revenue demand. On the other hand, there was almost no evidence that formal change in ownership had led to any physical change in the management of land. It appeared, rather, that the auction system had in effect shoe-horned one more interest into an already extended agrarian hierarchy. The new owner had to be given a share in the profits of agriculture. What the change did lead to was frequent litigation over the rights and duties of ownership and tenancy. Often the courts were used in an aggressive capacity by the hew owner, who was thereby putting pressure on the formally ousted owner so as to lay the basis for a practical compromise over income sharing.

The single largest volume of land cases was in the rent jurisdiction of North India, particularly in the province of Bengal. On the eve of the British departure from India the annual number of rent suits in Bengal amounted to well over half a million, and it had reached these heights half a century earlier. These cases arose from the particular character of the land administration in the so-called *zamindari* areas. *Zamindars* in Bengal were not only landlords in the usual western sense of this term, but also revenue intermediaries. In the Permanent Settlement of 1793 *zamindars* had been recognised as the parties from whom the annual revenue demand would be levied. They were authorised to collect rent from different classes of tenants within their revenue holding, and to live off the margin between what they could collect and what they had to pass on to the British rulers in Calcutta. But it was always difficult to collect this rent. Hence, the *zamindars* routinely took their cases to court.[11] This was only one of a variety of tactics they might employ. Force was another. More often than not the tenant did not turn up in court to defend the action; frequently, they were not even informed of the litigation by a highly defective institutional apparatus.

Even this too-brief discussion must suggest that the 'litigiousness' of the Indian population is not a self-evident proposition. If litigiousness means an unreasoning and irrational resort to litigation, then 'rational self interest' would seem to be a better guide to much of the litigation than 'litigiousness'. A very large proportion of the land litigation was in effect forced upon persons of ordinary rationality.[12] But it is important not to go too far in the other explanatory direction. At the very least, there was a remarkable lack of cultural resistance to the new judicial institutions established by the British administration. If a large proportion of the litigants were propelled (either as plaintiffs or defendants) by forces substantially beyond their control, in other cases there was considerably more choice. And by no means all the conflict over land was attributable to initiatives of the British. Disputes within families—brothers quarrelling over their patrimony, for example—are one example of conflict that was certainly not invented by the British. Disputes over the location of boundaries between fields is another perennial form of conflict that inevitably found its way into the new judicial institutions.

Land litigation may have dominated the colonial courts, but it did not monopolise them. A large body of litigation derived from the attempts of the *raj* to protect an established social order under threat from forces unleashed by its own policies. Thus Galanter has discussed a rich vein of cases of individual caste communities using the courts to defend their own exclusiveness. To give just one celebrated example, in 1908 the Privy Council upheld the argument that a particular temple had a right to exclude from its premises the upwardly mobile but ritually untouchable Shanar community. The temple was even awarded damages to defray the costs of its ritual purification following Shanar incursions.[13]

With one major exception, litigation deriving from commercial life was not a major occupation of the Anglo-Indian courts outside the largest cities. The exception was suits brought by moneylenders for the return of principal or interest. Again, the motivations of these plaintiffs are not difficult to reconstruct. They were simply resorting to institutions best calculated to protect their investment. Indeed, the provision of new judicial institutions was a *sine qua non* of the vast expansion of money lending under the British. Despite the small number of other commercial cases, relatively large commercial suits were a staple of the leading advocates of Bombay and Calcutta. Commercial litigation and general commercial practice was also the dominant business of the small number of solicitors' firms in Bombay, Calcutta and to a lesser extent in Madras. The role of these firms today will be discussed below.

This brief discussion of litigation during the colonial period is designed to point to the limited nature of the practical jurisdiction of the Anglo-Indian courts. Aside from the criminal law, it was only litigation to do with land that affected large numbers of people.[14] Much of this litigation was strategic and tactical rather than decisional in character. While negotiated as opposed to decisional justice may be universal to due process systems of justice, the habitual lack of enforcement of judgments in British India is at the extreme end of the continuum. It is clear that the Anglo-Indian courts were an important machinery by which many of the dislocations provoked by British policies were mediated. No doubt we could say the same thing, *mutatis mutandis*, about the role of tort law in 20th century Britain, the USA or Australia. In these societies, tort law has been a mechanism for adjusting the rights and interests of a variety of parties—manufacturers, public authorities, road users, and so on. But in India of the 19th and 20th centuries, the process of adjustment through litigation has been less frank and less transparent. It has not usually been clear to either the participants or the apparent orchestrators of the system—the British *raj*—just whose interests the whole complicated scheme of litigation was serving. Moreover, the legal process has been carried on entirely through litigation rather than extra-curial processes of the official legal system: this is a theme we will return to below.

Much of the basis of litigation has shifted in the post-Independence period, and the present legal order is profoundly different from the colonial order. At the same time, there is a crucial continuity between the two epochs. What links them is the *culture* of the law, by which I mean essentially two things: a commitment on the part of Indian opinion makers to the ideology of the rule of law; and secondly, the maintenance of a legal profession whose outlook and character were formed over the period of the *raj*. Since it is lawyers who are in charge of legal production or 'law', the continuity in their character is a basic limitation on the extent that divergence between post-colonial and colonial law is possible. It is context rather than essence that will dictate whether it is the departure or the continuity that is stressed.

Indian Law Since Independence

The Constitutional Basis of the Regime

India gained its independence from Britain in 1947, and a Constituent Assembly proceeded to draft a new Constitution that was adopted in 1950. As with most other post-colonial nations, India modelled its government on that of its former colonial master. But unlike most of these cases, India has retained its original form of government and its *Constitution*. India's variation on the Westminster or 'responsible government' model follows the example of Canada and Australia in dividing legislative and administrative power along federal lines. The head of state is an indirectly elected President with sweeping Constitutional powers, but these powers were intended to be merely ceremonial and formal after the example of the British monarch. While there have been points of conflict between the President and Prime Minister, there has been no constitutional crisis of the dimensions of the Australian conflict of 1975.

One major departure from the Westminster model was the power given to the President (effectively the Prime Minister and Cabinet) to proclaim an Emergency at national or State levels for reasons of war or 'internal disturbance' (Art. 352). Such proclamation enables the suspension of most civil liberties otherwise guaranteed by the Constitution. In addition, the President was authorised to take over the government of individual States in the event of the 'failure of constitutional machinery' (Art. 356). Although they departed from Anglo-American constitutional norms, these provisions were in broad conformity with India's own experience under colonial rule. The imposition of President's rule under Art. 356 has been employed on many occasions. But at the national level, there has been only one Proclamation of Emergency for reasons other than external aggression. Indira Gandhi's Emergency of 1975–1977 was proclaimed because the Prime Minister had lost control of national politics and had been convicted of electoral malpractice. Much of the constitutionalism of the last two decades has to be read in the context of the trauma occasioned by this period of authoritarianism. The adverse reaction to the Emergency at an elite level does not guarantee that a comparable period of authoritarianism will never again be inducted. But it does suggest that no Government will again believe that it can turn on and then turn off such an Emergency at its own discretion. Any future Emergency of the Indira Gandhi kind is unlikely to lead to a resumption of old constitutional forms.

The most progressive parts of the *Indian Constitution* are the Fundamental Rights and the Directive Principles of State Policy. The Fundamental Rights are judicially enforceable, and some are of a universal kind—equality before the law, freedom of speech and religious practice, for example. Others, like the abolition of untouchability, have point only in the Indian context. Protection of property was a specific Fundamental Right until it was revoked in 1978, but the revocation has not served to remove all protections on property ownership. (The *Indian Constitution* can be amended by relatively simple legislative action, though the Supreme Court has found a 'basic structure' to the Constitution which is not subject to alteration.[15]) The Directive Principles are not judicially enforceable, but constitute a blueprint for the creation of a fair and progressive society. Thus all Indians are declared to have a right to education and to work and receive a living wage, and the state is adjured to promote the interests of disadvantaged sections of Indian society.

Litigation Since Independence

The pattern of litigation in post-Independence India has changed fundamentally. Some of the old categories of legal action have disappeared altogether, while new jurisdictions have taken form. One entirely new area is the judicial enforcement of Fundamental Rights. Complaints of breach of right proceed by way of 'writ petition' to the High Courts or to the Supreme Court; this is a simpler, cheaper and sometimes more rapid procedure than ordinary suit. A large part of the vastly enhanced administrative law of India has been developed by way of the writ petition. Many thousands of the grievances of government servants regarding the terms and conditions of their employment—essentially labour law—have proceeded through this mechanism. More conservatively, the implementation of land reform legislation was delayed in the 1950s through writ petitions claiming a breach of Fundamental Rights; the effect on the availability of land for redistribution was nothing short of catastrophic. In the period since the end of Indira Gandhi's Emergency in 1977, the writ petition has been the basis of a wholly new 'public interest' or 'social action' litigation in the Supreme Court and the High Courts. The rights of prisoners under trial, rape victims, bonded labourers, child workers, pavement dwellers; and issues arising from environmental abuse, electoral malpractice and official corruption—these are just a few of the categories of public interest litigation that have transformed the jurisprudence of the Supreme Court over the last two decades.[16] The Supreme Court has been busy, albeit episodically and far from consistently, constructing a body of principles fit for a poor nation seeking to find paths of appropriate development. In many ways, this intensely democratic jurisdiction is the great adornment of post-Independence law. The Court has broken new legal ground in being prepared to entertain writ petitions whose form is nothing more than a human cry captured on a scrap of paper.

Perhaps the greatest change in the subject matter of post-colonial litigation is the radical decline in judicial contests over agricultural land. This has come about for several reasons, the most important of which is land reforms undertaken by the state. The single most important measure was the abolition of revenue intermediaries (*zamindars et al.*). In Bengal, Bihar and other areas of North India, all landholders were brought into a direct and unmediated relationship with the state. This measure was combined in some areas with appropriation of lands surplus to prescribed maximum holdings, though the amount of land so appropriated was painfully disappointing. The abolition of intermediaries removed with one stroke of the pen the many hundreds of thousands of rent suits that annually went to the courts. Since the intermediary no longer existed, how could he (it was always he) go to court to extract what was due from his tenants? Nor did the state succeed to the position vacated by the intermediaries: the revenue (taxation) demand levied by individual States against landholders has declined to the point of insignificance, and collections are not pursued with any vigour.

There has also been a steady decline in other judicial contests over agricultural land, including over ownership rights, boundaries and so on. Here, the cause of the decline is not so clear cut. One strong reason is that there are fewer causes of genuine uncertainty in relation to ownership of land. By now, land has been surveyed and settled so many times that relatively little ambiguity is possible in relation to ownership and control. Since most judicial disputes have a genuine basis in perceived right, any decline in ambiguity of right will be reflected in reduced litigation. Just as important, the ambitions of the old rural elite have increasingly been redirected from the village to the cities. In many regions they have been prepared to sell parcels of land to the rising peasantry in order to fund the marriage of a daughter, the education of both sons and daughters, and the purchase of urban property. Given these changing ambitions, there seems to be a declining propensity to litigate: for example, the epic contests within landholding families are largely a thing of the past. This is by no means to say that demand for land has decreased. Indeed, heightened consciousness on the part of landless labourers suggests that the very opposite is true. But nowadays the hunger for land tends to be expressed less in individual and judicial terms, and more in the language of class and politics.

If litigation over agricultural land has declined, there has been a phenomenal rise in litigation over urban land. The context of this litigation is rapid growth in the size of Indian cities and towns over the last half-century. Demand for urban property has risen sharply, and supply has failed to keep pace. The result has been rapid inflation in the value of urban land, to the point that prices for some land in Bombay is said to be considerably higher than for property in Manhattan.[17] This situation is not wholly an outcome of simple equations of supply and demand. A further factor is rent control, which was first legislated as a British wartime measure to secure the cheap garrisoning of troops. Rent control was retained after Independence, ostensibly as a welfare measure to protect tenants in the private rental market. Whether it ever worked to this end is questionable—one of the universal effects of rent control is to restrict the supply of stock. In any case, what has grown up is an increasingly distorted ratio of land values to rentals. The latter have not kept pace with inflation. Landlords have found it difficult to eject tenants so as to occupy property themselves or to sell or rent to someone else. The issue of ejection is the centrepiece of the so-called rent jurisdiction, which constitutes by far the largest single source of litigation in Bombay and the other major cities of India. We will return to this form of litigation shortly, since it is a prime constituent of the present crisis of the overall system.

The judicial scene is now quite rapidly becoming more varied. For example, the incidents of marriage have been transformed into a regular rather than strictly marginal concern of the courts. Reliable statistics are not available, but in cities like Bombay and Delhi the rates of divorce are rapidly rising (from what is admittedly a low base). This phenomenon presents women with special difficulties in a society still strongly biased towards male rights, particularly in the matter of property. The Indian norm is that the wife becomes a part of the family of her husband, and as such she is entitled to physical support from the family. This support is often underwritten by the payment of dowry. But in both cultural and legal terms, women have no clear entitlement to any share of either the ancestral property of her husband's family or even property acquired during the marriage out of the earnings of the husband.[18] This issue tends to become a live one in the event of the husband's death or the couple's separation or divorce. The problem may be compounded by the woman's lack of cultural entitlement—here there is a contradiction between culture and law—to share in the estate of her deceased father. So a divorced or separated woman is often shut out of any share in the property of her father's and her marital household. In the event that the woman has responsibility for children, her situation can easily become desperate. Characteristically, the legal profession is busy devising its own ways of mediating the clash between the interests of a divorcing woman and the strictures of a patriarchal society. Thus, there is a good deal of exploitation of recent changes to the criminal law which have been enacted to combat oppression of women in relation to dowry. Section 498A has been inserted into the *Indian Penal Code*, and this allows gaoling of the husband and his parents as a preemptive measure in cases of apprehended violence arising from a dowry issue. By common consent, lawyers have been fabricating cases of apprehended violence as a way of generating pressure towards a suitable property settlement. Nor is such action rare. This and other issues arising from marriage now constitute an estimated 30 per cent of all the criminal work in the lower courts of one region of New Delhi.[19] Again, I will return to this issue of marriage litigation ahead.

Negligence and other tort litigation is far less developed than it is in the other major centres of the common law world. There is no single reason for this lacuna, though perhaps it has to do with relative stages of development—including the slow growth of the insurance industry—and varying attitudes to the moral economy of compensation. But there are the bare beginnings of litigation over medical negligence. And there are a couple of flourishing tribunals: one dispensing compensation throughout the country in relation to motor accident victims, another deals with consumer complaints. These bodies parallel tribunals in a number of other common law countries, and their early years suggest considerable promise.

The Present Crisis of the Legal System

The essential characteristics of the present crisis of the Indian legal system are not new; they are precisely the failings that have been identified for at least a century. What has changed is the whole context in which the legal system has to operate. The crisis has deepened precisely because the legal system has been insufficiently transformed in the years after Independence. Old patterns of litigation may have withered and new patterns bloomed, but there has been no comparable transformation of the institutional, professional and cultural underpinnings of the law. While citizens and observers of India are used to its institutions muddling through, it is now somewhat doubtful that the legal process can continue as it has done in the past. Change will not come about from within the profession—this is not the way law or legal services are transformed anywhere. If change is to come, it will be a response to broader economic and social developments. Perhaps the most potent of these developments, if not necessarily the broadest-based, will be the internationalisation of the Indian economy.

The most obvious manifestation of the present legal crisis is extravagant judicial delay brought about by a huge backlog of cases. For example, an urban property suit initiated 30 or 40 years ago is likely; only now to be reaching finality. There are said to be some 20 million cases pending in Indian courts—close to 100,000 are pending in the Supreme Court, and 2.4 million in the High Courts.[20] An obvious reason for the pattern of delay is the sheer level of demand for judicial action, but this is by no means the only factor. Like litigation over agricultural land in colonial India, the subject matter of some contemporary litigation lends itself to long drawn-out struggle. We can return here to the example of landlord-tenant disputes in Bombay. Typically, the landlord is anxious to get rid of a tenant in order to resume control of the property for self-occupation or for sale. The tenant, on the other hand, wants to retain the property or pass it on to another tenant for a large consideration. It is in the interest of the tenant to delay a resolution where he or she wants to remain in possession, and in the interest of the landlord to expedite the matter. This clash of interests provides the ideal basis on which profusely protracted litigation can take place, ably assisted by a legal profession which makes more money the longer the case goes on. Sometimes, it is true, a more-or-less rational outcome is achieved outside the courts precisely because the courts are unable to deliver justice themselves. Thus in Bombay and a number of other cities a system has developed whereby the outgoing tenant, the incoming tenant and the landlord all collude so that no-one goes empty-handed. The incoming tenant is obliged to pay a consideration (called *pagri* or 'turban' for some obscure reason) for taking over the rent-controlled tenancy. This *pagri* is split in the ratio 2:1 between the outgoing tenant and the landlord. Although the landlord is by law able to stop the transfer of a rent controlled tenancy, it will take him or her perhaps 40 years to prove the point. And even then the outcome is uncertain. For this reason, many landlords settle for a share of the *pagri* rather than endure endless and uncertain litigation. But such 'rational' outcomes are by no means invariably to be had, and the overall legal impasse has been a prime cause of the stunted and corrupt character of the land market of Bombay. This, in turn, has had disastrous implications for economic activity in Bombay, India's premier commercial city and the lynch-pin of liberalisation. Very little building activity is taking place in Bombay—there is an acute shortage of hotel beds, for example—as a direct consequence of the difficulties in effecting transfers of land. To cite another example, the senior partner of a firm of solicitors at the very centre of liberalisation explained to me that his booming firm would now be three times its present size if they had been able to acquire premises to house the extra staff.

Perhaps surprisingly, there is an important parallel between the problem of urban land relations and the issue of contemporary marital litigation. In both cases, the legal regime has comprehensively endorsed the values and interests of one of the two parties to the conflict. Whereas urban property law systematically favours the tenant at the expense of the landowner, the law of marriage reflects the dominant male voice of Indian culture. Spokesmen for high caste, respectable Hindu society will not easily concede the claims for greater justice to be done to the increasing numbers of divorcing or separating women. Culture as well as property are at stake. So we can confidently predict that judicial conflict about marriage will increasingly be dragged down the same path of delay and subterfuge that is now characteristic of the urban land jurisdiction.

Law reform in India is not merely a matter of removing inappropriate value biases that compound the problems of the judicial process. There is a much broader project of law reform for the promotion of economic development. Some of the legislation that is now commonly argued to be either outdated or otherwise deficient is the Indian Telegraph Act of 1885, the Indian Post Office Act of 1898, the Transfer of Property Act 1882, and a mass of labour legislation. While bodies like the Law Commission have published many reports recommending specific legislative change, a great many of the changes have never been seriously contemplated. The legal and legislative drafting sections of the national and State governments are generally weak and lacking in prestige. All of this contributes to the creaky and outdated quality that marks much of the substance of Indian law. It is not just a case of freeing economic activity from the dead hand of government control, though this is necessary in many areas. But in other areas what is needed is more rather than less control. For example, the regulation of the stock exchange needs to be tightened up so that investors can have confidence that corporate governance is strict and appropriate in India. Without this confidence, India will be hampered in its search for foreign capital. It is a bad error to imagine that liberalisation in India will proceed best with less overall institutionalisation.

The Legal Profession and Liberalisation

Important though reform of property, marriage and many other areas of Indian law may be, such reform does not constitute the single key to reform of the Indian legal system as a whole. Reform of the notoriously imperfect profession is just as important an objective. Much of the problem is structural. India is different from most other common law countries in that the overwhelming majority of its lawyers are advocates paid to litigate, not solicitors paid to advise. An ineluctable consequence of this structure is that lawyers tend to have no interest in bringing about a speedy settlement of litigation. While tactical as well as narrowly forensic skills are the stock-in-trade of the legal profession everywhere, in India there is a special premium on the deployment of such skills. But lawyers cannot be asked to shoulder the whole blame for the development of sharp professional practices. For example, we have seen that in litigation over rent controlled property the tenant habitually has an interest in delaying proceedings. This platform of interest daily encourages lawyers to develop sharp tactical skills.[21] But whatever the ultimate cause, too many members of the profession fail to reach acceptable standards of competence and probity. The profession's low social reputation is evident from the lack of competition to enter it. Incoming members of the bar are to a large extent drawn from the families of present practitioners. Legal training in the universities is less than sophisticated, and it does not seem to be improving.

Economic liberalisation represents both an opportunity and a huge challenge to the legal profession. If liberalisation is to succeed to a high degree, the expanding economy will need to be supported by new and more sophisticated legal services. Many of these services will have to come from solicitors and not advocates. In colonial India, solicitors were exclusively centred in Bombay, Calcutta and to a lesser extent in Madras, and they did not take part in the great bulk of litigation that arose outside these cities. Solicitors' clients were mainly the larger companies—initially British, but the Indian houses too when they developed. The tasks were generally routine, and included drawing up prospectuses, drafting notices for statutory meetings, preparing security documents, conveyancing land, instructing advocates for litigation, and so on. Solicitors enjoyed less respect and less pay than the leading advocates of colonial India.

This character of the Indian solicitor has only very recently begun to change, and it is directly attributable to the influx of foreign investment in the form of joint ventures and equity uptake. The greater part of this change has taken place during the liberalising period since

1991, and the recent Enron deal is a good example of what is driving the change. The American Enron Corporation has entered into a joint venture to build the first private power station in India. Aside from the well publicised political controversy surrounding the project, it has been notable for the complexity of legal tasks entailed in the transaction. The demands imposed in relation to finance, property, relations between the joint venture partners, technical specifications, regulatory approvals and so on have engaged the attentions of a battery of lawyers. Most of this work has been done by American and British lawyers engaged by the Enron Corporation, while Bombay solicitors have been retained for the work that can only be done in India. For example, conveyancing of property must be entrusted to Indian lawyers, as must certification that the relevant regulatory approvals have been obtained. This kind of interaction between First World and Asian lawyers is commonplace in various developing countries of Asia, and of course Indian lawyers too have had relations with foreign lawyers in the past. But ventures like the Enron power project are thoroughly new in their scale and complexity. Indian lawyers who have participated in the project believe themselves to have acquired crucial experience and new skills, and their hope is that such experience will constitute a platform from which they will be able to assert a more central role in future projects. Of course, this question is part of the larger dynamic of First World–Third World relations. But aside from this, there needs to be rapid change within the Indian profession for such possibilities to eventuate. Some of the change will come relatively easily: for example, the enhanced premium on talent is likely to throw up important new opportunities for women. But while there is no doubt that the new work demands will bring about important changes for solicitors—they will have to change if they are to compete for the lucrative new work— the more uncertain question is whether there will be any great impact on the much larger body of advocates.[22] As yet experience is insufficient to venture an opinion on this, but any major effect is likely to be relatively slow to develop.

The Courts

The Indian population has substantially lost faith in all but the highest of its courts of law. In the popular mind, the courts are riddled with corruption from the lowliest clerk to the judge on the bench. Occasionally, action is taken against individual judicial officers. In 1990, four judges of the High Court of Bombay—perhaps the most prestigious court in India after the Supreme Court—were forced to resign by the Bar Association. The judges were pronounced to have failed to discharge their office 'with integrity and impartiality'.[23] One member of the Bar declared that the task of the Bar Association was 'to uphold the rule of law which had been threatened by corruption amongst Judges ... [T]he rot must be stemmed'. In 1995 the Association moved again, this time against the Chief Justice. He was allegedly seeking to launder bribe money through claiming it to be royalties from the publication of scholarly books, and again he was forced out of office. This action of the Bar was attended by considerable controversy. Some of the Bar took the view that the judges were denied natural justice through being condemned without trial. One member declared that the action was akin to a bill of attainder. And the Supreme Court later condemned the Bar Association for what it took to be an abuse of power. But the incidents do demonstrate that corrupt practices are still subject to resistance.

The precise extent of illicit dealing on the part of judges is quite impossible to assess. Despite the events in Bombay, it would seem that unethical practices are more characteristic of the lower than the higher courts. Certainly, there are powerful incentives for junior judges to accept money that is habitually on offer from litigants. The lack of symmetry between salary and responsibility is often extreme for these judges. Their poverty can lead to quite absurd predicaments. There is currently an industrial court judge unable to afford the rent of a Bombay flat of suitable quality for an official of his standing. This man is forced to commute daily from the city of Pune, where rents are much less, thereby incurring a train journey of some four hours each way. In circumstances such as this, the temptation to take bribes must be immense. Nonetheless, the incidence of such wrongdoing is likely to be considerably less than rumour would have it. But the perceptions are themselves a problem for the judicial system.

Distrust of the lower judiciary is one of the factors that encourages extravagant resort to appeals. The one court that still commands almost universal respect is the Supreme Court, and an extraordinary proportion of litigants seek to get their case heard by the highest

authority. Two full days of every week are devoted to the task of deciding which cases to admit to the Court's list, and even then the business
of admissions spills over onto other days. Given the backlog of cases
and the immense pressure on its time, the decision to admit a case is
often tantamount to a favourable decision for the admitting party. For
a routine case of no national importance, it will be many years before
the admitted case can be finally decided by the Court. The judges are
fully aware of the consequences of their decisions on admission, and
they routinely use the process as a way of doing rough justice. Nor is it
only the Supreme Court that artfully uses the fact of backlog as a way
of doing justice in impossibly congested circumstances. The recent outcome in the Kentucky Fried Chicken case was of precisely this genre.

As a powerful symbol of economic liberalisation, in 1995 Kentucky
Fried Chicken (KFC) was allowed to open two outlets in India. But
no sooner had its first Delhi outlet opened than it was shut down
by administrative order of the (Hindu nationalist) BJP Government.
The ground of the closure was that a couple of flies had been found
on its premises. KFC immediately sought an injunction in the Delhi
High Court to stay enforcement of the order, and it was duly granted.
The restaurant reopened for business. By the time the case comes up
for final resolution, the dirty flies will presumably be lost in the mists
of time.

What should we say about KFC's victory? To the eye of an American
or Australian lawyer, it is passing strange that an interim injunction
could stay in force for years. But given the massive backlog of cases, the
device preserves some capacity for decisive judicial action. Presumably
in this case the judge could see ideological motivation in the decision
to close down premises on the flimsy ground of discovering a couple
of flies—the action had caused national hilarity, given the profuseness
of Indian flies. The judicial outcome is hardly ideal in terms of a model
of due process, but it is probably considerably better than allowing the
grandstanding Delhi administration to have what would in effect be the
final word on KFC's right to trade. Indeed arguably the case is a neat
example of the continuing capacity of Indian justice to carry through
decisions independent of, and indeed opposed to, the Government of
the day. Is this not a crucial constituent of the 'rule of law'?

To return to the role of the Supreme Court, the period 1995–1996
has seen an upsurge in the activism of the Court. It almost seems as if

the Supreme Court has become a court of last resort for the nation as
a whole. In a series of decisions on social action cases brought by way
of writ petition, the Court has issued stringent orders to industrial pol-
luters of the Yamuna river; ordered interim compensation to be paid to
a woman accusing a university lecturer of rape; taken some tentative
steps towards expanding women's property rights; ordered an inquiry
into unlawful allocation of government houses; and demanded that the
CBI pursue corruption charges against a large number of politicians
in the 'hawala' bribery scandal. These are just a few of the Court's
recent decisions, and its activism has provoked inevitable controversy
about the proper limits of judicial power. But the Supreme Court has
clearly won the popular battle to be seen as the proper custodian of
decency, morality and fairness in public life. At a time of mounting corruption, institutional decline, and the steady criminalisation of politics,
the Court has encouraged the nation by affirming old-fashioned values
of morality and decency.

Conclusion

The image of law sketched in this chapter is one of considerable
underlying strength but weak institutional performance. India is no
China—she has not had to invent a legal tradition during the period
of the present regime. Law is not merely a symbol of modernity for
India, nor a mechanism for the attraction of foreign capital. The idea of
'the rule of law', with all its ambiguities, is deeply inscribed in Indian
society. But the institutions of the law, as with so many other public
institutions, seem to be declining rather than gathering new strength.
India remains poorly served by its legal profession, though this is by
no means solely the fault of the profession itself. The court system
is working less efficiently than it ought to be, a circumstance apparently recognised by low public confidence. On the other hand, the
highest court in India commands the greatest confidence of any Indian
institution.

It has become almost a cliché to suggest that India will be an
increasingly attractive destination for foreign capital and joint venture
operations by virtue of its strong and familiar legal order. No doubt
there is some truth to this, but there is little comfort to be drawn from
this circumstance. Foreign business houses are above all concerned that

their contracts can be enforced, and they will often prefer institutions of international arbitration rather than submit themselves to judicial institutions such as those of India. India can quite easily meet the basic legal needs of foreign corporations without any systematic change in its legal apparatus. But more importantly, liberalisation represents a once-only opportunity for India to reform and strengthen its laws and institutions for the overall development of economy and society—not merely for the encouragement of greater global engagement. Liberalisation is sparking a national mood change in which it becomes possible to imagine the rebuilding of institutions whose shortcomings are evident to everyone. The legal system is so important an Indian institution that it will inevitably have a great influence on the overall character and development of Indian society. Parts of the Indian profession are greatly fearful that their livelihood will be threatened by the appearance of foreign lawyers on their shores. But the proposition suggested here is that the new openness has a greater capacity for benevolent change to the structure and practice of the law, if not to every professional component of the system. There is just the hint that the system is beginning to take itself more seriously than it has for years, and that it sees a future other than burial in an ever-growing mound of undecided cases.

Notes

1. Part of the research for this paper was conducted in India during the period October 1995–January 1996, with the support of La Trobe University.
2. Alan Gledhill, *The Republic of India—The Development of Its Laws and Constitution*, 2nd edition (London: Stevens & Sons, 1964), p. 212.
3. See J.D.M. Derrett, *Religion, Law and the State in Modern India* (London: Faber and Faber, 1968).
4. On Macaulay and the Indian Penal Code, see V. Dhagamwar, *Law, Power and Justice: Protection of Personal Rights under the Indian Penal Code* (Bombay: Tripathi, 1974); and Eric Stokes, *The English Utilitarians and India* (Oxford: Clarendon Press, 1959), pp. 184–233.
5. A British revenue official, quoted in Elizabeth Whitcombe, *Agrarian Conditions in Northern India—the United Provinces under British Rule 1860–1900* (Berkeley: University of California Press, 1972), p. 206.
6. Martin Chanock, *Law, Custom and Social Order: The Colonial Order in Malawi and Zambia* (Cambridge, 1985).

7. The literature on the land system of British India is voluminous. For an introduction, see Eric Stokes, 'Agrarian Relations. 1 Northern and Central India', in Dharma Kumar (ed.), *The Cambridge Economic History of India* (Cambridge, 1982). One of the most illuminating collections of essays is Robert Frykenberg (ed.), *Land Control and Social Structure in Indian History* (Madison: University of Wisconsin Press, 1969).

8. D.A. Washbrook, 'Law, State and Agrarian Society in Colonial India', *Modern Asian Studies* 15(3) (1981), pp. 651–2.

9. Ibid., p. 654.

10. B.S. Cohn, 'Structural Change in Indian Rural Society, 1596–1885', in Frykenberg, *Land Control and Social Structure in Indian History*, p. 69.

11. For a discussion of this issue, see Oliver Mendelsohn, 'The Pathology of the Indian Legal System', *Modern Asian Studies* 15(4) (1981), pp. 823 at 846.

12. For a fuller discussion of this question of the psychology of Indian litigants over land, see ibid., pp. 823–63.

13. Marc Galanter, *Law and Society in Modern India* (Delhi: Oxford University Press, 1989), p. 148.

14. The subject of criminal prosecution lies outside the present chapter. But it can be noted that a large proportion of prosecutions were themselves incidents in a larger conflict over land.

15. The leading text on Indian Constitutional Law is H.M. Seervai, *Constitutional Law in India* (Bombay: Tripathi, 1995–96).

16. For a discussion of social action litigation, see Upendra Baxi, 'Taking Suffering Seriously', in R. Dhavan (ed.), *Judges and Judicial Power* (Bombay: Tripathi, 1985). It cannot be assumed that beneficial results will flow from favourable decisions of even the Supreme Court. For a detailed discussion of a celebrated case about bonded labour, see Oliver Mendelsohn, 'Life and Struggles in the Stone Quarries of India: A Case Study', *Journal of Commonwealth and Comparative Politics* 29(1) (1991), pp. 44–71.

17. The discussion of litigation and the overall legal situation in Bombay is based on interviews conducted in Bombay in December 1995.

18. For an accessible discussion of the issue of female inheritance in India, see Madhu Kishwar and R. Vanita, 'Inheritance Rights for Women: A Response to Some Commonly Expressed Fears', *Manushi* 57 (March–April 1990), pp. 2–15.

19. Interview with judge at Patiala House, New Delhi, 14 November 1995.

20. Bibek Debroy, *India Today* (31 December 1995), p. 148.

21. For a good discussion of lawyers' tactics, see R.L. Kidder, 'Courts and Conflict in an Indian City: A Study in Legal Impact', *Journal of Commonwealth Political Studies* 11(2) (1973), p. 121; and a collection of papers in *Law and Society Review* 9(1) (1974).

22. For an account of the way in which Australian firms of solicitors changed in response to pressures that arose from foreign corporations as well as domestic developments, see Oliver Mendelsohn and Matthew Lippman, 'The Emergence of the Corporate Law Firm in Australia', *University of New South Wales Law Journal* 3(1) (1979), pp. 78 at 98. There appear to be important, if far from complete, parallels between the Australian experience and what is now happening in India.

23. This discussion is based on minutes of meetings of the Bombay Bar Association, 12 June and 21 June 1990, and 22 February and 1 March 1995.

6

THE INDIAN LEGAL PROFESSION,
THE COURTS AND GLOBALISATION*

There are two distinct, even contradictory, narratives about the value of the Indian legal system to the development goals of the Indian regime. On the one hand the two-century tradition of Anglo-Indian law is regularly portrayed as one of the great advantages possessed by India in its drive to raise standards of living and improve the overall standing of the nation. The other narrative is one of outmoded and corrupt legal institutions and a profession poorly adapted to the demands of either the common people or modern, increasingly global, commerce.[1] Given the intensity and longevity of these two seemingly opposed accounts of the Indian legal order, it would be too great an ambition for the present article to attempt to rehearse the narratives and reach a simple verdict on their respective claims. The more limited object here is to discuss some recent developments within the Indian legal system, particularly in the legal profession but also in the courts and related institutions. This discussion will be relevant to the larger question as to the fitness of the Indian legal system to the contemporary demands of development.

Lawyers and the Litigation Syndrome

In India the practice of law is more synonymous with litigation than in perhaps any other jurisdiction in the world. In most other countries,

* This chapter was originally published in *South Asia: Journal of South Asian Studies* 28(2) (2006), pp. 301–20.

and certainly in other common law jurisdictions such as Britain and the US, the majority of lawyers neither appear regularly in court nor are directly engaged for the bulk of their employment in relation to actual litigation. In India lawyers are generally employed only if there is litigation before the courts, and this has been true for the whole two hundred years or so of the existence of the modern Anglo-Indian legal system. It was only the Presidency towns of Calcutta, Madras and above all Bombay that developed a significant branch of the profession that did not derive its income from arguing cases in court. These lawyers were called attorneys (or later solicitors), and they prepared the case for advocates in the highest courts and also performed a range of other legal services outside the context of litigation.[2] Bombay, Calcutta, and to a lesser extent Madras, were the Indian centres of international commerce, and a large proportion of the solicitors were employed by British or other foreign companies engaged in trade and manufacturing within India. In time the larger Indian businesses came to see the value of legal advisers in contexts other than litigation, as did some rich individuals, but private resort to solicitors has remained relatively rare.

During the colonial period the great bulk of litigation and criminal prosecution took place in rural areas. Only cases of very high value deriving from a rural area would originate in the High Court and therefore potentially involve an attorney. Most cases were relatively small affairs and a large proportion of them revolved around the administration of agricultural land. British policies in relation to land, above all the severity of their taxation demands, were the single greatest factor producing litigation in the courts the British themselves established. This became dramatically clear in retrospect, when the effective abolition of taxation on agricultural land after Independence caused the immediate disappearance of hundreds of thousands of cases annually in Bengal and other parts of eastern India. These cases were an aspect of the intermediary (*zamindari*) system, whereby the *zamindars* used the courts as a tactic to extract rent from their tenants; much of this rent had then to be passed on as a tax to the state.[3]

There was no other policy that generated large numbers of civil cases in colonial India, since British policy was to tread lightly in relation to the regulation of family and social life in general.[4] For example, they did not set up an administrative system to make marriage a contract requiring institutional validation and thus litigation in case of dispute.

In short, the exposure of ordinary Indians to legal institutions and legal professionals was highly limited. If they had to go to court they were either unrepresented—this seems to have been true of a great many defendants in particular—or represented by a *vakil* comparatively low in the professional hierarchy. Few of them encountered a barrister, the elite among the advocates, and fewer still an attorney (solicitor). On the other hand, in local courthouses throughout India there tended to be (and still are) notaries available to prepare official documents (including affidavits, sworn statements and other declarations required by the administration). What has never developed in India is ready resort to a category of skilled professionals for the purpose of making wills, transferring property and discharging other legal matters. Such matters have tended to be discharged privately (in the case of wills, for example) or by official record keepers approached more directly (in the case of land transactions). Only in what have become the great cities of India did a class of lawyers, the attorneys, develop to handle some of the complexities of real property transactions.

Despite the quite limited subject matter of cases that came to the courts, from the 1870s British officials became ever louder in their denunciation of what they took to be a frivolous Indian indulgence in litigation.[5] Indians were, in the eyes of their British masters, a litigious people. Attendance to the detail of Indian court action does not support this psycho-cultural construct. The basic Indian motivation for the initiation of litigation both historically and today appears to be self-interest.

Although litigation over agricultural land is far less today than during the colonial period, the contemporary Indian legal system has come to be typified by its mountain of unresolved litigation and therefore massive delay in decisional justice. Government figures suggest that there are millions of cases pending, although officials privately concede that there is no accurate measurement of cases in the system.[6] This problem of 'arrears', as it is officially termed, is widely seen as the most pressing problem of the Indian court system. It has become a dominating concern of some of the most respected Indian judges and of the international institutions that hold so much influence in India today. So the Bombay High Court, the most prestigious court in India after the Supreme Court, has now determined to take relatively radical steps to reduce 'arrears' (see ahead). And the Asian Development Bank has commissioned a major study of the Delhi courts so as to formulate a scheme for their institutional reform.[7] Although rarely expressed in print in such disparaging terms as during the colonial period, there still seems to be a view within India that a large proportion of litigation is without merit. Curiously, the British idea of the litigious Indian is not without support within India more than half a century after its Independence.

It is clear that other categories of litigation have at least partly filled the void left by the decline of cases to do with agricultural land, and there is now less skewed a pattern of litigation than was true fifty years ago. What is not so clear is whether the number of cases coming forward every year is genuinely beyond the capacity of a properly functioning system to handle. Marc Galanter and Jayanth Krishnan have recently argued that Indian litigation might actually be too low when the per capita numbers are compared with those of reasonably comparable countries such as Malaysia.[8] Galanter has long argued that Indians are disadvantaged by the failure of the legal system to have developed a pattern of torts litigation which could lead to reasonable compensation for the victims of negligence or simply accident. The appalling example of Bhopal is a case in point. In short, we need to be careful not to fall into assumptions about the over-use of Indian courts and into crude and probably erroneous characterisations of why people go to court.

Importantly, it is clear that in post-Independence India there continues to be a huge volume of litigation that is peculiarly the creation of particular and dubiously progressive schemes of public administration. The outstanding example is the litigation that flows from rent control in the great metropolises of India, Mumbai, above all. This may be the largest single source of litigation in post-Independence India, though it is less in volume and certainly does not have the same social impact as litigation over agricultural land in colonial India.[9] A short consideration of this litigation will usefully frame our later discussion of changes within the solicitors' branch of the profession.

The Problem of Rent Control, Particularly in Mumbai[10]

'Rent control' is the shorthand term for a series of measures regulating the relationships between landlord and tenant in the cities of India. The measures have their origin in the concern of the British authorities to secure cheap accommodation for their soldiers during World War I,[11] but have developed into an apparatus that systematically favours the tenant over the landlord, on the rationale that demand for urban property grossly exceeds supply and therefore the vulnerable tenant needs to be protected. So the rent of tenants is controlled and their tenure secured, such that they can be ejected only on highly restricted grounds. Protection of tenure is not merely for the original tenant, since the tenancy is also heritable under the legislation.[12]

Although there is surprisingly little scholarly discussion of the regulation of urban tenancy in India, its major impact has clearly been in the period since Independence. This coincides with the great growth in the population of Indian cities and thus radically increased pressure on housing and commercial premises. Perhaps paradoxically, but in line with the arguments of opponents of rent control, this shortage of accommodation has partly been brought about by rent control itself. The argument is that there has been too little incentive for developers to invest in housing and commercial buildings.

In 1992, as an aspect of liberalisation of the Indian economy, the Government of India circulated model legislation to reform the old rent control laws. Intensely partisan debate on the issue ensured that there was no rapid or radical change in the law, but Maharashtra is one of four states to have proceeded to develop new legislation at least partly along the lines of the central model.[13] Fully seven years after a bill was prepared, the *Maharashtra Rent Control Act* 1999, was finally enacted. The difference between the intent of the *Bombay Rents, Hotel and Lodging House Rates (Control) Act* 1947 and the Act of 1999 can be gathered from their respective preambles. The 1947 Act states that this is a law 'relating to the control of rents and repairs of certain premises ... and of evictions....' The Act of 1999 repeats these words but goes on to add the object of 'encouraging the construction of new houses by assuring a fair return on the investment by landlords....' The specific changes in 1999 are to the manner in which rent is fixed, allowing a more realistic rent to be charged by the landlord (sections 8 to 12); enhanced grounds for ejection of tenants (section 16); and improved mechanisms for the landlord to proceed against recalcitrant tenants (Chapter VIII). Large commercial tenants including multinationals are now exempted from the operation of the Act (section 3), in effect stripping these entities from any protection under rent control principles. But importantly, the new principles more favourable to landlords are applicable only to future tenancies: the determinedly cautious nature of the reform is evident in this protection of existing tenants (often including their heirs). Accordingly, any impact of the new legislation will be slow.

Rent control in India has worked at all only because of the device of *'pugree'* (literally, turban). This is the system whereby, upon transfer of tenancy from one person to another, a sum of money, or *pugree*, is payable by the incoming tenant to the outgoing tenant and to the landlord. Under the original *Transfer of Property Act* 1882 the transfer of such amounts was lawful (section 105) but it was made unlawful by rent control legislation such as the Maharashtra Act of 1947 (section 18). As the gap between the controlled and the market rent widened, the payment of increasing amounts of *pugree* became an invariable part of the transfer of tenancy. *Pugree* represented the only way a landlord could gain anything approaching a reasonable return on capital. But in order to persuade a tenant to quit a cheap rental, the tenant too had to be dealt into the transaction. Indeed, the larger share of the *pugree* went to the outgoing tenant: in Bombay, the outgoing residential tenant customarily received two-thirds of the *pugree*, the landlord one-third. The sums of money involved were very large, since the trade in rentals became an ersatz market in land. Upon payment of the *pugree*, the incoming tenant was virtually guaranteed of a ridiculously cheap and secure tenancy in a market where accommodation is highly scarce.

Since *pugree* was illegal under the rent control legislation, it represented 'black' money. As such it was neither taxable by the state nor available for many legitimate economic activities. Again as part of liberalisation of the Indian economy, *pugree* was made lawful by the *Maharashtra Rent Control Act* 1999 (section 56). While *pugree* will continue to be an important part of tenancy transfer for many years to come, over time the establishment of market as opposed to artificially low rents will reduce its significance in land transactions. More immediately, the legalisation of the premiums represented by *pugree* will greatly reduce the scope of the black economy in India and will work to strip away some of the advantages to be gained from some of the more ruthless exploitation of the courts as a weapon in tenants' fights to retain rent-controlled premises.

We can now turn more directly to litigation over rent control. It is impossible to quantify all litigation in the city of Mumbai and to apportion the litigation into type and subject with any precision. That said, it is clear from an analysis of the number and the jurisdiction of the civil courts in Mumbai that litigation arising from rent control has been by far the largest single source of litigation in the city for many decades in the post-Independence period.[14] Thus in 2004 there were 36 Small Causes Courts in Mumbai, four of them appeals courts (comprised of two judges), and rent control matters were the exclusive jurisdiction of all but two of these courts. So thirty-eight judges were exclusively taken up with rent control matters. There were also certain additional quasi-judicial officers, officially termed 'the Competent Authority', who deal with comparatively minor contests in the rent control jurisdiction. By contrast, and leaving aside the specialised Family Court (comprised of only seven judges), there were only eighteen judges (less than half the number of rent control judges) in the Bombay City Civil Courts to hear the myriad of matters other than landlord–tenant disputes. But even in these Civil Courts, there are a large number of suits to do with landed property and rent control in particular. For example, the Civil Court is the appropriate court for a plaintiff claiming possession of premises and disputing a claim of tenancy by the defendant, as well as for disputes over actual title to property. Finally, above all these courts stands the Bombay High Court, the second most prestigious court in India after the Supreme Court. There is no regular appeal on rent control matters to the High Court but many such matters get there through a couple of procedural vehicles. Thus suits claiming damages greater than Rs 50,000 can be brought within the original jurisdiction of the High Court, and it is an ordinary tactic of some litigants to adjust their claim accordingly. And secondly, the device of a writ petition to review (as opposed to appeal from) a decision of a lower court brings many a determined landowner into the embrace of the High Court too. Indeed, cases to do with urban property—and within this category 'rent control' matters are by far the most numerous—appear to be the largest single body of litigation in the Bombay High Court. In sum, the institutional apparatus of the Bombay judiciary reveals a heavy preponderance of landlord–tenant or rent control matters.

The basic reason for this profusion of litigation arising from rent control is the situation sketched above. In a word, it is in the interest of most tenants to hold on like grim death to their premises, whether these are for residential or for commercial purposes. Equally, it tends to be in the landlord's interest either to eject the tenant or to allow transfer of the tenancy and thus a share of the *pugree*. Given the sharp antagonism of these interests in the context of growing land scarcity, it is in no way surprising that landlord–tenant relations have become such a fertile source of judicial (and extra-judicial) contest.

It is worth beginning with an oral account of such a contest, which can be called *the case of the law lecturer made by rent control*.[15] The location of the matter was the city of Delhi but the rent control legislation there was broadly similar to that of Mumbai. My informant's grandfather had been a refugee from what became Pakistan in 1947, and he set up business in rented premises in the old cloth market of Delhi. The family lived above the shop in the same premises. Rental was for a fixed period of time but the family stayed on following lapse of the contract. The grandfather thus became a 'statutory tenant', with somewhat lesser protection than is available to a contractual tenant under the law. A statutory tenancy was heritable only if it were commercial and not residential in nature. Accordingly, the landlord of the premises initiated litigation after the grandfather's death to secure eviction of the family on the ground that the premises were for residential rather than commercial purposes and therefore the statutory tenancy was not heritable. In 1970 the High Court of Delhi found in favour of the landlord and ordered the family to vacate the premises but my informant filed an appeal before the Divisional bench of the High Court, thereby staying the effect of the order. That appeal was still pending at the time of interview in 1995, though the matter had long since been settled. Meanwhile the cost and complications of the litigation were so great that my informant decided to study law and be admitted to practise, so as to conduct the family litigation himself. He found he enjoyed law so much that he eventually gave up his commercial occupation and became a lecturer in law.

The matter was ultimately settled quite outside the arena of the courts. The landlord of my informant's premises lost heart during the protracted contest and finally sold the building to another landlord. The new landlord came to my informant and offered him a handsome sum (analagous to *pugree*) to vacate the premises. The now law lecturer agreed to this offer, but only because it could bring to an end another body of litigation in which he and his family were the plaintiffs as landlord of the property in question. In 1947 the grandfather had not only rented premises but had also purchased a building, and in August of that year he began court proceedings to eject the tenant. This tenant was just as determined to stay in the building as was the law lecturer's family in their rented premises. It was only in October 1977, when my informant used the money he had gained from his own landlord to make an offer to his recalcitrant tenant, that the latter agreed to vacate the ground floor of the building and retreat to the first floor. In this way, through compromise brought about by exhaustion and reasonable reciprocity, my informant was able to occupy at least part of a building his grandfather had purchased thirty years previously.

This account quite neatly epitomises the clash of interests at the heart of the rent control imbroglio that has developed in post-Independence India. It shows, for example, the sharply opposed legal tactics that need to be employed depending upon whether one is plaintiff (typically the landlord seeking possession of the property) or defendant (usually the tenant seeking to remain in the property). For the defendant tenant, there is no urgency to the judicial contest; indeed, the longer the proceedings last, the better it will be for the party in possession. The validity of the tenant's case for staying on will not need to be tested until the case comes up for final decision. So the lawyer for the defendant will seek to take advantage of every legitimate (and all too often, illegitimate) opportunity to delay ultimate resolution of the matter. It is now a matter of notoriety that the Indian judicial process is terribly vulnerable to such tactics. The most valuable aid to the recalcitrant defendant is the 'arrears' of litigation that over time has stretched decades into the future. With every year that passes, the problem gets worse: most courts decide far fewer cases than new ones are admitted. Even if a new matter were not deliberately delayed by one of the parties, it would be many years before it came up for decision by the court.

If it is typically in the defendant tenant's interest to delay resolution of a landlord's suit for ejection, then this interest coincides with that of lawyers for both defendant and plaintiff. The longer the matter goes on, the more they will be paid. No doubt this cools the passion for expeditiousness in many a plaintiff lawyer, though active efforts to delay proceedings will remain the responsibility of the defendant's lawyer. Opportunities for delay are abundant. Leaving aside the passive and always increasing effect of the mountain of arrears, the Indian judicial process is particularly fertile ground for the production of delay. Adjournments are freely given—both for good and for seemingly quite flimsy reasons. For example, all too often adjournments are granted because the lawyer for one side cannot be present for the hearing (sometimes because he/she is appearing in another case). Even less defensible, the judge is frequently absent from duty for one reason or another. An adverse decision will automatically lead to any available appeal or review. It is also routine that the one issue spawns a number of parallel judicial actions as a tactic to produce delay and mount pressure on the other side.

Although the example I have used above is a case where legal right was more likely on the side of the landlord than the tenant, this is not to suggest that the tenant is usually in the wrong in rent control contests. On many occasions landlords are trying to divest tenants of possession for their own reasons (redevelopment of the property, for example) quite outside the narrow grounds for ejection laid down in the statute (own need for occupation, non-payment of rent, sub-letting without permission, unauthorised construction, and several other grounds). And no doubt it is true that social justice is frequently on the side of the tenant rather than the landlord. Presumably, a large proportion of the tenants in the old chawls (apartment buildings) of Mumbai could simply not afford to pay the market rent for their small apartment.

The above example of *the law lecturer made by rent control* is not intended to be a summary of litigation over landlord–tenant matters in contemporary India but simply an example to demonstrate the complex histories such matters often develop in the particular context of the Indian judicial process. By the time rent control became a major issue in post-Independence India, the character of both the legal profession and the judicial process more generally was fully formed. The Indian legal process often appears as an extreme example of the faults seen generally in common law legal systems, that is, the systems that owe their broad characteristics to the original British model. So, if false witness is a problem for courts throughout the common law world, then it appears to exist in epidemic proportions in the Indian courts. And if lawyers everywhere can sometimes be seen to engage in sharp tactics, then in India such tactics (like deliberately procuring seemingly endless delays) are commonplace.

Various kinds of explanation have been attempted of the particular form litigation has taken in India. In an early post-Independence view that still recurs quite frequently, Bernard Cohn argued that the legal system introduced by the British is unsuited to the values of traditional India. Cohn claimed that the winner-take-all character of litigation in Anglo-Indian justice conflicted with a culturally ingrained preference for compromise and group solidarity.[16] Faced with this clash of values, Indian litigants had no respect for the courts and were prepared to give false witness and generally manipulate the process. Against this view, Robert Kidder could see no rejection of the values of the court system by litigants who happily came to the court seeking comprehensive victory rather than compromise.[17] Litigants simply learnt from their lawyers to do whatever it took to win, or at least not to lose. For Kidder the character of Indian litigation was largely formed by the legal professionals themselves. Indian lawyers have simply mastered the possibilities inherent in a due process system of justice.

It seems to me now, as it did many years ago, that Kidder was closer to the truth than Cohn.[18] But there remains a missing factor in accounts like that of Kidder which focus almost exclusively on the institutions and processes of the law. Granted that lawyers, judges and other functionaries have built a distinctive variation on the original British model of a legal system, we still need to explain the popular toleration of a system that is so unsatisfactory to so many people. Why do people put up with it? The answer is that it does in fact suit a category of litigants who appear before the courts. In other words, it is the interests of the litigants as well as the behaviour of the legal professionals that has driven much of the distinctiveness of the Indian legal system.

A moment's reflection on the above case of *the law lecturer made by rent control* can make this point quite neatly. Why did both parties to the two parallel sets of litigation put up with it for decade after decade? The answer is because the stakes were so high for both parties. The disparity between the market rent and what was due under the rent control legislation was the material issue that drove the litigation so powerfully for so many years. Any manipulation by legal professionals that may have occurred along the way, so as to prolong the litigation, was logically secondary to the core issue. It was the litigants themselves, rather than their lawyers, who ultimately drove the conflict. In any case, after a time my informant became lawyer and client in one. The parties only came to an agreement when they became exhausted with the contest.

On another level, however, these litigants were not at all in control of their conflict. The whole affair had been brought about by the rent control legislation. This law has so ignored market realities as to pit a legion of tenants against their landlords. There are important parallels between this situation and the litigation over agricultural land that was dominant in the colonial period and the early years after Independence. It was economic rationality too that drove most of those many hundreds of thousands of cases, but this rationality was created by a British land administration that had substantially destabilised agrarian relations.[19]

In short, rent control has been a perfect jurisdiction to perpetuate the kind of legal practice that became entrenched in India many decades ago. The phenomenal growth of 'arrears', in large part brought about by rent matters themselves, has only made worse a system long unable to produce rapid decisional justice. It is clear to every serious observer that major reform of the litigation system is necessary, with the object of modernising court processes and helping improve the performance of judges, court functionaries and lawyers. But the specific point being made here is that such reform will be effective only if the laws themselves—rent control is now the leading example—do not deliver a vast quantity of litigation that positively encourages abuse of process. Just as British land revenue policies had a strong part in shaping the legal system that developed in colonial India, so rent control laws in independent India have helped to compound the worst aspects of that system.

For seemingly the first time, there does now seem to be a degree of commitment to the twin goals of law reform and institutional reform. This is most notable in Mumbai. We have already noted the significant reforms to the rent control legislation that can be predicted to reduce, albeit gradually, the scope for conflict between landlord and tenant. On an institutional level, the Chief Justice and other senior judges in Mumbai are actively committed to filtering certain categories of cases, including rent control matters, through alternative dispute resolution processes.[20] Indeed, there would appear to be considerable scope for alternative dispute resolution in India. On the other hand, as argued above, in any diversion of rent control cases to other forums there needs to be adequate awareness that the defendant party in possession habitually has a strong interest in delaying proceedings if the plaintiff is seen to have a strong case. Justice A.P. Shah, the second most senior judge in Mumbai, is well aware of this problem and proposes that certain matters be referred to alternative bodies without opportunity for appeal or referral to the courts.[21] The objective of such an approach is to proceed immediately to the substantive issue in rent control matters and to defeat delays arising from tactical manoeuvres. It remains to be seen whether reforms such as this one will speed up judicial or quasi-judicial decision making, thereby reducing some of the pressures exerted by the mountain of arrears.[22]

There does seem to be a new ferment within the legal profession of India, particularly in Mumbai. I have earlier argued that this ferment has arisen from the general phenomenon of globalisation of the Indian economy, which has brought new international business and new ways of doing business to India.[23] Toleration of the terribly dispiriting manner in which litigation proceeds in India is waning. Thus there is a great deal of anecdotal evidence of the horror with which multinational business views the prospect of becoming embroiled in litigation in India—a horror so visceral that they habitually bind their Indian partners to accept international arbitration processes rather than be vulnerable to Indian litigation. And critically, in the fifteen years or so since the beginning of liberalisation of the economy, a branch of the legal profession has begun to reinvent itself along lines developed decades earlier in other capitalist economies.[24]

The Emergence of the Corporate Law Firm in India

At the beginning of this article we noted that most Indian lawyers are litigators and that this has been the case since the inception of the Anglo-Indian legal system. It was mainly in Calcutta, Madras and Bombay that 'attorneys' were to be found. Perhaps from their inception and certainly by late in the nineteenth century, some of the attorneys of Bombay had close connections with British business houses that traded or manufactured in India. These attorneys were more likely to have formed themselves into firms, rather than practising individually, and their principals were of British origin. And even today, some of the Mumbai firms bear names that reflect their true origins: Little & Co, Payne & Co, and Crawford Bayley are examples. The first Indian was admitted as an attorney before the then Supreme Court of Bombay as early as 1858, and Indian firms of attorneys—many of them with Parsee or Gujarati principals—were formed in the succeeding decades. Eventually, though, Indians took over the British firms, in a number of instances in the years immediately before or after Independence. Thus the Parsee firm of Mulla & Mulla merged with a British firm in 1953 to become Mulla & Mulla & Craigie Blunt & Caroe, now perhaps the largest law firm in India. Because of their Indian origins, until recently Mullas did not have a significant association with British or other foreign commercial houses. Whereas Crawford Bayley had clients such as the Imperial (later the State) Bank, Grindlays and Lloyds, as well as large British shipping companies, Mulla & Mulla built their business through Indian clients that included the Nizam of Hyderabad, the Maharaja of Baroda and what became the dominating business houses of Birla and Tata. Even today the old British firms tend to have a higher concentration of foreign clients than do the long established Indian firms.

Despite their connection with commercially important British and later European and American companies, the solicitors of Bombay had to fight the perception both within the profession and among many clients that their existence was illegitimate and worked to increase the cost of litigation. While this attitude was also to be found in Britain and other common law jurisdictions (though not the US with its unified profession), the solicitors' struggle for legitimacy was especially sharp in India by virtue of the small number of solicitors and their lack of contact with even middle class India. Since popular involvement in legal practice was overwhelmingly confined to the experience of litigation (conducted in court as it was by a barrister or vakil), many clients found it difficult to understand the point of the involvement of another branch of the profession. It was largely their connection with powerful foreign interests that underwrote both the business and the legitimacy of the solicitors of Bombay. And it was the growth of Bombay into the undisputed commercial capital of India that pushed the Bombay solicitors into a more solid and wealthier position than their counterparts in Calcutta enjoyed; the Madras branch of the profession was always far smaller.

Indian solicitors have emerged as the most dynamic branch of the profession at the very time that their existence has formally been abolished. By way of a 1976 amendment to the Advocates Act 1961, the dual profession was ended. All lawyers were thereafter styled 'advocates', and common requirements for education and admission to the bar were set down. In practical terms, this legislative change has meant very little. It has certainly not ended the practice of advocates on the original side of the High Court being instructed by a solicitor. 'The Bombay Incorporated Law Society', the organised body of solicitors formed in 1894, remains in existence today and continues to lay down standards of practice; prescribes education and training; and sets examinations for aspirant solicitors, as it did prior to the fusion of the profession. What has happened, somewhat unexpectedly, is the migration of some erstwhile advocates into the profession of solicitor. Given that in formal terms there is now only one category of lawyer, the 'advocate', it is now possible to do the work of a solicitor without having to become an articled clerk or pass any examinations set by the Law Society. Increasingly the law firms, that is what used to be the firms of solicitors, are seen as the practitioners of 'transactional' law, as opposed to litigation. Transactional practice is gaining the reputation of being financially well rewarded and less frustrating than advocacy before the clogged, inefficient and often corrupt courts.

The volume published in 1995 to celebrate the centenary of the Bombay Law Society in 1994 notes that there were 660 solicitors at that time, 147 of them women, and 232 law firms.[25] By then, and much more so now, there were many other lawyers doing the work of solicitors but not eligible for membership of the Law Society. Probably the great majority of solicitors are overwhelmingly engaged in property matters. The solicitors are not so heavily involved in rent control matters as are the advocates, because rent control matters begin in the lower courts where the involvement of a solicitor would be unusual. But the bread and butter of the solicitors is conveyancing—in this sense they are like their counterparts in London or Sydney, though Mumbai lacks any modern title system run by the state. And certainly there is heavy involvement of solicitors in litigation over land, which arises in many contexts other than in rent control matters. Succession contests, for example, are common in contemporary India, and often the largest issue is landed property.

Of course, the dynamic character of the solicitors of Mumbai has not arisen from their involvement in property matters. Rather, this quality is lent by the emergence of a small section of the profession as indispensable players in the new, increasingly globalised, economy of India. The most important date in this transformation was 1991–92, when the Indian economy entered its phase of liberalisation under Rajiv Gandhi and Finance Minister, now Prime Minister, Manmohan Singh. As a way of pointing up the change in the legal profession of Mumbai, it will be instructive to begin with the career of one person.

Zia Mody is the founder and principal of AZB & Partners, Advocates and Solicitors. Ms Mody is not herself a solicitor, having begun her practice as an advocate rather than serving the apprenticeship that would qualify her for membership of the Law Society. Her education in law was at Cambridge and afterwards an LLM at Harvard. For five years she worked at the law firm Baker & McKenzie in New York, and then came back to work as junior advocate to a practitioner who was once her father's junior; her father is the former Attorney General of India, Soli Sorabjee.[26] After her professional experience in the US, Zia Mody had found her work at the Bombay bar less than fulfilling and she gradually drifted into a style of practice which she now calls 'transactional and corporate'. Her clients are overwhelmingly foreign corporations, and initially they began coming to her largely on the basis of recommendations from the American firms Baker & McKenzie and Simpson Thacher.

In 1995, when I first interviewed Zia Mody, she described her practice as 'an unholy mix'.[27] She was still conducting a lot of commercial litigation—the proportion was down from ninety percent in her years of full-time work at the bar to about thirty percent. She was also doing a lot of what she now call transactional work—involvement in joint ventures between foreign and Indian corporations, setting up mutual funds to raise capital for both Indian and foreign ventures, facilitating direct investment, and the like. In relation to foreign mutual funds raising capital in India, for example, she handled regulatory approvals, prepared documentation, advised on corporate and taxation issues, and was generally available to see the matter through. The broad character of this work was typical of corporate legal practice in New York or

London but it was new to Bombay at the time. Zia Mody's own experience in New York had made the work thoroughly familiar to her, even if the institutions and legal culture of India differed sharply from that of the US. Since she had only four juniors with her in 1995, there were limits to what she could take on. Much of the litigation was conducted by the juniors, leaving her to deal direct with the foreign corporations.

In 1995 Zia Mody's small office in Dalal Street—the street that houses the Bombay Stock Exchange—was furnished more stylishly than any of the solicitors' firms. She noted that foreign clients derive confidence from well furnished rooms, whereas Indian clients are uncomfortable because they tend to assume that they are paying for the decoration themselves. Since most of her clients at the time were foreign corporations (as they still are today), her style of office was appropriate.

By 2004, when I interviewed Zia Mody again, her firm had become AZB & Partners (the 'A' and 'B' being two of her senior partners' initials) and now occupied the whole twenty-third floor of a prestigious building looking out over the Arabian Sea.[28] There were now 14 partners in the firm, five of them women. In April of 2004 she had merged with a Delhi firm, putting her 40 lawyers in Mumbai together with 25 in Delhi. Her firm had already set up in Bangalore in 2003 and there were now 15 lawyers there. So there were a total of 80 lawyers in the firm by the end of 2004. Zia Mody herself was now doing very little litigation, concentrating instead on management of the practice and general corporate work but including appearances before SEBI (the securities regulator). The firm retains its own litigators, while briefing senior counsel at the bar in important matters. This combination of both solicitor's and barrister's practice within a single firm—some individual lawyers doing both forms of work—is just one of the marks of innovation in AZB & Partners.

The firm's business is general corporate law, with a particular specialty in mergers and acquisitions. This latter specialty entails multiple tasks including finance raisings, the arrangement of proper flows of intellectual property, labour approvals, customs and other regulatory approvals, and even the acquisition of premises. Aside from such incidental involvement in property transactions, AZB & Partners is distinctive among the Mumbai firms in not having partners or a whole department devoted to property matters. Within its general corporate work, the firm has been a leader in raising capital on foreign equity markets. And they have been heavily involved in project finance for major infrastructure (ports, airports) and power projects.

In short, within about a decade Zia Mody has established in Mumbai a modern corporate law firm of the kind found in New York, London or Sydney. What is so distinctive about the firm is the short time period in which it has been created and the extent to which one person has driven its rise. Unlike the long established law firms in Mumbai, the age profile of her law firm is young: the two oldest members of the firm are herself at forty-eight and one of the other senior partners at fifty. This youthfulness has been a major factor in the firm's ability to take advantage of the new opportunities for corporate legal practice available in Mumbai.

If AZB & Partners is a singular example of what an individual lawyer of drive, imagination and relevant experience both in India and abroad can accomplish in the newly deregulated world of Indian business, the more general story of the solicitors' profession is quite different. The major practitioners of corporate law in Mumbai are the long established firms, a number of which have been performing such work since well before Independence. Strong relationships were built up with individual companies, both foreign and Indian. For example, for many years the largest client of Crawford Bayley was the Imperial Bank (which was renamed The State Bank of India and nationalised in 1955). Often, a partner of one of the Bombay firms was asked to join the board of individual companies. Thus the senior partner in one firm has for many years been a director of what is now the largest corporation in India, Reliance Industries. In another of the largest and oldest firms, a partner held ninety directorships at the height of his practice, and even in 2004 this partner (by then aged sixty-six) was on fifty boards.[29] A position on the board has long been seen by the firms to be extremely valuable in generating legal work for them, though some solicitors now see this as an outmoded way of doing corporate law.

If the argument being developed in this article is that the solicitors are the most dynamic branch of the legal profession in Mumbai and probably in India as a whole, this is not to conclude that the firms have in general shown any marked capacity for rapid and imaginative change. Nor, to repeat, are most of the Mumbai solicitors engaged in corporate law at all; they are largely preoccupied with mundane property transactions. It is true that by now there are a considerable number of individual Mumbai lawyers equipped with skills appropriate to the new environment of global business, but even in their own firms, overall adaptation to the new business environment has been slower than it might have been. Much legal business that could appropriately be done in Mumbai continues to be discharged by foreign lawyers. This is partly because of preconceptions on the part of foreign clients but also because the firms have failed to transform themselves sufficiently rapidly so as to develop the full range of services demanded by transnational corporations.

Curiously, one of the reasons for the slower than desirable transformation of the Mumbai solicitors is the advantage they have derived from rent control. As with many other commercial ventures in the business district of south Mumbai, most of the old solicitors' firms occupy rent-controlled premises. Many venerable and respected law firms are still to be accessed only through shabby and dilapidated corridors and steep staircases because the landlord has failed to maintain the public parts of the building and sometimes not even kept the elevators operating. Since the landlord cannot charge extra rent by spending money on the building, it is left to slowly rot. Sometimes the tenant solicitors have refurbished the interior of their premises at their own expense, presenting a ludicrous contrast between the public and the private areas of the building. But in many cases even the interiors are far shabbier than in buildings that are not rent controlled. It is difficult to escape the conclusion that the bonanza of rent control for established tenants like the old law firms has made some of them complacent and insufficiently focused on the need to change. The firms that have made capital improvements in their premises have to work harder before showing a profit, but in the long run these will be the firms that prosper.

One of the more striking aspects of conservatism among Mumbai law firms is the continuing practice of nepotism in many of them. Sons and now sometimes daughters have followed their father into many of the firms and later into the partnership without necessary regard to merit. In Australia, by contrast, the firms that transformed themselves into corporate law firms in the 1970s were often old family firms that had begun to cut the ties of nepotism as early as the 1940s. The Australian firms that had been built on talent were in a position to take advantage of new opportunities when the Australian economy began to open from the late 1960s. Other firms that failed to make the appropriate structural and cultural change fell by the wayside. In Mumbai, the ties of family have lasted far longer in the context of a closed Indian economy. But hiring and promoting staff strictly on the basis of talent will become an irresistible demand in firms that are going to prosper. Almost certainly, formerly significant firms that fail to modernise their internal workings will decline quite rapidly.

Not only will there be increasing competition within Mumbai, but under the General Agreement on Trade in Services (GATS) annexed to the WTO, India is supposed to open up legal practice to international competition. The greater part of the profession (but not including the organised body of solicitors) is deeply opposed to the entry of foreign lawyers in India.[30] Whether or not there will be a strong and direct foreign presence in the market for legal services in India, there can be no doubt that transnational expectations will bear down increasingly on the practice of law in Mumbai. The firms will find that they need to modernise all aspects of their performance if they are to prosper in an environment that imposes new pressures for performance, as well as offering new opportunities for financial and professional reward. Thus far the firms have been protected by their considerably lower bills for the same services offered in New York or London, but while price differential is an aspect of competition, it cannot be a long-term alternative to modernisation. It is not enough that the most talented of the Mumbai solicitors are able to meet the highest standards of international practice. The whole sector needs to improve its performance, and this will involve a much more thorough transformation of structures and processes than has taken place thus far.

Conclusion

This article has juxtaposed two parts of the Indian, more particularly the Mumbai, legal scene—litigation over rent control and changes within the solicitors' branch of the profession. Litigation is the defining characteristic of the Indian legal system, and rent control has become its centrepiece over the last few decades. Much of this litigation appears tactical rather than decisional in character and it grows out of the highly artificial world created by rent control legislation. Once the sharply antagonistic interests of landlord and tenant were delivered into the hands of a legal profession that had already thrived on other distorted social relations for many decades, the result has been dispiriting and seemingly endless litigation. An extended example of such has been discussed in this article.

On the other hand, the dynamism of some of the solicitors of Mumbai has been a response to new opportunities thrown up by globalisation of the Indian economy. Whereas rent control merely compounds the problems of the Indian legal system, the developments within corporate law circles point to a productive new kind of legal practice. The brightest law students in India, many of them studying in the new national law schools, have been quick to sense the change. They are increasingly attracted to what seems an exciting and up-to-the minute form of professional practice, as against the socially disreputable and empty work of litigation over matters like urban property.

It is possible therefore to argue that the example of corporate law practice in Mumbai is in some ways the best hope for the Indian legal system. Of course, I would not want to suggest that the whole Indian legal system should be remade in the mould of corporate legal practice. In a poor nation of over a billion people, three-quarters of whom still live in rural areas, such an idea is fanciful. Rather, what is valuable, I think, in the new practice of corporate law in Mumbai is the discipline imposed by having to meet international standards of professional practice. The argument is that if one branch of the profession is beginning to raise its performance under external stimuli, then it is likely that higher standards will progressively spill over into the profession more generally. But for the moment, reform of the system remains largely in the future.

To return to the two narratives sketched at the beginning of this article, it would be quite impossible to claim that the Indian legal system is a straightforward advantage to the nation in its concern for development. Attendance to the dismal world of rent control litigation must prevent such a conclusion. On the other hand, it would be possible to argue that other parts of the legal system not discussed here have indeed made a major contribution to the development of India. Thus the highest court of India, the Supreme Court, has had some significant success in reviving public morality through its embrace of 'public interest' or 'social action' litigation.[31] This has been a jurisprudence for the poor and for the defence of democracy itself. And yet such intervention by the Supreme Court may scarcely have balanced the great reputational damage to Indian justice caused by the proven corruption and the professional incompetence of a number of judges (particularly at lower levels). Clearly these are matters that go to the larger question of the relation of the legal system to the 'development' of India—but they are matters for discussion elsewhere. The more limited argument developed here is that changes within corporate legal practice in Mumbai represent a sorely needed modernisation of a segment of the legal profession. 'Globalisation' may suggest to many Indian lawyers that their livelihood is under threat, but to this writer such a scenario is unlikely. Another more positive scenario is that globalisation of legal services can induce improved standards of service into the Indian legal profession. The ultimate beneficiary of such change would be the Indian citizen.

Notes

1. See, for example, Arun Shourie, *Courts and Their Judgments* (New Delhi: Rupa, 2001). For a critique which concentrates on the deficiency of the laws themselves, see Bibek Debroy, *In the Dock—Absurdities of Indian Law* (Delhi: Konark, 2000).

2. 'Barrister' was only one, albeit the most exalted, term for those lawyers who appeared before the British courts in Bombay, Calcutta and Madras. Barristers were also often called 'advocates'. These were distinguished from mere vakils, an Indian term, or 'pleaders', the lawyers who worked both in rural areas and in the great towns. The latter group, perhaps invariably Indian rather than British in origin, were in constant battle with barristers (originally exclusively British in origin) throughout the nineteenth and twentieth centuries as to the right to argue in the highest courts. As one way of underlining their own superiority, barristers in the highest court of the Presidency towns—these were called the High Court after 1861—insisted on being briefed by another lawyer. In original matters, that is, matters originating in the High Court rather than coming there on appeal from a lower court, it was usually the attorneys (solicitors) who performed this function. High Courts were later established in other provincial capitals (Allahabad and Bangalore, for example), and some solicitors established themselves in Bangalore at least. But it is doubtful that the dual system established itself in these other centres, such that barristers demanded to

be briefed by solicitors rather than taking briefs direct from the public. For an account of the legal profession in Madras, see John J. Paul, *The Legal Profession in Colonial South India* (Bombay: Oxford University Press, 1991). The best account of the development of the High Court in Bombay is P.B. Vachha, *Famous Judges, Lawyers and Cases of Bombay: A Judicial History of Bombay During the British Period* (Bombay: N.M. Tripathi, 1962).

3. The basis of this conclusion is argued in Oliver Mendelsohn, 'The Transformation of Authority in Rural India', in *Modern Asian Studies*, 27(4) (1993), pp. 805–42.

4. For a good discussion of the limits of British intervention through law, see D.A. Washbrook, 'Law, State and Agrarian Society in Colonial India', in *Modern Asian Studies*, 15(3) (1981), p. 651.

5. See Elizabeth Whitcombe, *Agrarian Conditions in Northern India—The United Provinces under British Rule 1860–1900* (Berkeley: University of California Press, 1972), p. 206.

6. Part of the problem of quantification is that cases characteristically mutate: for example, an application for a temporary injunction might be decided but the substantive case will persist for ultimate resolution.

7. Professor Marc Galanter was one of the leaders of this project. Some of his findings are reported in Marc Galanter and Jayanth K. Krishnan, 'Debased Informalism: *Lok Adalats* and Legal Rights in Modern India', in Erik G. Jensen and Thomas C. Heller (eds), *Beyond Common Knowledge: Empirical Approaches to the Common Law* (Stanford: Stanford University Press, 2003).

8. Galanter and Krishnan, 'Debased Informalism: *Lok Adalats* and Legal Rights in Modern India', p. 98.

9. It has certainly been the largest source of litigation in a number of the largest cities of India. And given that litigation over agricultural land has declined over the same period, there has clearly been an historic shift in the centre of gravity of Indian litigation from the countryside to the urban centres. But weak official statistics and the difficulty of categorising all litigation must make us cautious in claiming any exact proportion of litigation represented by rent control cases.

10. Bombay changed its name to Mumbai in 1996.

11. Kiran Wadhva, 'Maharashtra Rent Control Act 1999: Unfinished Agenda', in *Economic and Political Weekly*, 37(25) (22 June 2002), p. 2471.

12. The different States have different Acts regulating tenancy, which is a matter of concurrent Union and State jurisdiction under the Constitution of India. Specific reference here is to *The Bombay Rents, Hotel and Lodging House Rates (Control) Act, 1947*, and to *The Maharashtra Rent Control Act, 1999*, the latter Act being a significant reform of rent control.

13. Wadhva, 'Maharashtra Rent Control Act 1999: Unfinished Agenda'.

14. There are some 45 magistrates courts throughout the city and suburbs of Mumbai, and their jurisdiction is exclusively criminal. No doubt landlord tenant disputes sometimes involve conduct prosecuted by the police but other than in this indirect way, the magistrates are not concerned with rent control matters.

15. For reasons of confidentiality, it is not possible to set down the name or employer of my informant. These details are, in any case, scarcely relevant, since the situation sketched here is representative of a great many such occurrences in the history of rent control in India.

16. This view was put most simply by Bernard S. Cohn, in 'Some Notes on Law and Change in North India', *Economic Development and Cultural Change*, 8 (1959), pp. 79–90. Reprinted in *The Bernard Cohn Omnibus* (New Delhi: Oxford University Press, 2004).

17. R.L. Kidder, 'Courts and Conflict in an Indian City: A Study of Legal Impact', in *Journal of Commonwealth Political Studies*, 11(2) (1973), p. 121.

18. See Oliver Mendelsohn, 'The Pathology of the Indian Legal System', in *Modern Asian Studies*, 15(4) (1981), p. 823; and in chapter 1 of this volume.

19. The story is far too complex to be retold here. For an account of the problem, see ibid.

20. The International Centre for Alternative Dispute Resolution (ADR) organised a conference in Mumbai on 20 November 2004 at which the Chief Justice of India, and the Chief Justice and Justice A.P. Shah of the Bombay High Court, all spoke about the promise of ADR for India.

21. Interview with Justice A.P. Shah, Mumbai, 22 November 2005.

22. There is no doubt that the problem of arrears is critical, but as we have canvassed above, it should not be assumed that the arrears arise because there is simply too much litigation in India. The problem has to do with the kinds of cases that come to the courts and the manner in which they are dealt with in the judicial process. Attention to this perspective will bring about quite a different remedial strategy.

23. Oliver Mendelsohn, 'From Colonial to Post-Colonial Law in India', in Veronica Taylor (ed), *Asian Laws Through Australian Eyes* (Sydney: LBC Information Services, 1997), pp. 297–315; and in chapter 5 of this volume.

24. It is instructive to compare what is happening in India today with what happened elsewhere much earlier. There are important parallels between changes in the Indian legal profession today and what happened in the legal profession of Australia from the mid-1960s. For a discussion of the transformations in Australia, see Oliver Mendelsohn and Matthew

Lippman, 'The Emergence of the Corporate Law Firm in Australia', in *University of New South Wales Law Journal*, 3(1) (1979), p. 78.

25. The Bombay and Incorporated Law Society, *Centenary 1894–1994* (Bombay, 1995), p. 59.

26. This pattern of following the father into legal practice would be quite typical of a large proportion of Indian practitioners, were it not for Zia Mody's gender.

27. Interview with Zia Mody, 13 December 1995.

28. Interview with Zia Mody, 17 November 2004.

29. Interview, Mumbai, 21 November 2004.

30. For a discussion of this issue see 'India Law and International Resources', in *Global Law Review* (GLR), available at: http:// www.globallawreview. com/forlawinin.html, last accessed 5 May 2005.

31. 'Social action' litigation is the term preferred by Professor Upendra Baxi, one of the original inspirations for this activist use of the courts for social change. His most influential article on this subject is Upendra Baxi, 'Taking Suffering Seriously: Social Action in the Supreme Court of India', in U. Baxi (ed), *Law and Poverty—Critical Essays* (Bombay: Tripathi, 1988), pp. 387–415.

7

LIFE AND STRUGGLES IN
THE STONE QUARRIES OF INDIA
A Case Study*

The characteristic face of poverty in India is still that of the landless agricultural labourer, but in recent years another image has insistently intruded itself alongside the familiar agrarian figure. This more recent image is of men, women and children labouring on roads, dams and quarries, carrying bricks in kilns or building sites, and living in 'dwellings' made of bits of scrap. The linage is a kind of distorted mirror reflection of the urbanisation and economic growth which India is now undergoing. Urbanisation holds out the prospect of a better life for tens of millions of people in the countryside but for the labourers (most of them from untouchable castes or tribals) who arrive from the villages to build the towns and cities, it usually represents another version of a familiar poverty. This article is a study of a cluster of stone quarries in Faridabad, near Delhi, and the struggle to improve the life of the labourers there. The struggle has been a substantial failure, but much can be learnt from understanding its nature.

The pivotal figure in the Faridabad struggle has been Swami Agnivesh, at once Hindu monk and unconventional politician. Agnivesh was born a Brahmin in Andhra and received his university education in law at

* This chapter was originally published in *The Journal of Commonwealth & Comparative Politics* 29(1)(March 1991), pp. 44–71.

Calcutta University. While he was in Calcutta he came into contact with the Arya Samaj and later moved to Haryana to be admitted as a *swami* or monk of the order. Partly inspired by Mahatma Gandhi, he has pursued his religious life through political action. Agnivesh joined regular opposition politics and was for a short time Minister for Education in the Janata government of Haryana in the late 1970s. He remained a member of the Janata party until his ouster in the course of bitter internal struggles during 1985. For Agnivesh, though not always for others, there has been no contradiction or necessary tension between his two roles as politician and activist in the field.

Swami Agnivesh adopted the Faridabad quarries as an important example of what he takes to be the much larger problem of bonded labour in India. In 1981 he had set up his *Bandhua Mukti Morcha* (Bonded Liberation Front) to expose bonded labour throughout India and to work for its liberation. His definition of bonded labour is simply that of the Bonded Labour System (Abolition) Act, 1976.[1] The Act defines bonded labour as 'any labour or service rendered under the bonded labour system'. This, to paraphrase and shorten the definition in the Act, is the system of forced, or partly forced, labour, whereby in return for an advance a labourer agrees to work for no wage or a nominal wage, or to forfeit freedom of employment or movement. Agnivesh's contention was that the stone quarries of Faridabad operate predominantly as a 'bonded labour system'. His principal object was to have the bonded labourers released, sent home to their place of origin and rehabilitated there by the relevant State government.

The Bonded Liberation Front took up the issue in early 1982 after an earlier involvement with the brick industry workers of Haryana and western Uttar Pradesh and the sand quarries of Delhi Territory. It is not at all difficult to see why a political reformer would find this site compelling. Here within some 20 km of the capital, workers labour in conditions which can only shock even the most inured observer of Indian industrial conditions. The area has apparently been mined for most of the present century and now appears as a kind of dreadful moonscape. Access is by way of what are now raised tracks separating deep canyons of mined rock with jagged cliffsides. At the bottom of the canyons the workers can be seen smashing large quartzite rocks into smaller ones with the aid of sledgehammers up to 13 kilograms in weight. The large rocks have been produced by blasting the cliffside, a job performed by the same rock choppers. They have to make a fast escape (usually barefoot) once the fuse has been lit, since the fuse is very short for reasons of economy. Smashed or merely injured limbs turn out to be a daily occurrence. Women and larger children work alongside the men, while smaller children play in the dust and dirty puddles. But what gives these quarries their almost surreal horror is the pall of snow-like dust that practically whites out vision when the crushers are operating. These are the large and primitive machines which shiver the small stones produced by the smashing process into still smaller stones for use primarily in road construction. There were in 1983 some 70 crushers operating within the one area and they produced an intense fog and level of noise which made speech difficult. Instinctively one could believe the claims of almost certain respiratory disease, including asthma and tuberculosis, for those who worked and lived here long. The houses of the labourers—a few of them relatively decent, others squat *kaccha* structures like piggeries, still others leaky shacks of iron scrap and plastic—are clustered throughout the quarries amid all the noise and dust.

Agnivesh's strategy has been built around a petition to the Supreme Court of India as part of an emerging 'public interest litigation' in India. This central judicial tactic has been buttressed by political action and by organising the workers industrially. Thus, almost simultaneous with initiation of the Supreme Court writ, a Stone Quarry Workers' Union was established in Faridabad in January 1982. This was an unusual union in that its primary object was not the improvement of industrial conditions but the liberation of workers such that they could leave the industry. Agnivesh recognised that some workers would freely choose to remain in Faridabad, so a secondary object was indeed the improvement of health and safety conditions and remuneration. Legal research revealed a number of pieces of progressive legislation relating to mining, inter-state migration, and health and safety standards which were apparently being ignored by the employers and by the Haryana and Union governments. Complaints of violation of this legislation were joined to claims under the Bonded Labour Abolition Act to constitute the legal basis of the writ petition to the Supreme Court.

By 1989, and despite a spectacular success in the form of the Supreme Court judgment, the Faridabad campaign had to be counted a failure. Very few workers had effectively been rehabilitated as bonded labourers; wages had risen only moderately; and health and safety conditions were scarcely different from a decade ago. Swami Agnivesh concedes this failure himself and has now abandoned organising in the quarries, though he persists with the residual litigation. The reasons for the failure are several but at root is a variation of what one always finds in relation to exploitation of the poor in India: the overwhelming power of large employers and the unreliability of the state as an ally of the poor, despite the good intentions of elements within the judiciary and bureaucracy. But Swami Agnivesh, senior bureaucrats in New Delhi and the Supreme Court played a part in the failure by adopting too pure a view of bonded labour which derived from the superficial nature of the Bonded Labour Abolition Act itself. It is now possible to see that the primary emphasis on the bonded nature of the labour rather than on its more generally exploitative character was an unhelpful analysis given the real life choices of the labourers. In short, it has not helped the Faridabad labourers to be deemed *bonded* because there is no realistic hope that the government will provide the material basis for a life outside the quarries. It might have been preferable to devote more energy to the more narrowly industrial struggle for improved wages and conditions within the quarries, though it has to be said that this struggle is also scarcely more winnable.

The present study uses the Faridabad struggle for several interlocking purposes. First, I wanted to draw attention to the severity of problems represented by the Faridabad quarries as just one example of the kind of migratory labour increasingly undertaken by untouchables, tribals and a sprinkling of people from other communities. The development of this so-called unorganised sector is rapidly changing the character of the Indian poor. Secondly, this example of an effort to organise a segment of the poorest Indian labour is worthy of attention on the ground of its rarity. And finally, the Faridabad struggle can lead us towards relevant perspectives on the Indian state—in its statutory roles of industrial regulation and welfare provision; in its judicial role through the Supreme Court, labour tribunals and other judicial bodies; and in the functioning relationships between the state (including the police), the quarry owners and the labourers.

The Supreme Court Action and Its Aftermath

Shortly after his decision to take up the Faridabad case at the beginning of 1982, Agnivesh instituted the Supreme Court writ petition to free the bonded labourers and to enforce the relevant welfare legislation (*Bandhua Mukti Morcha* v. *Union of India and Others* or the Quarry Workers' Case).[2] From a legal standpoint the case was an important example of what has come to be called 'public interest litigation', a kind of judicial activism inspired by but not directly patterned upon models in the United States.[3] This litigation was the joint creation of certain activist legal practitioners, academics and several receptive justices of the Supreme Court. Cases of abuse of underprivileged persons have been taken up in the form of writ petitions alleging breach of fundamental rights under the Constitution. For its part the Court was happy to ignore procedural niceties and even accept petitions written on scraps of paper. For a few years and in marked contrast to its previous history, the Court appeared at least in this jurisdiction to be more an instrument of the weak than the strong.[4]

When the Court delivered judgment in the Quarry Workers' Case on 16 December 1983 it already had the benefit of a 'socio-legal investigation' of conditions in the quarries performed by an academic sociologist (Dr S.V. Patwardhan of the Indian Institute of Technology) specially appointed by the Court. This device of appointing a fact finding agent had been employed in previous cases, though it remains controversial by virtue of what is seen by the defence to be the creation of biased evidence unchallengeable through the regular court procedures.

Dr Patwardhan duly reported at great length on what he took to be a dreadful situation of systematic law-breaking by the proprietors of the quarries.[5] He found that there were indeed many bonded labourers and that the welfare provisions of the Inter-State Migration Act among many other pieces of legislation were not being enforced. The bonded nature of the labour flowed from the advances paid to the workers, usually through intermediary *jamadars* (labour sub-contractors), before they left their homes to come to the quarries. These sums were strictly repayable before their departure from the quarry. The workers therefore lacked freedom of movement. Their vulnerable position led to exploitation of many kinds, including underweighing of stones for which they were paid on a piece-rate basis. The benefits they were legally entitled to as migrant labour and miners—proper housing, clean water, washing facilities, schooling for their children, creches, health facilities, sick pay—were systematically denied to them. The conditions of work—the dangerous physical presentation of the site, the lack of safety procedures and equipment—were extraordinarily bad and quite unlawful under the Mines Act and other legislation. The many government authorities required to take action under the relevant legislation were almost completely neglectful of their duties. In sum, the quarries 'show full signs of a reckless drive for stone extraction.... In several places there the quarrying is nothing short of slaughter mining'.[6]

The Supreme Court agreed, contrary to the representations not only of the quarry owners but also the Governments of India and the State of Haryana. The major judgment was handed down by Bhagwati J.; the other two judges, R.S. Pathak and A.N. Sen J.J., did little more than express their agreement. Bhagwati J. was scathing in relation to the efforts of the State of Haryana to have the case thrown out on jurisdictional grounds. The Haryana argument was that even if what was alleged were true it would not justify a writ petition under section 32 of the Indian Constitution, since no breach of fundamental rights under the Constitution was at issue.

> We can appreciate the anxiety of the mine lessees to restrict the writ petition on any ground available to them, be it hyper-technical or even frivolous, but we find it incomprehensible that the State Government should urge such a preliminary objection with a view to stifling at the threshold an inquiry by the Court as to whether the workmen are living in bondage and under inhuman conditions ... [T]he State Government ... is, under our constitutional scheme, charged with the mission of bringing about a new socio-economic order where there will be social and economic justice for everyone and equality of status and opportunity for all...[7]

These are unusually strong words directed from the bench to a government whose legal representative is engaging in the usual lawyerish pursuit of the technical, and demonstrate the extent to which particular members of the Court saw public interest litigation as distinct from ordinary kinds of adversarial litigation between private parties. Bhagwati J. was here enunciating a view of government in India as a kind of trust for the downtrodden. Moreover, he was clearly disturbed that the Bonded Liberation Front had as its judicial opponents not only the quarry owners but also the State and even the Union governments.

The Court rejected the contention of the Government of India that the concerned workmen were not migrants under the Inter-State Migrant Workmen Act because they came to the stone quarries 'of their own volition and they are not recruited by any agent for being migrated from any State'.[8] Bhagwati J. said that ordinarily he would be prepared to accept such a contention from so responsible a source as the Government of India, but in the face of an empirical report from Dr Patwardhan he could not. The judge concluded that many of the workers had been brought to the quarries by a *jamadar* (sub-contractor of labour) and as such they were clearly inter-state migrants within the meaning of the Act and therefore entitled to its protections.

As to whether the labourers named in the petition were bonded labourers within the meaning of the Bonded Labour Abolition Act, the judge did not feel competent to decide this central issue; he delegated the task to an official who could make on-the-spot inquiries. Instead, he limited himself to laying down some legal guidelines on the matter. Regrettably, these guidelines appear to be quite beside the point. Following some argument of the Haryana government, Bhagwati J. seemed to regard the central problem as the evident difficulty of discovering whether an advance had been given by the employer to the worker. Without such an advance there could be no bonded relationship, and he assumed that the employer would effectively cover up the existence of the loan. To meet this problem he laid down a rule that if a worker were obliged to provide forced labour, it could be presumed that the force proceeded from some economic relationship and that the labourer was therefore bonded. This rule would obviate the necessity to prove the fact of a loan in individual cases—the loan or other relationship could be induced from the fact of forced labour being extracted. But while Bhagwati J.'s presumption is reasonable enough, it quite fails to reach the central difficulty. The real problem is one of deciding just what constitutes *forced* labour in the first place, rather than whether the forced labour could be said to derive from a loan. Is the labour *forced* wherever the labourer owes money to his employer? Or is it possible to be so indebted and still not to be unfree within the legal meaning? Bhagwati J. is silent on this question, which is the very core of the problem.

On perhaps the most natural reading of the Act's very broad definition, all loans from employer to worker do give rise to the relationship of bonded labour. The reason for saying this is our assumption that no labourer would ordinarily be free to leave his employer for another without having first discharged his debt. In terms of the language of the Act, such lack of freedom deriving from this economic source could easily be said to constitute an example of 'the bonded labour system'. Is this what the court intended? Bhagwati J.'s judgment gives no answer. Instead, he turned over what he took to be the merely technical task of discovering whether the labourers named in the petition were in fact bonded to the Director-General (Labour Welfare) of the Government of India. It is this official rather than the judge who provided the definition of what was *forced* labour, as we shall see shortly.

The judge directed that if any workers were found to be bonded, they should be asked whether they wished to go back to their home. If they did, the District Magistrate of Faridabad was to make the necessary arrangements for their release and transport home. The Director-General (Labour Welfare) was also to inquire into which particular employers were *prima facie* bound by the Migrant Workmen and Contract Labour Acts. The judge went on to observe that

> the problem of bonded labourers is a difficult problem because unless, on being freed from bondage, they are provided proper and adequate rehabilitation, it would not help to merely secure their release. Rather in such cases it would be more in their interest to ensure proper working conditions with full enjoyment of the benefits of social welfare and labour laws so that they can live a healthy decent life. But of course this would only be the next best substitute for release and rehabilitation which must receive the highest priority.[9]

This passage suggests that Bhagwati J. was troubled by the extent to which it would prove prudent to move the workers out of the quarries, in view of the village situation from which they had originally come. This doubt was realistic and we will return to it later.

Finally, the Court ordered the Union and State governments to secure compliance with those legislative provisions requiring the employers to ensure safe working and living conditions. In all, the Court issued

21 directives for action into matters including the spraying of water over the crushers so as to reduce dust emissions; the provision of adequate supplies of clean drinking water, latrines, proper medical facilities and creches; and inspection of truck capacity to ensure that workers were not required to supply the contractor more stone per load than the 150 cu.ft they were paid for.

Clearly this was a great judicial victory for the Bonded Liberation Front. The victory was given substance when the Director-General (Labour Welfare), Laxmi Dhar Misra, went on to name 295 workers to be bonded within the meaning of the Act and to order their release by the Haryana government. These workers were among 352 who had been interviewed out of a total working population estimated by the Regional Labour Commissioner at Chandigarh to be 4,130.[10] (The union's estimate of workers was up to three times this figure.) Mishra states that he was only able to interview a small proportion of the potentially bonded population: constraints of time and resources inhibited a more thorough job. As to the determination of who were 'inter-state workmen' within the meaning of the Act, he found that all his interviewees would qualify.

The approach taken by this Labour Department official was a highly expansive one. His criterion for the existence of *forced* labour was simple:

> If you are working with or under or for me and owe me some advance money, you are tied to me and have no freedom of movement or freedom of choice of alternative avenues of employment until and unless the advance money has been fully liquidated. What better ingredient of the worst form of bonded labour system could there be than this?[11]

This construction is consistent with the definitions in the Act, as we have seen above, and its effect is to make a very large proportion of migrant workers legally bonded, as well as a very high proportion of agricultural labourers. Most seasonal workers who travel from one part of India to another require an advance from their employer for their expenses. In law, at least part of this advance is not repayable but is a legitimate charge against the employer under the Inter-State Migrant Workers' Act. In fact, the common practice of employers is to recover advances of all kinds from the employees; without repayment it is no doubt difficult and perhaps impossible for the worker to leave his employer. The same would apply to the common practice of making occasional loans to employees—this creditor-debtor relationship is endemic in agricultural labour.

What Laxmi Dhar Mishra has done here is to supply the definition of 'forced labour' which the Supreme Court did not. He has done so in the spirit of a judgment highly favourable to Swami Agnivesh's organisation and in a way that seems to make sense of the Act. But the interpretation is in fact far clearer than the Act itself and, if it were to be generally adopted, would convert the legislation into an instrument of extraordinary breadth. The Department official has in effect assumed that all labourers indebted to their employers are bonded labourers.

So far as the struggle was concerned, the matter did not end with the Mishra Report. On 31 October 1984 the Bonded Liberation Front petitioned the Court (Civil Miscellaneous Petition 3700 of 1984) that seven months after the Mishra Report the 295 labourers had still not been released or rehabilitated. Indeed the Front claimed that the labourers' situation was worse, in that that they were no longer being given work and were being 'terrorised' by the contractors. On 29 November 1984 the Court ordered inquiries to be made into this and if some of the labourers deemed bonded were still there and desired to go home, 'the District Magistrate will promptly make arrangements for their repatriation to their respective homes at the cost of State Government'.[12]

This directive brought some action and on 16 December 1984 a total of up to 106 families were put into the charge of the authorities of Banner District in Rajasthan by the District Magistrate of Faridabad. But on 30 January 1985 the Front was back in the Supreme Court with a petition complaining that many of these families had wrongly been classified as not being 'bonded' but only 'inter-state workers' and therefore presumably not entitled to the benefits of debt cancellation and rehabilitation. There was also a recital of the failure of the State authorities to provide adequate housing or other facilities to the families, such that already three of the children had died in the cold of January. No action seems to have flowed from this petition.

Release of the Banner labourers at the end of 1984 effectively marked the end of the Front's success in relation to bonded labour. Many of the other labourers deemed bonded by Laxmi Dhar Mishra seem to have stayed on in the quarries, presumably for want of any satisfactory alternative.[13] Contrary to the instructions of the Supreme Court, no further inquiry into bonded labour was undertaken until the Court appointed its own Commissioner once more in 1989; by then it seemed too late to affect the situation favourably. No additional labourers have been declared bonded. Overall, then, the practical success of all the judicial action was meagre in juxtaposition to the soaring rhetoric and expansive legal definitions deployed by Bhagwati J. in his judgment.

Indeed, the fate of the 'liberated' labourers makes the practical achievement even less to celebrate. I was able to follow the Rajasthan contingent back to where they had been sent in January 1985; my own visit was in April of that year. Ninety-five families had been taken to Banner District—the other Rajasthanis from Faridabad must have gone elsewhere. These families were from a single tribal community, the Bhils, and they had been dumped into a place with which they had no more than a casual connection.[14] Before 1947 they had been part of a large nomadic community in what is now Pakistan but on partition, they had migrated to India and were arbitrarily located in Banner District. They had had to be fed for some time at public expense but soon a Punjabi contractor had picked them up and taken them to the Delhi area. Over the years they had been moved around various quarries in Haryana. They had not left the quarries since their arrival there and had certainly not been back to Banner. So they had no roots whatsoever in the area to which they were now 'repatriated'.

The families had been split into two almost equal parties and settled in different locations near the town of Balota, one 6 kilometres from the town and the other 11 kilometres in a different direction. When I encountered them, their condition was deplorable. They had been delivered there some four months earlier, given a sum of Rs 500 plus some 'building materials' and basically left to fend for themselves. The first settlement was on a sandy, windswept plain where no-one would willingly choose to live. The winds of mid-April were already distressingly hot and dusty. Their 'houses' were flimsy structures made of grass, almost completely permeable to the weather. It had been bitterly cold in this arid desert when they arrived four months previously, and many of the children fell ill with pneumonia; one child was diagnosed with this condition in my presence. A tuberculosis patient had not received medicine since his arrival here. As to employment, they were able to get a bit of labouring work here and there. One of the sources, ironically enough, was a nearby small quarry. Others found some work at a brick kiln, while some travelled the six kilometres into the growing town of Balotra to try to pick up some lifting or carting work. Everyone was eating poorly and they were unable to purchase the medicines which they now needed more than ever. Bad as their condition had been in Faridabad, they were unanimous that it was far worse in Rajasthan.

The other settlement told similar but worse stories. The major difference was that they were further from the town of Balotra and therefore unable to take advantage of labouring opportunities there. Their major source of income came from the (illegal) collection of sticks from a hill some distance away. They were able to sell bundles of these twigs in Balotra for use as fuel; the going rate was Rs 3 for a head-load. In order to earn this sum they had to walk 11 kilometres to Balotra and 11 kilometres back. They left at 4 a.m. and returned by 1 p.m. The bus was far too expensive to afford. One, two or three people from each family made the trek every day, while others went in search of the sticks. Again these people had suffered many illnesses since being brought to Banner and they produced large bills for drugs they were forced to purchase. In my presence a doctor in Balotra examined one of their sick babies and pronounced the illness to be 'either simple fever or malaria. I cannot make an exact diagnosis due to inadequacy of facilities.' Good medicine was further from their reach than ever.

These people were bonded to their employer by virtue of their borrowing from him. The figures they quoted as debts were mainly small sums of around Rs 1,000 but since they would not have been allowed to leave without repaying these amounts, they were clearly bonded within the meaning of the Act as interpreted by the Director-General (Labour Welfare). Moreover, they presumably received less than their due under prevailing piece rates—the deductions for their loans would have ensured this. But equally clearly, when I saw them rootless out in the Rajasthani desert they had by their own and anyone's reckoning been positively disadvantaged by having been declared bonded.

I have no direct information on what has become of these Bhils in the succeeding several years. But in the latest report on the Faridabad situation prepared in February 1989, yet another commissioner appointed by the Supreme Court reports one of his informants saying that all the Banner labourers were now back working in the Faridabad quarries.[15] This information may not be authoritative but it is credible. It is difficult to imagine, even with some sincere effort on the part of the government of Rajasthan (such as the provision of livestock and better housing), that the Bhils could have survived, let alone thrived, in the physical location to which they had been led. The most logical outcome is that they would return to the life that they knew in Faridabad.

Undoubtedly the body that has to take primary responsibility for this sad story is government at both central and State levels. But this experience is scarcely unusual. Government performance in relation to the 'weaker sections', as they are termed, can be seen to range from lukewarm assistance through indifference to callous opposition. This knowledge has simply to be factored into any programme undertaken for these people by activists outside government. We will return to this case after a discussion of several other cases which have not been the subject of judicial action but which are useful as a point of comparison.

Some Further Enquiries into the Labourers of Faridabad

The Case of Ram Prasad[16]

Ram Prasad is a Raegar, an untouchable leather-working caste, and was 38 years old when I talked to him in February, 1985. He was born into the quarries—his father worked there too—and he has been breaking rocks for the last 25 years. His family is from Jaipur but he does not know the particular locality or when they left for the quarries. He has never been to Jaipur and was therefore no longer really a migrant worker. Ram Prasad is married with four children, the eldest of whom is a 12-year-old boy studying in school. He wants to send the younger three children to school too—including the one daughter—but this possibility now seems beyond his economic reach. The reason is that Ram Prasad suffers a physical disability following an accident in the quarry. About a year before our conversation a rock fell on him, breaking his leg and smashing his foot. The foot is now permanently and seriously damaged, and he can no longer perform physical labour to the extent that he previously could.

It seems that Ram Prasad's employer paid for the operations on his foot and for the drugs and dressings he received during the period of his convalescence. But he received no money at all as compensation for his injury. Accordingly, his economic circumstances were now ruined. For seven months he could do no work at all and afterwards could work with only a shadow of his former vigour. He says that he and his wife together can now earn only Rs 300 a month, a sum quite inadequate to the family's needs. In order to live during the period he was unable to work, Ram Prasad was forced to borrow Rs 5,000 at the interest rate of '3 rupees' per month, as he puts it, or 36 per cent a year. His monthly payments are thus Rs 150. The loan is from a fellow Raegar in Delhi; he was forced into this loan because no other source was available to him. He made the connection with the lender through his wife, who originally comes from Delhi. 'Big people', he noted, do not lend to people of his kind. The rate of interest is quite standard for loans in the quarries, even for loans made by fellow quarry-workers, though not all such loans are made at these usurious rates. Indeed, it is not uncommon to find rates of '5 rupees' or 60 per cent on an annual basis.

Some three years before our interview Ram Prasad's wife had fallen ill and remained so for about two years. Since she could not work in the quarry—women are mostly employed to excavate earth from the site so as to expose the rock—they were forced to sell all her jewellery except for some light silver anklets and toe-rings. Barely had she recovered from this illness than Ram Prasad suffered his accident. After repayments on the loan, they now have about Rs 150 a month to live on. This is far too little for anything but the most meagre survival, if that. Ram Prasad was very bitter indeed but his wife was more resigned to their lot. The children were well fed and it was easy to believe Ram Prasad's statement that he denied himself for the sake of the family. Their one asset was a goat, but they were just about to sell this. The goat was bought with money from the Rs 5,000 loan and it will now fetch from Rs 300 to 350. The family had consumed all the goat's milk themselves as an accompaniment to tea, but they could no longer afford to keep the animal. In addition to bits of grass they could collect for it, they had had to purchase millet in the market. When I asked why he had not applied for a bank loan/subsidy under the Integrated Rural Development Programme, Ram Prasad said that none of the Raegars had any knowledge of such schemes.

Ram Prasad's case may not be entirely typical of the cases I collected in Faridabad—his situation was more immediately desperate than many, and he had waited impatiently to tell it to me. But the case does reliably represent the precariousness of life in the quarries. With good health and strength, it is possible to live up to and sometimes beyond the level of ordinary labourers in villages. But if a rock rolls the wrong way or if the cliff face slips, then life becomes even more of a nightmare than is usual among the very poor of India. And such accidents happen all the time; this is not an occupation of only ordinary danger. Even without catastrophic accident, the chance of sustaining good earnings over a long period of time is slight.

Despite the severity of Ram Prasad's situation this is *not* a case of bonded labour, for the reason that Ram Prasad borrowed money from a caste fellow in Delhi rather than from his employer. Presumably the employer would not have been prepared to make a loan to someone who could not be relied on to pay the instalments, and Ram Prasad's injury made him a dubious proposition. Since Ram Prasad was not a migratory labourer, he did not receive an annual advance to bring him back to Faridabad. But the source of Ram Prasad's loan was not necessarily advantageous to him. A loan from his employer might have made him vulnerable to being cheated further out of his legitimate returns for his piece-work, but this is not certain.

When I left Ram Prasad his outlook appeared to be one of unrelieved misery. More than a year later I learnt that he had become a *jamadar* or sub-contractor of labour. Since this position is usually an exploitative one, Ram Prasad may now be yet another example of those oppressed people who through cunning or necessity connive at the exploitation of their fellows. Ram Prasad would not have chosen such a role willingly. He had ambitions for his children; he did not want them to grow up to be as driven down as himself.

The Case of Jagdish

This is a case of no great complexity and is offered as an example of a quarry labourer for whom nothing has yet gone wrong. Jagdish is from the Balai caste of untouchable weavers, and his home in Rajasthan is only several hours away from Faridabad by bus. He is 29 years old, married for four years without children yet, and has worked in the

quarry for nine years. His father worked here before him for 25 or
30 years, he says. Jagdish had already passed tenth standard school
before coming to Faridabad. By then there was insufficient money
for him to continue study and he was unable to get a regular job.
Although he was very sad about coming to the quarries, there was
no alternative.

Jagdish's wife works alongside him, clearing earth to expose the
stone. She is paid Rs 10 a day for this. When I talked to him she had just
come back from his village, where she stayed for a month. He himself
goes home twice a year for four or five days at a time. Otherwise he
works all year round, including the rainy season. He does not need
advances from his employer to make these short trips. But he has borrowed Rs 1,200 in his village at the favourable rate of 30 per cent a
year. He took out this loan at the time of his marriage, four years previously. He services the loan at the rate of Rs 30 a month, which means
that he is doing no more than paying interest. Since there are four or
five at home, including his mother and father and a young brother who
is studying in school, he has to send money back to the village. None
of the family at home is earning, though they possess a little bit of
unirrigated land which produces some millet if there is rain. Jagdish's
45-year-old father, now retired from the quarry, does the agricultural
work. Four or five of Jagdish's extended family work in the quarry
too; it seems that perhaps three-quarters of the able-bodied Balais of
his village work outside the village. There are 21 Balai houses in the
village and most of the residents are either old or children; some of the
old people still do a bit of weaving. Agricultural work is no longer available in the village, since the caste Hindu cultivators have turned to
tractor cultivation.

This, then, is a favourable case. Neither Jagdish nor his wife has
suffered major illness or accident. Their position is not improving
because of the burdens of the modest debt they incurred for their
marriage and the support they provide for the remainder of his family.
But thus far, and without children, they have not slipped into a decline.
Of course this is also a sad case, typical of untouchable poverty. Jagdish
attained a fair measure of education and had hopes. Now he is the
most menial of labourers, living in a hut and an environment not fit for
human habitation.

The Case of Shiv Lal

This case is again unremarkable except that it appears to be a case of bonded labour, whereas the two earlier ones are not. Shiv Lal is from the Vade community, a scheduled tribe rather than caste in Maharashtra. He is 30 years old, married with three children. He has four brothers, three of whom work in the quarries too; the fourth brother is only eight years old. Shiv Lal's wife and the wives of his two married brothers work alongside their husbands. The men are well educated, three of them to matriculation standard. This is the second generation of the family to work in quarries owned by their employer, a man named R.L. Sharma, one of the three major contractors of Faridabad. Their father had worked in a number of the Sharma family quarries in Maharashtra, Andhra Pradesh and Gujarat. Such a career is apparently common, since it is said to be the policy of large-scale contractors to move their workers around wherever possible in order to minimise the chance of labour organisation.

Shiv Lal and his brothers had hopes of getting a position 'in service' after their schooling and had not expected to be doing the same work as their father did. But there were simply no other opportunities and no agricultural land to fall back on. The youngest brother is said to be very bright and they have high hopes that he will go to college. The next youngest also has active plans to go to college and his brothers speak of him as if he is not really working in the quarry at all—he had been there only six months at the time of interview, but the likelihood of his escaping his brothers' fate seemed slight. Shiv Lal himself had been quarrying since 1973 and in this particular location for three years.

The whole family returns to the village in Maharashtra during the summer and rainy seasons, a total of some four months. They usually take with them a total of about Rs 1,200 which they have accumulated during the previous eight months—this works out at about Rs 200 per working person. This is insufficient for their needs during their stay at home and they try to supplement it with whatever labouring work they can find in the village. Shiv Lal says they can usually manage only 10 or 15 days' work throughout the four months. Invariably he is forced to take an advance usually from Rs 200 to 250, to come back to Faridabad. This year he is further in debt to his employer, since he had borrowed Rs 150 to send to his parents in the village. The advance and any loans must be repaid before he can leave for home. In addition to these debts, Shiv Lal and his brothers say they are invariably in debt to Maratha or Muslim money-lenders in their village. This money is borrowed during the rainy season at rates of interest as high as 120 per cent. It is usually about four months after their return to Faridabad before the various loans are repaid and saving can begin. Hand to mouth as the cycle is, Shiv Lal and his brothers' situation would be far worse if there were serious accident or illness among the workers. They pointed to another man present at the interview who had had to pay Rs 2,000 over a period of time for treatment of his wife's tuberculosis.

A major difference between Shiv Lal and both Ram Prasad and Jagdish is that Shiv Lal has to travel a great distance at considerable expense to return home. Ram Prasad's home, such as it is, is now in the quarry itself. Jagdish can be home by bus within a few hours. Also, Shiv Lal's language and culture is different from that of Haryana and this may prompt his group to spend a longer time at home in Maharashtra. Since there is little work at home, the family group invariably has to take an advance in order to return. And the fact of taking this advance is sufficient to constitute Shiv Lal and his brothers bonded labourers within the meaning of the Act. By virtue of his debt Shiv Lal can be assumed to lack the freedom to change employers or to 'move freely throughout the territory of India'. On an ordinary reading of the Act, this is sufficient to constitute the state of being bonded. But presumably Shiv Lal is a bonded labourer for only a portion (usually four months) of the year, the period when he is actually in debt to his employer.

Forfeiture of freedom of action through the advance system is pernicious, though people like Shiv Lal tend to regard it as so standard as to be unworthy of comment. Some feeling did emerge when we got on to the subject of the *jamadar*, a man from their own community. The *jamadar* performs the task of annual recruitment by disbursing sums of money either from his own pocket or (more usually) as an agent of the contractor. He has a continuing role in the quarry as intermediary between contractor and labourer. Usually the contractor pays the *jamadar* for the crushed rock and he then passes the money on to the labourer, less his own deductions for commission and any debts owed to him. The precise relationship between *jamadar* and labourer varies. In one instance I found a harmonious relationship between labourers from Madhya Pradesh and their *jamadar*, who professed to be closer to the labourers than to the contractor. He had taken what seems to be the characteristic path to becoming a *jamadar*, first working as a labourer himself. As this man (Prakash) told it, other people in his area asked him to arrange employment for them and his contractor agreed to take them on. When they came to work for the contractor, Prakash was made their *jamadar*. Prakash, rather than the contractor, provides advances to his workers to enable them to return to the quarries after their period at home. The advance is usually Rs 400 or 500, which is repaid (without interest, he claims) out of their wages. For his labour management in the quarries, Prakash is entitled to 10 per cent of the wages bill. He takes and passes on orders from the contractor as to what is to be done, but his workers are experienced and therefore the task is not onerous. Several years previously Prakash had apparently invested his own funds to build some mud brick housing for his workers. He did this in order to make work more attractive in the quarries—since he is paid on a percentage basis he has an interest in maximising his workforce. The houses may be an attraction to the workers but they are so small that one has to stoop low to enter them and sit or lie rather than stand up inside. The land on which the houses are built is owned by a nearby Gurukul (monastery) of the Arya Samaj, which charges the occupants Rs 5 per month for the privilege of occupying the site.

The Question of Bonded Labour

The above are only three of many cases I collected in the quarries but they will suffice to present a picture of individual labourers. Only one of the three cases can be seen to reveal bonded labour within the meaning of the Act as it was interpreted by the Labour Department official, and an obvious question is whether this is the 'worst' case. Pretty clearly this is not so, at least in the absence of any documentation of particular exploitation arising from the creditor-debtor relationship between Shiv Lal and his employer. Thus on its own the case of Shiv Lal would not warrant being placed in a category separate from that of Ram Prasad or Jagdish. My more general suggestion is that the

term 'bonded labourer' as it is defined in the act and interpreted by
the Court and particularly by the Director-General (Labour Welfare)
will not always do service in identifying the most downtrodden labour
in India. Degrees of exploitation cannot be fixed with the definitional
purity of legal language. And the worst examples of bonded labour
do constitute some of the very worst labour situations in India. But
Shiv Lal and his brothers work at the margins of what is a very broad
category, and it may not greatly advance our understanding of their
position to think of them first as bonded labourers rather than as ordinary migrant workers in the quarries.

Behind the questions of technical law lie crucial questions for public
policy and political action. Just what is the principal condition which is
sought to be cured? If the starting object is not simply the 'liberation'
of bonded labourers but rather the more diffuse effort to maximise the
welfare of poor and often migrant workers, then the emphasis of action
may sometimes shift. Part of the shift may entail a less doctrinaire
outlook on the matter of employers lending money to their workers.
No doubt exploitation is facilitated where workers borrow from their
employers, but it cannot be assumed that the initiative for the loan
always comes from the side of the employers as a way of entrapping
the dependent and ignorant worker. Often the employer may be the
only source of a needed loan. Thus I discovered labourers in the Bhati
sand mines of Delhi who responded very warmly when asked whether
they were better off following nationalisation of those mines.[17] They
claimed they were actually worse off, citing their inability to get loans
from their new employer. This was clearly a major issue for them.
Undoubtedly they would not be persuadable that expenditure (and
therefore borrowing) for marriage, death and other 'unproductive'
activities was undesirable and that the government was really helping them by not encouraging such frivolous waste. True, employers do
not lend to their employees out of altruism but the example of Ram
Prasad shows that outside creditors may be no better. In the absence
of cheap institutional credit for necessities (including marriage and
death), it is not necessarily progressive to demand a cessation of all
credit relationships between employer and employee in the name
of ending bonded labour. The nature of these remarks should not be
misunderstood. This is certainly not an argument for the benevolence
of the exploitative quarry owners, only a caution about 'progressive'

stands which turn out to be rooted in somewhat elitist assumptions about the way poor people should lead their lives.[18] Moreover, there is a danger that the very concept of bonded labour will be trivialised if it is to be reduced to the routine case of a credit relationship between employer and labourer.

The larger subject of bonded labour in contemporary India has not been approached at all uniformly by recent scholars. Naturally, most who have written on the subject are appalled by the indebted poverty of many Indians in the area of agricultural labour and related spheres such as brick factories. And since there is abundant evidence of bondedness and even outright slavery in the recent past, there is a tendency to conflate present conditions with this past. Jan Breman has recently delivered a sharp criticism of such thinking.[19] Breman wants to delineate the contemporary condition of the Halpatis of South Gujarat from their historical status as bonded labourers. These people's very caste name, Halpati, reflected the *hali* system of bondedness which characterised the community. In return for small sums often taken out at the time of marriage, the *halis* became bonded to their employers for life. Usually the bonded relationship extended to wife and children as well, such that the whole family worked without pay for the bondsman. In return they got bare subsistence amounts of food but also a small plot of land and some *noblesse oblige* entitlement to care in adversity.

Breman says that this *hali* system is now a thing of the past and that it died sometime in the post-independence period. In his telling the system has been destroyed by the development of a capitalist labour market in the agriculture of South Gujarat. It no longer suits landowners to give labourers security by tying them as they did in the past. Now they play one set of labourers off against another. In particular, they have increasingly drawn on incoming migrant labourers from other regions of Gujarat in an effort to drive down wages. These developments have actually made the Halpatis even worse off than they were under the old order. Their situation is one of increasing *pauperisation*, whereby they live at increasingly sub-poverty levels without even the chance of a handout.

More generally, Breman notes that 'it is the conditions accompanying the debt, rather than the debt itself, which constitutes the coercive character of the service bond.'[20] So he wants to distinguish the farm servant tied to an employer for a particular period from the bonded relationships of earlier times in South Gujarat and elsewhere in India. Breman's view is that labour in South Gujarat today is *free* rather than *forced* or *bonded*.[21] His concept of freedom is not, of course, unlimited freedom to choose between desirable options. Rather, freedom is the absence of a particular style of coercion. 'I shall regard as unfree only that form of debt-labour which is rooted in non-economic coercion.'[22] Breman wants to see the essence of the old order residing in a relationship of personal subjection and dominance which now lies in the pre-capitalist past.

Precisely the opposite view is put by Utsa Patnaik in her introduction to a book of essays on both historical and contemporary examples of the problem of bonded labour and slavery.[23] Patnaik notes that

> No other society in the world, perhaps, is as burdened by the memories and material survivals of its ancient past, as is the Indian; anachronistic precapitalist social relations and ideology form an incubus on the new society painfully attempting to chart a capitalist path of development. Marx's prescient observation of a century ago remains as true today as then, that Indian society suffers not only from the development of capitalism, but also from its insufficient development.[24]

The several essays in the above volume proceed on the basis that the contemporary forms of debt bondage—for example, in the brick kilns of Muzaffarnagar; Bihari labourers in Punjab; agricultural labourers and weavers in South Arcot—are instances of a more general and long-standing Indian form of bondage.

This article is not the place to consider at any length the divergent views represented by Breman and Patnaik, since it would take us too far away from our primary object of drawing attention to workers like those in Faridabad. Suffice it to say that Breman is on firm ground in pointing to the change from non-economic to merely economic coercion as characteristic of labour relations in the countryside.[25] This view coincides with some of the present writer's observations over a number of years in different parts of India, particularly Rajasthan and Bihar. The conditions for the old patterns of subordination are no longer generally present, though there are no doubt areas of persistence in various parts of India.[26] One of those conditions which has eroded is the lack of strong resistance on the part of the subordinated people themselves. To give one important example, the oppression represented by sexual access to women from the subordinate families by local dominants is now widely resisted.[27]

Secondly, there is a naivety in many of the accounts of contemporary 'bonded labour' (including that of the Bonded Labour Abolition Act itself) which seem to proceed on the basis of too sharp a distinction between tied or long-term contractual labour and more casual labour relations. This distinction may often be based on an idealised conception of the possibility of achieving significant wage rises in an open labour market. But as Breman and many others have shown, overall income for the labourer (as distinct from per diem wages) can fall in the 'free' market too. The contractual arrangements which often bind landowner and field labourer together for a year are, of course, exploitative. Characteristically, the labourer has to work longer hours than he would if he were being paid on a daily basis.[28] But the conditions of casual labourers are only marginally rather than dramatically better and they always receive less, usually very much less, work than the tied labourer. The labourers themselves know this. It is beyond question that many labourers deliberately opt for a tied relationship to a landowner which strips them of their capacity to sell their labour at high prevailing rates at peak periods of agriculture (chiefly harvesting). They choose this option because they value the security of a higher overall income.[29]

At the same time, the views represented by Patnaik's essay are not to be dismissed out of hand. It is one thing to deny, as we are doing here, that it is possible to see the routine cases of bonded labour (using the legal definition) as contemporary examples of patterns of servitude prevalent a century or more ago. And yet the transformation of social relations within India has not yet proceeded systematically along individualist lines apparently familiar from European experience. Some contemporary exploitation in India appears familiar by virtue of its incorporation of incidents from an earlier time. Thus borrowing money from his employer by a labourer to stage his wedding was both a common historical practice in India—it was the basis of the bonding of the Halpatis, to give just one example—and continues today in many situations, including the Faridabad quarries. What is different is the consequence of such a loan today. Although the loan may be difficult to pay off as a practical task, its terms allow for its discharge on an arithmetically calculable basis. Bonding for life, or even into the next generation, is not a consequence today for most such debtors and clearly not for the labourers of Faridabad.

From the perspective of political action, it does not seem crucial to adopt one view or the other of labourers such as those in Faridabad. I have tried to suggest here that any doctrinaire treatment of the problem should be avoided in favour of a more pragmatic approach. It turns out to be extremely difficult to 'rehabilitate' exploited migrant labourers by sending them back to their home village, and it does not matter for this purpose whether the labourers are to be termed 'bonded' or not. The case of the Banner labourers is admittedly not a fair test, since these labourers did not have a home village to return to. But it does seem likely that 'rehabilitation' at home will seldom work. First, any reliable observer of village India can see that dynamic forces are at work pushing/pulling people out of villages and into a variety of labouring situations connected with a developing capitalist India. This process of change will clearly continue. And secondly, no government can be relied on to put in place conditions which will guarantee the material well-being of large numbers of people selected for rehabilitation as bonded labourers. In these circumstances it would seem prudent only to attempt to rehabilitate the very worst examples of exploited migrant labour which can reasonably be thought capable of reinstatement at home (with resources such as the provision of land).

The Union Struggle in Faridabad

Even before the Supreme Court had handed down its decision at the end of 1983, Swami Agnivesh had broadened his activities in Faridabad to encompass the health and safety conditions, wages and social amenities of the labourers in Faridabad. He took on this role despite a marked reluctance to see himself as union organiser rather than liberator of bonded labour. In Agnivesh's own account, the change came about partly because of the 'moral embarrassment' of not being able to secure proper rehabilitation for labourers released prior to the Rajasthan group.[30] The later experiences of the Rajasthan people cannot have increased his confidence. It is not clear how long-term a role he envisaged for the union; perhaps originally it was conceived as little more than a short-term activity while the main business of discharging labour was proceeding with the aid of the Supreme Court. In the event the Court took almost two years to hand down its decision and almost another year elapsed before the Barmer labourers finally went home. By then Agnivesh was committed to continuing action on wages and conditions for the labourers who chose to remain in the quarries. This gradually wound down in the late 1980s as solid progress proved elusive.

The union organisers were badly harassed by the contractors in the early period but as they achieved legitimacy through their association with the highest court in India and with Agnivesh's flair for publicity, the situation gradually eased. The workers became increasingly confident about asserting their claims, and Agnivesh regards dissipation of the 'fear psychosis' in the quarries to be one of the major achievements of the union activity.

By early 1985 there were said to be 1,500 financial members of the union paying dues of Rs 12 annually. Four organisers were paid a monthly wage of Rs 400 out of these dues but the principal organiser was paid directly by the Bandhua Mukti Morcha (which derives its operating expenses from a variety of sources, including foreign assistance agencies). The total cost of the union activity was said to be Rs 30,000, leaving a shortfall of Rs 12,000 between dues and expenses. Apparently this shortfall was made up from donations by members of the union. Some of the workers gave a monthly sum of Rs 5.

The progress of the union may more easily be understood by saying a little about the organisers. The principal organiser in the mid-80s was a 29-year-old man named Bharat Lal. He comes from a peasant caste and village background in Haryana, and was educated to MA standard in Political Science and Hindi. Bharat Lal had separated from his family in 1977 and has had little contact with them since—he says his values diverge from those of his father. He first encountered Agnivesh in 1977 and through him got a job managing an Arya Samaj hostel. He joined the Lok Dal, an opposition party, in 1980 and in 1981 he began working for the Bandhua Mukti Morcha. From July 1981 he began organising the union, which was officially inaugurated in January 1982 with Swami Agnivesh as President and Bharat Lal as General Secretary. Unlike the other organisers, Bharat Lal did not live at the quarry site but at Agnivesh's headquarters in New Delhi. He commuted daily, except when there was work at the Court, on a motor cycle.

The other organisers have come and gone—none of them has been an actual quarry worker, though this was an ambition of the leadership. Some have been more and some less likely union organisers, perhaps reflecting the difficulties of attracting outsiders to work and live in such unpropitious circumstances. For example, Krishnaji is an older man of adventurous spirit. In true Hindu fashion, he has now separated himself from his wife and grown-up children—he says he loves them in the same way that he loves all humanity. Krishnaji is a former employee of the Rajasthan Electricity Board, with which he was in bitter conflict for years. He says he would not connive at the corruption that was endemic there. In 1977 he rode his bicycle from Rajasthan to Kanya Kumari at the southern tip of India and later cycled to Kathmandu. In 1978 he became a *saddhu* and wandered around India for six years when he happened to meet Bharat Lal, who recruited him for his then position several months before our meeting. When asked why he had abandoned his religious search, he explained that he was now engaged in *jan sewa* (service to the people), which is a branch of religion.

Scarcely surprising, the issue that has caused the greatest conflict with the contractors is wages. The Union's strategy in this area has been a variant of its approach on the issue of bonded labour, viz. to use the appropriate judicial tribunal, which in this instance was an industrial arbitration body. This strategy has reflected Agnivesh's perception that what they had on their side was a body of progressive legislation and procedures and the necessary knowledge to take advantage of them. So in 1984 the Stone Quarry Workers' Union made a claim for increased wages before the Central Industrial Tribunal, Chandigarh. The matter started out in the conciliation jurisdiction of the Tribunal with the Union making application for a rate of Rs 100 over the allegedly current Rs 71 to be paid for every 150 cu.ft of broken stones delivered to the contractor. This amount was to be paid in addition to supplying the inputs—explosives, detonators, wicks and so on. It is not clear just what part the contractors played in proceedings but clearly they played at best a minor part. Their tactic seems to have been largely one of avoidance. The tribunal made a determination on 10 September 1984 which seemed to be even-handed—it rejected the Union's claim for Rs 100 but decreed that the deductions by the employers for the inputs was unlawful as determined by the Supreme Court in the Quarry Labourers' Case. In short, the workers were to get Rs 71 net of all costs.

The Union was jubilant at this result. In fact, the employers were paying amounts far less than Rs 71 (Rs 48 and less was standard) and deducting significant further amounts from this to cover the cost of the input. So in putatively confirming the amount of Rs 71 and also decreeing the cessation of deductions, the Tribunal was actually benefiting the Union twice over. It is not clear whether the figure of Rs 71 came from the employers' or the Union's side—it may have been a tactic on the part of the Union in order to achieve a confirmation of this amount but with no allowable deductions.

The employers, needless to say, did not accept this result. In a response to litigation initiated in the Supreme Court by Agnivesh's organisation, R.L. Sharma claimed that his Company had been disbanded and was no longer working in the Faridabad area. Indeed, Sharma does seem to have taken some legal steps to terminate his company and form a new one. But the object was not to effect any physical change or cessation of operations but to be able to claim that the corporate body against which the industrial award was made no longer existed. This issue does not seem to have reached the stage of decision by the Court. Meanwhile, the Pioneer Crushing Company (another of the contractors) moved the High Court of Punjab and Haryana on 3 May 1985 for a writ quashing the award on a number of grounds, including breach of natural justice to the contractors by virtue of having been insufficiently heard. But on 27 July 1985 the Court declared this action premature, since it was available to the contractors to move the Industrial Tribunal itself that the award be set aside.

No further legal action directly on this matter took place, though there is still a matter pending in the Supreme Court which could conceivably overturn the award. But again, the favourable legal outcome did not lead to any large rise in the rates of pay for the quarry workers. The employers simply declined to pay the rates enjoined on them by the tribunal. Agnivesh says that privately the Arbitrator advised them to negotiate and fix on a mid-way point between the prevailing rate and the Rs 71 with no deductions decreed in arbitration. But Agnivesh does not seem to have taken up this suggestion, perhaps for a number of reasons. As we have suggested, Agnivesh has always been uncomfortable in the role of union leader—despite the other organisers on the ground, all the policy decisions have been made by him. He is not the person to sit down with employers for whom he has no respect and proceed to hammer out a compromise. Moreover, as a lawyer he is bemused by the almost impotence of even the highest court in the land on the matters he has battled for over such a long period.

On a number of occasions throughout the years of the struggle there have been serious clashes between workers and the employers. The Union has staged several strikes and numerous marches. In one clash a worker was killed early in 1985 and in the ensuing processes Agnivesh himself was arrested in apprehension of a breach of the peace. Characteristically, Agnivesh instituted another Supreme Court action following these events alleging contempt of court on the part of the employers for their several failures to conform to the orders of the Court. Regrettably delays resulted in the retirement of Bhagwati J. before this petition reached judgment, and it has had to be started afresh.

In the second half of the 1980s the workers' struggle has slowly been disintegrating. The principal union organiser, Bharat Lal, left amid recriminations, and the lack of dramatic improvement has tended to rob the movement of enthusiasm. Agnivesh noted in an interview in June 1989 that he was no longer going to the quarries because in conscience he could no longer ask the workers to undertake any action.

From the beginning, his most vehement denunciations have been reserved for governments at the centre and State levels. Early on it seems to have come as a surprise to him to learn how callously indifferent the authorities appeared to be in the face of the lawless exploitation of labour in the Faridabad quarries. His analysis has proceeded on the basis that there was collusion between the contractors and the highest level of the state government of Haryana, such that in return for favours to the ruling party the state government would not cooperate with even lawful directives favouring the workers. The central government has not been seen to be quite so tightly connected to the contractors but it has also been negligent in failing to discharge many of the duties it has under national legislation. He has been critical of even the Supreme Court. Though this body has been favourable to the workers' cause when it has handed down judgments, these have often taken so long to come out that the workers' movement has been robbed of momentum.

For their part, the employers too have been critical of the central government. Their persistent complaint has been that the system of quarrying rights conspires against good management and the capacity to pay higher wages. The prevailing system has been to auction quarrying rights for a period of three years, and this tenure is said to be too short to justify major investments needed to improve profitability and therefore amenities in the quarries.[31] Since there are no figures readily available, such claims are difficult to evaluate. It may well be that a period of three years is too short for economic efficiency, but this is clearly not the root of the problem in the quarries. Agnivesh is likely to be far closer to the truth in his claims about the relationships between contractors and political parties and the awful neglect of legal duties on the part of officials for a number of reasons, including sheer moral indifference.

The Concrete Achievements

After some eight years of struggle in Faridabad, the gains have been meagre. The latest commissioner appointed by the Supreme Court reported in February 1989 that 'the mine lessees and the crusher owners and others have failed to implement' the original twenty-one directives of the Supreme Court, 'which is reflected in the sub-human conditions in which the quarry/crusher workers of Faridabad find themselves till date'.[32] This finding stands in the face of evidence submitted to the Court by both the Haryana and Union governments showing substantial compliance with the Court orders. The commissioner reports that there has been little or no improvement on matters like the provision of fresh water, toilet facilities, safety equipment, health facilities, the reduction of dust emissions, and so on. Perhaps the judgment of the commissioner is somewhat too sweeping—there is now, for example, a bit more fresh water available than there was before the struggle. Evidence tendered to the Court by the central government suggests, too, that sprinkler mechanisms have been installed on the crushers, though it may well be true that these have not actually worked to reduce dust emissions significantly. The commissioner's own report together with information from Swami Agnivesh's organisation shows that there has been a modest rise in wages paid to the labourers over the period—presumably at least partly due to the strenuous activity of the union. But there is no doubt that these improvements are strictly marginal.

A table reproduced but not commented on in Commissioner Jain's report suggests that none of the above is the major change to have come over the Faridabad quarries during the 1980s. Table 1 of the report shows that the quarry workers have been reduced from 4,050 in 1984 to 1,300 in 1988. These are said to be official figures obtained from the Department of Mines Safety and the Labour Enforcement Office, Ghaziabad. During the same period the number of crusher workers has risen from 480 to 639. The most likely explanation for the reduction in quarry workers is that the old quarries have become increasingly unproductive and that operations have started to move elsewhere. But it is barely possible that the major effect of the union activity and the modest government measures aimed at securing compliance with the Court orders has been to drive the contractors away.[33] Either way, the workers have clearly not gained from the change.

Conclusion

This account of the Faridabad struggle is offered as a case-study of some of the conditions of migratory labour (most of it untouchable and tribal) and also of the difficulty of intervening to ameliorate these conditions. Perhaps the most remarkable aspect of this case is the abject failure of the Supreme Court to have its decrees enforced: nothing much has changed in the quarries as a result of the Supreme Court's decisions.

The contractors have had everything but law on their side, and law is simply deficient in the face of that degree of power. The workers may have come closest to some kind of victory when they staged a strike in 1984, but almost inevitably they went back to work without having achieved any solid results. Severe poverty in the context of a state government favourable to large contractors defeated them. In this and other encounters the Haryana police force was not neutral but rather an obedient servant of the contractors' interests. The workers could be portrayed as disturbers of the peace and selected workers and organisers imprisoned at strategic moments. Nowadays Swami Agnivesh suggests that the workers will not get anywhere until they administer a 'brushing' (beating) to the employers and their 'muscle-men'. But it takes a climactic moment after a long struggle for the workers to reach this point of boldness. The possibility of reaching such a moment is now long past. Clearly the actions of the reformers cannot be immune from criticism. Their major institutional success was the release and 'rehabilitation' of the Banner labourers, but this success was transformed into a pathetic failure by their eventual return to Faridabad. I have come close to suggesting that the Banner exercise was doomed from the start, given the special nomadic history of this group and their lack of any but a fleeting connection with the area they were sent back to. And throughout I have adopted a severely critical—some might think cynical—stance in relation to government in its dealings with the poor. But, of course, it is too easy to be critical of organisations like that of Swami Agnivesh. He himself was genuinely optimistic that, with the support of the Supreme Court in its new 'public interest' jurisdiction, the tide could be turned against a group as powerful as the quarry contractors. And he has had to learn as a painful discovery that government (particularly the bureaucracy) has a severely limited willingness/capacity to intervene decisively in support of the workers.[34] It should be said that Bhagwati J. of the Supreme Court of India seemed to evince the same optimism that government could intervene effectively.

Organisation of the Faridabad workers was also flawed, as Agnivesh recognises. He attributes part of the problem to the sheer difficulty of organising migrant workers who are far less secure than workers living at home. Many of them come and go, destroying continuity of organisation. And clearly their capacity to absorb the hardship of loss of income during industrial action is specially limited away from home. But clearly there were also faults that arose from Agnivesh's less than enthusiastic role as union organiser and his pursuit of a wider political agenda as a national opposition figure. Still, it would not be appropriate to dwell on these limitations. What Agnivesh accomplished was to make migrant workers like the Faridabad quarry labourers visible for the first time. And he pursued with admirable and skilful energy a strategy of judicial, political and industrial action which looked immensely promising for this particular group of workers. In the end it is highly doubtful that any other organisation could have achieved more.

What stands out above all is the sheer difficulty of intervening in processes like that represented by the Faridabad quarries. Effective intervention entails an elaborate and energetic effort by government to enforce admirably progressive health, safety and labour legislation. The employers must be forced to pay the transport costs of their workers without deducting these costs from future earnings of the workers. Most important, means must be found to provide loans to poor workers so that they can spend modest amounts on life-cycle events such as marriage and death without becoming hopelessly indebted at usurious rates of interest. The mainstream Indian trade unions need to be interested in areas of labour other than the most organised and most privileged; it is not reasonable to expect makeshift organisations such as that of Swami Agnivesh to undertake the arduous long-term process of industrial organising. Such a list is obviously forbidding and represents an antidote to naive optimism. At the same time, it is unreasonable cynicism to believe that no useful intervention is possible. It seems to this writer that the task becomes more feasible in the context of an overall political culture (like that of Kerala) which places a high value on organising the poor. Kerala, after all, is the only State where there is an effective union of agricultural labourers.

Notes

1. This legislation was enacted during the so-called Emergency of 1975–77. Liberation of bonded labour and a renewed emphasis on land reform were two of Indira Gandhi's '20 points' programme of economic and social policy which were designed to demonstrate a seriousness about attacking poverty. The Bonded Labour Abolition Act was not strictly necessary to outlaw the bonded labour system, since section 23 of the Constitution had already abolished all forms of slavery and forced labour. It was essentially a symbolic affirmation of official concern, though it had some small concrete core in purporting to extinguish all bonded debts and providing a legislative basis for rehabilitation of the affected labourers.

2. AIR (1984) SC 802. Henceforth the 'Quarry Workers' Case'.

3. For an account of this litigation, see Upendra Baxi, 'Taking Suffering Seriously: Social Action Litigation in the Supreme Court of India', Upendra Baxi (ed.), *Law and Poverty: Critical Essays* (Bombay: N.M. Tripathi, 1988).

4. One of the most famous of these cases was the Asiad Construction Workers' Case (AIR (1982) SC 1473) which arose from the feverish construction of stadia and facilities for India to stage the Asian Games of 1982. The Court (again with Bhagwati J. as principal judge) pronounced

in the language of outraged morality as well as law against the labour practices of the construction authority. This body was found to have infringed numerous legislative provisions, but by the time the judgment was handed down, the construction was complete and the Games were over.

5. Unpublished report submitted to the Supreme Court, 28 June 1982: social action litigation in the Supreme Court of India's *Third World Legal Studies*, Ann. (1985), pp. 107–32.

6. Ibid., p. 74.

7. 'Quarry Workers' Case', p. 811.

8. Ibid., p. 821.

9. 'Quarry Workers' Case', p. 829.

10. Unpublished report of Laxmi Dhar Mishra (27 February 1984), p. 5.

11. Ibid., p. 15.

12. Unpublished order of Court.

13. In an affidavit to the Supreme Court, 1 July 1988, the Government of Haryana stated that 93 of the 295 labourers declared bonded by the Mishra Report were 'not willing to go'. Of the others, 73 were declared to have been 'released and repatriated' and 124 to have 'left of their own'. The latter note seems particularly unsatisfactory, since it suggests that these people were given no help despite being declared to be bonded. Their later experience can safely be assumed to have been unfortunate. (Copy of affidavit reproduced in Mahaveer Jain, 'The Stone Quarry and Crusher Workers of Faridabad—A Study of Their Condition and the Implementation of the 21 Directives of the Supreme Court', unpublished report commissioned by the Supreme Court under writ petition 2135 of 1982, New Delhi, February 1989, Appendix II.)

14. No community census has been done for the Faridabad quarries but clearly the untouchables (scheduled castes) far outnumber the tribals (scheduled tribes). Together, these two groupings account for the great majority of quarry workers in Faridabad.

15. Mahaveer Jain Report, p. 179.

16. This and the following names of quarry workers and union organisers at Faridabad are fictitious, to save possible embarrassment.

17. I was taken to the Bhati mines by Inder Mohan, whose help I gratefully acknowledge.

18. For an argument along these lines, see Nirmal Sengupta, *Destitutes and Development: A Study of the Bauri Community in the Bokaro Region* (New Delhi, 1978).

19. Jan Breman, *Of Peasants, Migrants and Paupers—Rural Labour Circulation and Capitalist Production in West India*, (Delhi, 1985), pp. 306–13.

20. Ibid., p. 307.

21. Ibid., p. 311.

22. Ibid.

23. See also Tom Brass, 'Unfree Labour and Capitalist Restructuring in the Agrarian Sector: Peru and India', *The Journal of Peasant Studies*, 14(1) (October, 1986), pp. 50–77. Brass sees 'debt bondage' (even where the debt has been voluntarily assumed by the employee) as 'a modern form of slavery'.

24. Utsa Patnaik, in Utsa Patnaik and Manjari Dingwaney (eds), *Chains of Servitude-Bondage and Slavery in India* (Madras, 1985), p. 25.

25. Two of the best accounts of slavery or agrestic servitude in the old order in the early European period in India are Benedicte Hjejle, 'Slavery and Agricultural Bondage in South India in the 19th Century', *The Scandinavian Economic History Review*, 11(1 and 2) (1967), and Dharma Kumar, *Land and Caste in South India* (Cambridge, 1965).

26. Cf. the view of the study conducted under the auspices of the Gandhian Institute in the late 1970s: Sarma Marla, *Bonded Labour in India* (New Delhi, 1981). This study purports to locate many hundreds of thousands of bonded labourers in India, but it does so on the basis of concepts and research which are questionable at many points. To give just one example, it has a category of labourers who have been bonded for 'less than one year'. In many regions a majority of the identified bonded labourers fall into this category. Now, there may well be strong normative arguments against the system of tying agricultural labourers to particular landowners' households, but it does not make sense to treat short-term (e.g. one year) contracts of agricultural service as if they follow in a straight line from, say, the slavery of the Pulaya caste of Kerala in the nineteenth century. In the State of Haryana (which the Sarma Maria team did not investigate on the ground that it was unlikely to find bonded labourers there) it is still common, though becoming less so, to find one-year labour contracts for field servants. Where these contracts entail a loan component, they would have to be regarded as examples of bonded labour. (Source: fieldwork in Kaithal District, Haryana, April 1985.) The field-servants of the irrigated districts of Haryana are among the best-paid labourers in India: in one case I found a labourer to be receiving Rs 2,400, plus some green fodder for a buffalo and 2 quintals of wheat and padi in both the kharif and rabi seasons. In addition, the landowner had supplied advance money of Rs 5,000 at 'nominal interest' (which amounted to about 18 per cent p.a.) so that the labourer could build his own pukka house. This loan was seen by the landowner as an extra benefit to the employee, who would otherwise have sought to claim a higher wage. Indeed, another labourer of this same owner received Rs 3,000 because he did not have access to the fringe

benefits of cattle fodder and loan. Of course, the loan in question would render the labourer bonded within the meaning of the Act.

27. At the same time as being committed to a view that there has been a fundamental change of outlook among the subordinates over a period of years (particularly following Indian independence), I would not want to discount the important perspective of James Scott articulated most fully in *Weapons of the Weak—Everyday Forms of Peasant Resistance* (New Haven, 1985). Scott draws a picture of poor-peasant resistance as ubiquitous across region and time, against a view centred on the necessarily rare acts of violent rebellion. The figure of the poor peasant as an essentially accepting figure disappears in Scott's account. It is possible to accept this view without abandoning an idea of historical growth in consciousness of exploitation.

28. I have used the masculine gender here because the tied relationship is arranged between the landowner and a male labourer. Sometimes the arrangement involves other members of the family but very often it does not.

29. This changes in those rare instances where there is effective labour organisation. Thus in Kerala union organisation has ensured the payment of high daily rates of pay and the local workers apparently refuse to work in any system which would reduce this rate. One of the consequences of this is that the Kerala labourers are consistently underbid by migrant labour (mainly from Tamil Nadu), where it is feasible for employers to utilise this. The influx of migrant labour contributes to the overall poor availability of employment in Kerala, which means that the income of agricultural labourers is much lower than in many other States.

30. Interview with Swami Agnivesh (12 March 1985), New Delhi.

31. This claim was made in an interview with Kartar Singh, one of the major contractors at Faridabad, and his assistant Mr Ojha, Faridabad (10 March 1985). It also appears in various representations of the employers. The period of the lease seems now to have been extended to five years: Mahaveer Jain Report, Appendix VII.

32. Mahaveer Jain Report, p. 196.

33. I have been advised by letter in November 1989 that the Faridabad quarries have recently been nationalised. Whether conditions for the workers will now improve is a matter for the future.

34. Agnivesh is by no means the only reformist politician to learn of the severity of the governmental system in relation to the poor. In an interview on what turned out to be the night before he died, Karpoori Thakur (sometime Chief Minister of Bihar and a leading opposition politician over many years) observed that what shocked him most about the situa-

tion in Bihar was the violence done to the poor by the state itself rather than other citizens. See Oliver Mendelsohn, 'Last Interview with Karpoori Thakur', *Times of India* (18 February 1988.) Substantially the same point was made by a renowned reformer within the Bihar cadre of the Indian Administrative Service, the elite body of bureaucrats. None of these three people is by nature a cynic but each has been genuinely disabused of his belief in the potential of government to intervene effectively in support of the poor.

8

THE SUPREME COURT AS
THE MOST TRUSTED PUBLIC
INSTITUTION IN INDIA*

The principal argument of this paper is contained in the title, viz. that the Supreme Court is now probably the most trusted major institution in India.[1] This appears to be quite a recent circumstance and largely an outcome of two other developments. The first development is the steep decline in the prestige of other institutions, above all politicians but also including the bureaucracy. But secondly, the Supreme Court has been responsible for its own rise in popularity by adopting an overall approach that has increasingly made it seem the only true fount of justice in India. The more the other institutions have declined in prestige and trust, the more the Court has risen. This paper, then, is a short interrogation of aspects of the first half-century of the Supreme Court's existence. Although I will make an effort to place this history into the larger context of Indian public institutions, my main concentration will be on the Court itself. But I will begin with some words about this larger context.

There is no simple judgment to be made about the half-century of Indian Independence. On the one hand there are conspicuous successes both at the material and constitutional level. The most frequently cited

*This chapter was originally published in *South Asia: Journal of South Asian Studies* 23(Special Issue) (2000), pp. 103–19.

material success is the tremendous increase in agricultural output, such that it is often said that 'India can now feed itself'.[2] In political and constitutional terms, one only has to look at the history of the rest of pre-partition India to appreciate the strengths of the Indian experience. There is now a vigorous debate, for example, about whether Pakistan should be placed in a new analytical category called 'failed states' (along with the USSR, apartheid South Africa and so on).[3] Whether or not such a category is useful, no serious observer would want to place India into it. Thus, India gave itself a highly detailed Constitution exactly 50 years ago, and this remains the Constitution which governs the country today.[4] Somewhat more controversial but still generally agreed,[5] India deserves credit for having remained a broadly open society and a democratic polity. In these respects India compares favourably with China. On the negative side, however, Indian poverty and inequality remain at appalling levels, sectarianism has been growing, official corruption and government lawlessness are rife and getting worse, and there is far more cynicism at every level of society than there was at the time of Independence.

Arguably one of the very worst symbols of what has gone wrong with Indian governance is the prosecution of former Prime Minister Narasimha Rao for official corruption. The veteran Congressman Rao was Prime Minister from 1992 to 1996, and the clouds of suspicion that formed around him in the last months of his rule culminated shortly after his fall in a cluster of prosecutions for the receipt of large sums of money in return for official favours. He was even arrested at one point. Nor was Rao the only leading politician to be accused of corruption. There was a whole slew of them, including L.K. Advani, then Leader of the BJP and current Home Minister. But while these prosecutions were an indication of the level of corruption that had overtaken India at the very top, they were simultaneously something of an indication of the strength of Indian governance. The prosecutions did not take the form of victor's justice after a change of Government—in this respect they can be contrasted with Pakistan, where a death sentence has been carried out on one former Prime Minister and the immediate past Prime Minister is currently under prosecution. Whatever the merits of the charges against these men, inevitably their prosecution has been tainted with suspicion of political bias. The Indian prosecutions, by contrast, were clearly nonpartisan in inspiration.

Indeed, and not without its own problems, the actual prosecution (as opposed to the adjudication) of Prime Minister Rao and a number of other ex-Ministers of his Congress Government owed a great deal to the intervention of the Supreme Court itself. In response to 'public interest litigation' (PIL) petitions brought by lawyers acting either for themselves or for larger coalitions of interested citizens, the Supreme Court demanded that several insufficiently active investigations by the Criminal Bureau of Investigation (CBI) be taken up with vigour against any person 'whosoever high'.[6] It was clear that the Supreme Court believed that the CBI was acting under Government pressure to go slow on investigating the flood of serious claims of official corruption during the period of the Rao Government. Following the lead of the Supreme Court, even the High Courts of the States began to concern themselves with the progress of criminal investigations and prosecutions.

This intervention of the Supreme Court of India into the affairs of a branch of the executive is highly unusual by the standards of the Westminster form. There has been no comparable occurrence in Britain or Australia, for example. In these constitutional systems, that of the United States too, such judicial intervention would be seen as a breach of the principle of the separation of powers. While it is possible for a court in a Westminster-style constitutional arrangement to direct an administrative body to make a decision that it has thus far failed to make, the Indian Court's energetic and multi-pronged directions to an investigative and prosecutorial authority such as the CBI go far beyond such practice. These interventions demonstrate just how far the Supreme Court has moved along the road of securing for itself a central part in Indian governance. The Supreme Court has become as powerful as any court in the world, perhaps more powerful than any other. This article will explore just how this has come about and what its implications are.

The Indian Constitution and the Emergence of the Supreme Court's Power

Before I sketch the development of the Supreme Court to its present position of power, it will be necessary to make some preliminary observations about the Constitution under which the Court works. The *Constitution of India* 1950 is a complex and lengthy instrument which cannot easily be characterised in terms of fundamental orienta-tion. On the one hand it embodies a statement of fundamental rights for individual citizens of India, rights which are capable of full enforce-ment in the courts. The rights follow what was by 1950 a relatively standard international pattern, including rights to equality, religious freedom and speech, and freedom from arbitrary imprisonment and from deprivation of property without compensation. Such a statement of rights was no more than fit and proper to a society newly emerged from colonial autocracy. But on the other side the Constitution seems to perpetuate that authoritarian legacy by laying down powerful mechanisms of governance for a society conceived to be always suscep-tible to disorder. So the Constitution provides the Government of the day acting through the President as head of state, a power to declare a state of emergency and thereby suspend the recognition of those very rights that have so forthrightly been enunciated earlier in the docu-ment (Article 359).

One of the most novel aspects of the Indian Constitution is its elab-oration of a set of 'directive principles of state policy'. These constitute a relatively radical set of prescriptions to bring about social justice but, unlike the fundamental rights, they are not enforceable in the courts. The directive principles include the right to an adequate means of livelihood; 'that the operation of the economic system does not result in the concentration of wealth and means of production to the com-mon detriment'; and that men and women receive equal pay for the same work (Article 39). Among the other goals there is to be free legal aid; provision for just and humane conditions of work and maternity leave; a living wage for workers; and provision for free and compulsory education for children. Despite the fact that the Constitution makes abundantly clear that these goals are not judicially enforceable, in recent years the Supreme Court has on occasion ignored the distinc-tion between directive principles and fundamental rights. Thus the Court has in effect rendered the right to education a fundamental right with full enforceability.[7] This has come about as part of the larger development of judicial activism, the subject of the present paper.

The Supreme Court did not begin its life as an activist court, that is a court dedicated to energetic intervention on behalf of the dispossessed elements of Indian society. Some of the most important early judicial battles were over land reform legislation, and a number of the Court's decisions invalidated crucial reform legislation and gravely injured the overall prospects of reform.[8] Indeed, it is arguable that for roughly the first two decades the Supreme Court tended to function as a support for the most powerful landed interests in India. This approach of the Court reached its apogee in the famous *Golak Nath* case of 1971.[9] The legal issue in this case was the extent to which Parliament had free rein to change the Constitution so as to restrict property rights. In an effort to acquire more land for redistribution, a Constitutional amendment (the seventeenth) had been passed by the Parliament to effect a certain technical change in the definition of an estate in land. On the face of it, the Constitution was freely amendable by simple Act of Parliament (Article 368). But the question raised in *Golak Nath* was whether this free power of amendment of the Parliament could be used so as to deny or abridge fundamental rights laid down in the Constitution as originally created. In a split decision the Supreme Court held that there was a 'basic structure' to the Constitution that included the fundamental rights and that this basic structure was not open to amendment by the Parliament. The Parliament (in other words the Government of the day) was thereby prohibited from amending the Constitutional right to property in a way that disadvantaged property owners. Although this was in one sense yet another profoundly conservative decision in favour of landed interests trying to avoid confiscation under reform legislation, at another level the decision has underpinned the whole subsequent growth of judicial power in India. What the court was asserting for itself in *Golak Nath* was the right to determine just what constituted the 'basic structure' of the Constitution.

In the subsequent case of *Keshavananda Bharati v. State of Kerala* (1973)[10] the Court overruled its decision in *Golak Nath* and held that fundamental rights were susceptible of amendment by the Parliament. But the Court retained the idea that there was in fact a 'basic structure' to the Constitution: it was just that this basic structure did not include fundamental rights or the right to property in particular. The Court said that the basic structure included provision for democracy, a secular state, federalism and a number of other aspects of the Constitution.[11] Beyond the particular issue of amendment of the Constitution, the Court's flexing of its muscles had shown the way to a broader judicial activism. This activism has reached its full flowering in public interest litigation.

Public Interest or Social Action Litigation

The First Phase

Public Interest Litigation (PIL) is an invention of the period after the great constitutional trauma of the post-Independence period, the Emergency proclaimed by Indira Gandhi's Government and lasting from 1975 to 1977. Like virtually all structures in India, the courts had no reason to congratulate themselves on the way they upheld constitutional norms during the Emergency. Self-examination by some of the judges led to a stance markedly more favourable to the assertion of both the classic or negative civil liberties and also the positive interests of those at the bottom of the Indian economic and social heap. Somewhat curiously, the leftist (albeit left-authoritarian) orientation of the early Emergency period was one of the factors that helped move the Court in its new direction. PIL was essentially an invention of certain judges of the Supreme Court advised by a handful of academics—one of them Professor Upendra Baxi of the University of Delhi—and lawyers.

The form of the PIL cases was a writ petition under Article 32 of the Constitution moving the Supreme Court to enforce one or more fundamental rights enunciated by the Constitution and argued to have been breached. Later, and far less importantly, PIL writ petitions were also accepted by the High Courts of the States under Article 226. This device of the writ petition was one of the great innovations of the Constitution, enabling individuals to take their cases directly to the Supreme Court or the High Courts of the States rather than on appeal from lower courts after the inevitable years of litigation. Such petitions had been richly used, for example, by civil servants complaining of events (or non-events, such as lack of promotion) in their careers. But in the post-Emergency landscape, the writ petition came into its own as a mechanism by which the Supreme Court could dispense popular justice. PIL writ petitions differed from earlier petitions and ordinary litigation by virtue of not being directed to the narrow self-interest of the petitioner or litigant. Indeed, in many cases the potential beneficiaries had neither conceived nor played any substantial part in the conduct of the case. Sometimes activist lawyers working substantially alone have taken up a cause and petitioned the Court for an end to abuse. In other cases lawyers have been assisted by civil libertarians of diverse backgrounds or by journalists or by activists (environmental, for example) working in a particular area of struggle.

The essential foundation of PIL was a willingness on the part of the judges of the Supreme Court, and later the High Courts too, to relax the ordinary strictness of procedural forms for litigation.[12] Crucially, the rules as to standing were relaxed: these are the rules that require litigation to be conducted by an interested party. As suggested above, one of the characteristics of PIL is that it is not directed to self-interest as this is usually conceived in the courts. But self-interest is what ordinarily gives a litigant standing—a litigant must not be a mere busybody. So the rules as to standing had to be varied to allow third parties—lawyers, 'social workers', journalists, academics and so on—to bring action in pursuit of a cause that the Court was prepared to see as their legitimate concern. The Supreme Court was also prepared to dispense with the accepted formalities of the admission process, such that on occasion it accepted as a legitimate petition something as informal as a mere postcard sent to a judge. (This came to be known somewhat grandly as the 'epistolary jurisdiction' of the Supreme Court.) This willingness to encourage public interest litigation proceeded side-by-side with the enormous overload and backlog of cases that has afflicted the Supreme Court for years and is constantly getting worse. Clearly the Court was saying that here is a vein of cases that is so important that way must be made for them without regard to form or burden of business.

There have now been many hundreds of PIL cases, far more than could possibly be discussed in a short article. All that will be done here is indicate the broad types of cases that have come to the Supreme Court, the distinct historical periods that can be discerned, some of the problems of the litigation, as well as several of the more important individual cases. Thus there have been two broad periods of intense PIL activity: the first period was from 1979 to the mid-1980s; and the second, from the early 1990s to the present. Between these periods there was much less activity. As to the subject matter of the litigation, during the first period there was a concentration on social injustice suffered by the downtrodden and powerless. During the second period, the thrust shifted to environmental and resource concerns; and, more recently, a major preoccupation has been corruption in high places.

The very first cases centred on the criminal justice system—prisons, the plight of prisoners supposedly under trial rather than sentence, the behaviour of police—and psychiatric institutions. Thus the very first case in 1979, *Hussainara Khatoon and Others* v. *Home Secretary State of Bihar*,[13] concerned prisoners who had been imprisoned without trial for periods longer than any possible sentence that could be handed down for the offences of which they were charged. The Court was prepared to entertain the petition despite the fact that it was filed by an advocate who had had no direct acquaintance with the case and had read of its circumstances in a newspaper. Imprisonment of what came to be known as 'undertrials' for years on end, for a period longer than any permissible sentence, was found to violate Article 21 of the Constitution: 'No person shall be deprived of his life or personal liberty except according to procedure established by law'. In what became characteristic of many PIL cases this matter came back to the Court on several occasions as the facts of the case were clarified and the stance of the authorities was ascertained, including any recalcitrance in the face of legal directives. In *Hussainara* the Court had no hesitation in issuing orders far broader than necessary to decide the particular case—this itself is not the form that higher courts adopt in the Anglo-American-Australian world, though of course in these jurisdictions too an important case has value as precedent and is expected to influence the actions of the executive. The difference in *Hussainara* and many subsequent PIL cases is that the Court was prepared to issue general rulings on the law. In this case the Court ordered that all undertrials had to be informed of their entitlement to bail and that they had to be released if the period of their imprisonment was longer than the maximum possible sentence for the offences of which they were charged.

Fuelled and to a large extent framed by cases such as *Hussainara*, undertrials became one of the great issues of the early post-Emergency period. One aspect of this was the disgraceful overcrowding and squalid conditions of jails, which became a national scandal right at the end of the 70s. The habitual confinement of prisoners with leg irons and handcuffs was explored in a number of PIL cases in 1979 and 1980, as was the circumstance of solitary confinement. Another case followed the most infamous event of all involving undertrials, the Bhagalpur blinding of 1980, when ten men in Bhagalpur Central Jail had their eyes punctured with sharp instruments and then filled with acid (*Anil Yadav and Others* v. *State of Bihar and Others*).[14] This case was filed in order to try and ensure that the investigation and prosecution would proceed in a speedy and orderly manner. Given the inflamed caste feelings that led to the event in the first place, such orderliness was inevitably difficult to achieve. A later case sought to secure vocational training facilities for some of the victims.

Closely related to the litigation of abuse within the criminal justice system, a range of cases was brought to the Supreme Court about the treatment of mentally ill inmates—some in psychiatric institutions, some in jails. For example, *Rudul Sah* v. *State of Bihar* (1982)[15] was a habeas corpus petition claiming that a man had been kept in prison for 14 years as allegedly insane following his acquittal at trial.

For reasons of space, I will pass over a large number of cases categorised by a recent work under the following rubrics: the police; the armed forces; injustices specific to women; children.[16] Though there are many important cases here, the broader perspective of this article can be anchored by cases drawn from other categories. Thus in this first flush of PIL there were several cases that seemed to open up whole areas of social life to the scrutiny of progressive opinion for practically the first time. One of the most important of these was *Olga Tellis and Others* v. *Bombay Municipal Corporation and Others* (1981).[17] Olga Tellis was a journalist in Bombay, and she and two pavement dwellers brought their action to fight the mass and forcible eviction of pavement and slum dwellers ordered and begun by the then Chief Minister of the State, A.R. Antulay. The Government's intention to beautify the city by ridding it of human eyesores continued a strong theme of the mid-1970s Emergency in a number of cities, notably the capital, New Delhi itself. Clearance and deportation of large numbers of people out of Bombay began early in the morning of 23 July 1981. In response Olga Tellis wrote to Justice Bhagwati of the Supreme Court and the letter was registered as a petition, later formalised and detailed by the advocate Indira Jaising.[18]

The radical argument in *Olga Tellis* was that there was a Constitutional right under Article 21 to squat on the pavements of Bombay. Of course, there was no such specific right articulated in the Constitution document. To repeat the words of Article 21: 'No person shall be deprived of his life or personal liberty except according to procedure established by law'. On the face of it and powerfully argued by the Bombay Corporation, squatting on pavements and erection of structures on public lands were unlawful. The Corporation argued that it had a duty to clean up the streets and the pavements to promote the orderly development of the city. But the argument of the petitioner was that the overwhelming poverty and deprivation of the people in question were the inescapable context of the petition. The pavement dwellers had not come to Bombay out of free choice but from necessity. To remove them abruptly and forcibly from their meagre existence in the city was to condemn them to a still worse and more dangerous life. The Court accepted this argument. The right to life in Article 21 was declared to include the right to livelihood:

> If the right to livelihood is not treated as part of the Constitutional right to life, the easiest way of depriving a person of his right to life would be to deprive him of his means of livelihood to the point of abrogation (at pp. 193–4).

Perhaps no case illustrates the extraordinary change in the stance of the Supreme Court during the early period of Public Interest Litigation than *Olga Tellis*. Acceptance by the Court of the proposition that there was a fundamental Constitutional right to squat on the pavements of Bombay was nothing less than stunning. Prior to invention of the PIL form there would have been no mechanism by which to bring a case like this, but the proposition itself is an indication of just how far the Court had come from its earlier, profoundly conservative, history.

This short discussion of the early period of PIL has no more than touched on the important range of problems addressed by the Supreme Court. The object has been to give an indication of the kind of issues to do with social justice that began to come to the court following the restoration of a functioning democracy after Indira Gandhi's Emergency. But I will return to this early period and discuss at least one more major case when a more evaluative approach to Public Interest Litigation is taken below.

Novel and important though these early PIL cases were as the major indication that the Supreme Court had ceased to be predominantly the servant of the rich and powerful in India, it is doubtful that they transformed the consciousness of the citizenry as a whole. By the middle-1980s the Supreme Court was probably still not generally seen as anything more than the highest court in India. It had not yet developed a reputation as the conscience of the nation. Two other developments have been the midwife to such a change. First, politics, politicians, the bureaucracy and even most of the courts of law have continued to decline in public estimation. And secondly, the Supreme Court has more recently taken up a different style of Public Interest Litigation. Once the Court began to pronounce on matters that affected the whole public rather than merely the underprivileged, the status of the Court began to rise accordingly.

There was a temporal gap of about a decade between the first phase of Public Interest Litigation sketched above and the second phase which continues even now. During this decade, roughly from the mid-1980s to the mid-90s, there were still a considerable number of petitions being taken to the Court. And in retrospect, the beginnings of the shift of subject matter to the contemporary pattern can be discerned from the litigation of this time. But the decade can still be said to constitute something of an interregnum by virtue of the considerably lower profile than was true of PIL either before or since. Explanation of the lull in intensity of PIL at this time is not self-evident. Perhaps the explanation has something to do with the state of political life—it was a turbulent period, with the assassination of Prime Minister Indira Gandhi, the succession of her son Rajiv Gandhi to the Prime Ministership, his electoral defeat, a short-lived Janata Dal Government, and then assassination of Rajiv Gandhi. Narasimha Rao took over leadership of Congress and was able to serve out a whole five-year term. Perhaps the return to considerable stability during this period was a contributing factor to the re-emergence of a more intense judicial activism. It may be that judicial activism is suited to relatively quiet political times.

Environmental Issues

By far the dominant pattern of PIL since the mid-1980s has been issues to do with the environment—including pollution of water, air and land; deforestation and inappropriate forestation (using species like eucalyptus); encroachment on wetlands; and a range of other matters such as the hunter gathering rights of tribal people. Unlike the earlier period when issues of social justice predominated, there have been no individual cases of special significance. Rather, what stands out is the pattern of litigation rather than any individual case brought by an environmental movement that was gathering strength from the mid-80s. The name of one particular Supreme Court advocate, M.C. Mehta, recurs through many of the cases from the mid-1980s on. This pattern reached its zenith ten years later in a flurry of decisions of the Court in which Justice Kuldip Singh gave judgment either alone or with one or more of his colleagues. Justice Singh became known as something of an environmental specialist, such judicial specialisation being yet another of the unorthodox aspects of PIL.

The environmental litigation that captured the public imagination was a series of cases brought by advocate M.C. Mehta on the industries polluting the air, water and land of Delhi. No doubt the fact that the subject of the litigation was the national capital contributed greatly to the impact of these cases. As early as 1985 Mehta had raised the issue of polluting industries in Delhi, but it was not until 1995 that the matter was taken up in earnest. In *M.C. Mehta* v. *Union of India* (1995) the Secretary (Environment), Government of India, stated that 8378 industries, including noxious and heavy industry, were operating in Delhi in contravention of the Master Plan for that city and relevant legislation including the *Factories Act* (1948). The Court ordered that notices be sent to the offending installations requiring their closure or relocation. It appears that this order was not intended to close down particular factories at that stage, but to prepare the ground for such closures. In a later order in the same case, the Court directed the Municipal Corporation of India 'not to register or give licences to any hazardous/noxious industry in Delhi'. In a third order, the Court directed the closure of 168 of the hazardous installations which were found to be operating unlawfully and in disregard of the Master Plan for Delhi. Delhi and the neighbouring States were ordered to provide assistance to the industrial units to relocate in a more suitable environment.[19] Following this decision and again prompted by advocate M.C. Mehta, the Supreme Court plunged deeply into the issue of pollution of the river Yamuna and also the Ganges into which the Yamuna flows. The Court made a series of orders in relation to sewerage disposal and the discharge of toxic flows from industrial establishments.[20]

The Probity of Public Officials

In quantitative terms, the judicial engagement with elected public officials has been a comparatively minor as well as recent preoccupation of the Court. But it is this engagement that has most clearly captured the public imagination and consolidated the Supreme Court's position as the custodian of public virtue. In a word, the issue is corruption. The acquisition of illicit money by both appointed and elected officials has long been a notorious element of public life in India and the general perception is that this phenomenon has been gathering strength over time. Normally, of course, any judicial engagement with this issue would be in the form of adjudication of prosecutions for breach of the criminal law. But, of course, the problem is that few cases involving corruption ever reach the stage of prosecution. In addressing this issue the Supreme Court has made its impact on corruption in the highest places.

The single most important case has concerned the 'Jain hawala' matter. This first received a public airing when a journalist and several Supreme Court advocates took a petition to the Supreme Court in October 1993 asking the Criminal Bureau of Investigation (CBI) to pursue allegations that the Jain brothers, businessmen, had given bribes to politicians in return for the award of government contracts and favours. The then Prime Minister, Narasimha Rao, was one of the politicians mentioned in the diaries as a participant in the unlawful activities of the Jain brothers. The petition stated that information had been laid before the CBI in 1991 but that because of the power of the suspects, the CBI was not pursuing the case with sufficient vigour. Progress of the writ petition was initially slow: one of the petitioners recalled that 'in the first year of the litigation, the Court seems to have had no clue to the case'.[21] But when a new bench headed by Justice Verma was constituted in November 1994, it immediately grasped the significance of the case. The head of the CBI was required to attend the next hearing and was roundly criticised by the bench for his lack of progress to that time. For more than a year this official was required to submit periodic reports on the state of the investigation, the reports taking the form of in camera meetings with the bench. This highly unusual secretiveness seems to have been adopted against the backdrop of the great seniority of those under investigation. Eventually, early in 1996, the first charges against tens of leading politicians under investigation (but not including Prime Minister Rao) were laid by the CBI. Narasimha Rao was not so fortunate in one of several other investigations involving him among others. In what became known as the

St Kitts Forgery case, Rao was not only charged but actually arrested before being granted bail. Again the charges had been brought against Rao only after the Supreme Court had taken up yet another PIL case arguing that the CBI had been going slow in its investigations of the then Prime Minister.[22]

Never before 1996 had the Supreme Court so directly and personally confronted politicians occupying the very highest positions of power in India. Just why the Court was prepared to act so forcefully at this time is a matter of some speculation. One obvious factor was the character of the judge leading the bench in the Jain hawala and several other cases, Justice Verma. Clearly this particular judge was prepared to be more resolute than other judges had been. But it is also true that Justice Verma was one of a unanimous bench of three judges in the Jain hawala case, so at best he was the prime mover rather than a solitary radical. And, as the cases on the environment have shown, even prior to this confrontation with politicians the Court had already entered into a new phase of activism. Indeed, it was 'the environment specialist' Justice Kuldip Singh, not Justice Verma, who at the time had the reputation of being the most activist of the judges of the Supreme Court. Deeper explanations therefore have to be sought in the institutional history of the Supreme Court, the Bar, constitutional politics and public opinion. Perhaps the most powerful explanation is to be found in the idea of an institutional momentum built up by previous judicial activism, together with an intensification of public distaste at high-level corruption and its political practitioners. When the Supreme Court intervened it rekindled a sense of probity and public morality that many had despaired of ever revisiting.

The Controversies Surrounding Judicial Activism

Despite the record of achievement that has been sketched above, the activism of the Supreme Court of India has not lacked attendant controversy. The criticisms have been of several different kinds. First, members of the legal profession have been concerned about procedural novelties of Public Interest Litigation. Secondly, questions have been raised as to the efficacy of PIL decisions of the Court: in a word, are the decisions implemented? And thirdly, there has been an argument from the standpoint of democracy to the effect that the Supreme

Court has usurped the political and executive privileges that properly derive from electoral trust of the people.

As to the first issue, there is no doubt that PIL has involved considerable departure from ordinary procedural forms. Some of the departures seem almost impregnably justifiable. This applies, for example, to the relaxed admission procedures which have by-passed lawyerish, procedural niceties so as to allow the hitherto downtrodden and mute to have a voice in the highest court. Other innovations are not so clear cut. For example, in a number of the more important cases the Court has appointed particular persons to provide research reports on the situation that obtains in the relevant industry or jail or slum colony. These reports have then become part of the basis of the Court's decision. But advocates for the defence have often taken objection to this process, pointing out that it confounds the ordinary rules of evidence. Ordinarily evidence is given orally rather than in writing and is subject to robust cross-examination by the opposing party. Such procedure is the very essence of the adversarial system of justice and is the principal procedural characteristic of common law, in contrast to the code-based systems of Continental Europe. By taking notice of commissioned research reports as if they were uncontroversially factual, the Court has effectively denied the defence an opportunity to contest the evidence in the reports. There has also been criticism of the frequent tendency in PIL to make judgments which are expressed in highly general terms rather than limited to the particular case in litigation.

The question of the efficacy of PIL decisions is a much larger and more important issue. It is not an issue that can be more than touched on here; I have looked at it in considerable detail elsewhere.[23] There can be no definitive answer to the question of just how much difference PIL decisions have made to the industries and areas of injustice or concern that gave rise to the litigation. Far more research work needs to be done to see what improvement there has been, for example, in the conduct of jails and psychiatric institutions, and in the cleanliness of the Yamuna and Ganges rivers. The present author conducted a study of one industrial situation, that of the stone quarry workers of Faridabad, close to New Delhi. This is an appalling industrial site whose workforce is predominantly composed of inter-state workers brought by middlemen to work for the operators of the quarries. The Faridabad stone quarries were the subject of one of the most important PIL cases, *Bandhua Mukti Morcha* v. *Union of India and Others* (1984).[24] This case was brought by an organisation founded by a political activist, Swami Agnivesh, with the object of having a large number of the quarry workers declared 'bonded labourers' within the meaning of the *Bonded Labour System (Abolition) Act* 1976. The Act had been passed during the leftist phase of Indira Gandhi's Emergency, and had been designed to liberate and rehabilitate workers who were forced to work with little or no payment for someone to whom they (or even their fathers or grandfathers) owed money. After a great deal of evidence, some of it in the form of a research report commissioned from a social scientist, the Court found that many of the workers in the quarries were in fact bonded within the meaning of the Act, and ordered that they be returned to the place from which they had originally been transported and that the State of Rajasthan rehabilitate them and their downtrodden families. This remains one of the greatest victories of the PIL movement. Unfortunately, close scrutiny of what happened on the ground leads to a considerably less celebratory account of the case. It turns out that the bonded labourers were dumped into a wholly unsuitable environment in Rajasthan where they had had only a casual connection almost forty years previously. The Government of Rajasthan made scant effort to provide these hundreds of people with the means to survive, let alone thrive. When I interviewed them in the desert of Rajasthan, they were unanimous that their present condition was far worse than it had been in the degraded circumstances of Faridabad. My argument in the paper was that this miserable outcome had arisen from faulty reasoning in the case and also the utter unwillingness and incapacity of State governments to commit themselves to rehabilitating some of India's most put-upon people. In short, the PIL victory in the stone quarry workers' case had simply failed to deliver measurable improvement in the lives of the quarry workers.

It is not possible to generalise from this one case of Public Interest Litigation to conclude that PIL has been an overall failure. There have been many cases and very few of them have been studied in a rigorous empirical way. But the findings of the above study must give some pause to too-naive hopes and claims that are made for PIL. It is far from a panacea. Any effectiveness that it may have will undoubtedly be vitiated by over-use. Moreover, it is vital that the judiciary have a sense of realism as well as goodwill to those in whose name litigation is waged. It was precisely that sense of realism which was lacking in the Stone Quarry Workers' case. On the other hand, it would also be wrong to suggest that the only measure of PIL is whether it has delivered concrete outcomes in individual cases. PIL has operated on multiple levels. On the one hand it has been directed to individual cases of injustice and wrongdoing. But simultaneously, if not always consciously, PIL has sometimes worked towards a general revitalisation of the moral foundations of Indian constitutionalism. This may be a difficult proposition to sustain empirically, but it is possible to argue— indeed I myself would want to argue this—that in its PIL jurisdiction the Supreme Court has been engaged in nothing less than the revival of Indian democracy. Again, this is not to suggest that the character and outcome of individual cases is not crucial to the quality of PIL. It is only to make the point that the subject matter and manner of considering PIL cases have had beneficial consequences for the larger project of Indian constitutionalism.

This latter argument connects up with the objections that have often been levelled against PIL and Supreme Court activism more generally, to the effect that they represent a challenge to and derogation from democracy. This argument is not novel to India but has been offered up wherever powerful apex courts have handed down judgments in areas of intense controversy. Thus, judicial activism in the United States has often been seen to have usurped power properly residing in the elected branches of the government—the President and Congress. This was an argument frequently levelled against the Warren Court of the 1950s and the Court of the 1960s with its path-breaking decisions on the rights of criminal suspects and electoral malapportionment. More recently, the High Court of Australia has been intensely criticised by social and political conservatives for its decisions on Aboriginal land rights in *Mabo* and *Wik* and for its 'discovery' of implied rights embedded in the Constitution. So it is not a matter of any wonderment that the Supreme Court of India has been criticised for pushing into areas where it has no real business. For example, the sociologist André Béteille has written:

> Judicial activism often stems from the best of motives, the desire to set things right in corrupt and decaying public institutions ... But it can also be argued that in a democracy, judicial restraint is a virtue not only in good times but also in bad times.[25]

There is no doubt that fine decisions must be made about the proper extent of judicial power. Surely the Supreme Court, an unelected, unaccountable body cannot be allowed to entertain and make decisions on whatever it chooses. This would not only represent a problem for the principle of a constitutional democracy in its Indian form, it would also lead to the possibility of judicial tyranny. But in my reading this is not what has been happening in India. Rather, at key times and in limited ways, the Supreme Court has moved to fill a constitutional vacuum left by a parliament and executive which have been unable to focus sufficiently on 'institutional decay', to use Béteille's phrase, and public squalor and spoliation (in the matter of the physical environment).

Conclusion

In less than twenty years the Supreme Court of India has done nothing less than re-invent itself. From an early post-Independence history of conservatism, the Supreme Court has emerged as the most admired and trusted of the major institutions in India. While the lower courts, the bureaucracy and above all the politicians have come into widespread disrepute or at least cynicism by virtue of their perceived corruption, the Supreme Court has been untouched by scandal or even innuendo. This reputation for honesty has underpinned the Court's novel departure from its own previous approach to litigation. The Court has emerged as a friend of the poor and of social justice in general, a protector of the physical environment, a defender of constitutional morality. True, not all the judges and not all the decisions of the Court can be viewed in this light. But nor is this reading of the Court a selective one. An apex court can establish a general mood, indeed a whole 'era', by a few major decisions that tend to have a ripple effect. In the case of the Supreme Court of India there have been more than a few decisions establishing the progressive trend sketched above.

In striking out in the direction it has, the Supreme Court has not only renovated itself but also made a crucial contribution to Indian democracy itself. From the 1960s a veritable slew of commentators asked the question of whether India could survive as a democracy and whether the army was likely to take an increased role in political life.[26] The long-term decline of the Congress Party, the rise of the BJP and the resurgence of Hindu-Muslim tensions are just some of the developments that have put great strains on public life in India. Less immediately apparent but more insidious has been the overall decay of public institutions in India—notably, schools, universities and the bureaucracy. In this climate of strain, decay and public cynicism, the rising prestige of the Supreme Court has been of inestimable value to the whole project of democracy in India. Democracy is not just about majoritarianism; it is also about minority rights and social justice. It is precisely in relation to these matters that the Court has been so valuable, and in the process of taking these matters seriously it has given heart to a wide section of Indian society. But courts are also unusually fragile institutions. Changes of personnel, threats by more powerful institutions (Prime Ministers, politicians in general, bureaucracy) can quickly undermine the courts' autonomy. So the continued vitality and progressiveness of the Supreme Court cannot be taken for granted. Its progressive role is both immensely fragile and worthy of concerted support. The Supreme Court is now one of the central strengths of Indian public life.

Notes

1. At one level this is a factual proposition, demonstrable or falsifiable by surveys of public opinion in India. Important though such surveys are as a general indicator, they are not the basis of the argument here. In any case, I am not aware of any public opinion surveys that isolate attitudes to the Supreme Court. I understand that the Centre for the Study of Democratic Institutions in New Delhi has conducted surveys that include attitudes to the courts in general, as opposed to the Supreme Court in particular—these show a low level of trust, a circumstance discussed below.

2. This claim is true in the sense that famine is not the scourge in Independent India that it was during the colonial period, and there has indeed been a powerful increase in food production. This is not to say that all, perhaps even most, Indians get enough to eat, let alone enough to eat of the right foods. For a broader discussion of this problem, see O. Mendelsohn and M. Vicziany, *The Untouchables—Subordination, Poverty and the State in Modern India* (Cambridge: Cambridge University Press, 1998), pp. 149–53.

3. See, for one example, Jeffrey Herbst, 'Responding to State Failure in Africa', *International Security*, 21(3) (1996–7), pp. 120–44.

4. In Asia, Japan and Indonesia seem to be the only other states which have retained their original Constitution for the duration of their post-War history. In the case of Japan this is a real source of that country's strength too, while the persistence of the Constitution in Indonesia masks at least one fundamental breach of constitutionalism in the form of a military coup.

5. An alternative view is put by Ayesha Jalal in a recent work, *Democracy and Authoritarianism in South Asia: A Comparative and Historical Perspective* (New York: Cambridge University Press, 1995), which throughout refers to India as a 'pseudo democracy'.

6. *India Today* (31 October 1996), p. 21.

7. *Unni Krishnan v. State of Andhra Pradesh* (1993) 1 SCC 645.

8. There is no exhaustive study of the Supreme Court's dealing with land reform legislation. But one useful discussion is Daniel Thorner, *The Agrarian Prospect in India* (New Delhi: Allied Publishers, 1976), pp. 18–31.

9. *Golak Nath v. State of Punjab* AIR (1967) SC 1643.

10. *Keshavananda Bharati v. State of Kerala* (1973) 4 SCC 225.

11. The present BJP Government has established a Constitutional Commission 'to examine in the light of past 50 years as to how far the existing provisions of the Constitution are capable of responding to the needs of efficient, smooth and effective system of governance and socio economic development of modern India and to recommend changes, if any, that are required to be made in the Constitution within the framework of parliamentary democracy and without interfering with the basic structure or basic features of the Constitution'. It is clear that the BJP and its associated bodies would like to read out of the 'basic structure' of the Constitution the principle of 'secularism'. Whether it will be able to accomplish this through the Commission and subsequent action remains to be seen. For a discussion of this, see Upendra Baxi, '*Kar Seva* of the Indian Constitution? Reflections on Proposals for Review of the Constitution', *Economic and Political Weekly*, 35(11) (11–17 March 2000), pp. 891–5.

12. The best short account of PIL or SAL is Upendra Baxi, 'Taking Suffering Seriously: Social Action Litigation in the Supreme Court of India', Upendra Baxi (ed.), *Law and Poverty: Critical Essays* (Bombay: N.M. Tripathi, 1988), pp. 387–415.

13. (1980) 1 SCC 81.

14. (1982) (1) SCALE 43.

15. AIR (1983) SC 1086.

16. Sangeeta Ahuja, *People, Law and Justice—A Casebook on Public-Interest Litigation*, 2 Vols (New Delhi: Orient Longman, 1997).

17. AIR (1986) SC 180.

18. There was parallel, less radical PIL on this same issue in both the High Court of Bombay and the Supreme Court. See Ahuja, *People, Law and Justice*, Vol. 1, pp. 352–6.

19. This series of cases is reported as follows: *M.C. Mehta v. Union of India* (1995) (4) SCALE 789; *M.C. Mehta v. Union of India* (1995) (7) SCALE SP 7; *M.C. Mehta v. Union of India* (1996) 4 SCC 351. The cases are summarised by S. Muralidhar in Ahuja, *People, Law and Justice*, Vol. 2, pp. 804–6.

20. See 'SC Gives Trend-Setting Verdict in Yamuna Case', *Times of India* (4 December 1995).

21. *India Today* (15 March 1996).

22. *Ankul Chandra Pradhan v. Union of India* (1996) 6 SCC 354.

23. See Oliver Mendelsohn, 'Life and Struggles in the Stone Quarries of India: A Case Study', *Journal of Commonwealth and Comparative Politics*, 29(1) (1991), pp. 44–71; reproduced as chapter 7 in this volume.

24. AIR (1984) SC 802.

25. Andre Béteille, 'Judicial Activism—Future of Institutional Autonomy', *Times of India* (12 December 1995). See also the debate between eminent Indian jurists Nani Palkhivala (critical of) and Soli Sorabjee (defending) PIL in the *Sunday Times of India* (3 and 10 December 1995).

26. One of the best known works sounding alarm about the prospects of Indian democracy was Selig Harrison, *India: The Most Dangerous Decades* (Madras: Oxford University Press, 1960).

9

LAW, TERROR AND THE INDIAN LEGAL ORDER*

I. Introduction

Two almost perfectly opposed views are ceaselessly presented following the destruction of the World Trade Centre in 2001. The first, predominantly American, view is that, 'everything has changed since 9/11'. This is the position almost daily presented by the Bush administration, which has declared a worldwide 'war on terror'. Arraigned against this view are those who see in the US response to the World Trade Centre attack and in the Iraq war the assertion of a self-interested and aggressive push for still greater American power, not an admirable defence of freedom and civilisation. In the latter account the rhetoric of millenarian anti-terrorism cloaks and rationalises the continuing effort to subordinate the Third World. It is to state the obvious that many of the regimes and much of the population of the Middle East subscribe to a version of the latter position. Situated somewhere between these polar positions are a great number of governments and people, including some overwhelmingly or at least predominantly Muslim nations in Asia—Malaysia, Indonesia and Pakistan are examples—often desperately trying to plot a middle way. Many of the people in these nations

*This chapter was originally published in Christoph Antons and Volkmar Gessner (eds), *Globalisation and Resistance: Law Reform in Asia since the Crisis* (Oxford: Hart Publishing, 2007), pp. 157–78.

subscribe to an aggrieved Islamic perspective on American and western power generally, while the regimes themselves have to manage a more complex world order in which the concerns of the United States must be taken seriously. Moreover, these Asian regimes know all too well that radical Islamic opinion can as easily be directed against themselves as against the United States and the West in general.

The position of India in the months since September 11 is distinctive.[1] India quickly signed up to the US-led 'war against terror'. The government of India was at the time led by the Bharatiya Janata Party (BJP), an aggressively pro-Hindu party, and it made immediate sense to them to join a cause directed against Islamic terrorists. Three months after 9/11, in December 2001, a small band of terrorists penetrated the Indian Parliament and detonated bombs which killed a number of officials. Militants engaged in the long-running military campaign in Indian Kashmir were charged, convicted and ultimately hanged for this attack. The militants' action could reasonably be pronounced to be 'terrorism' and easily linked both to the persistent military actions of Pakistan-backed dissidents in Kashmir and to the World Trade Centre attack. And although Pakistan became an admired assistant to the United States in confronting Al Qaeda and the Taliban in Afghanistan, relations between the United States and India have drawn considerably closer in the three years since September 11. India has succeeded in depicting itself in American eyes as one of the great victims of terrorism, a much more reliable ally for the United States than Pakistan.[2]

The US-led campaign against terror thus suited the BJP-led government of India, since it made their preoccupations more respectable. Indeed, American approval may even have emboldened the government in its descent into opportunistic political violence within India. Thus the most violent Indian event for years was the slaughter of some 2,000 Muslims in Gujarat State in February 2002.[3] This was superficially a spontaneous popular action but the better view is that it was orchestrated, certainly exploited, by elements within the BJP government of Gujarat following the death in a train fire of some 59 Hindu activists.[4] The activists had been returning by train from a gathering that had sought to revive the movement to dismantle the Babri Masjid, a mosque in the State of Uttar Pradesh that was allegedly built over a pre-existing Hindu temple. A confrontation over the mosque in 1992 had provoked the most bitter political struggle between Muslims and Hindus since partition of the sub-continent in 1947. The death of the Hindu activists in Gujarat in 2002 was claimed to have been deliberately brought about by Muslim zealots, and the official explanation of the ensuing riots was that they were a spontaneous response to the cruel train murders (themselves reminiscent of appalling incidents on trains during partition).[5] The rise of the BJP as a political force in India at a time of unprecedented international anxiety about 'Islamic terrorism' has led to the public expression of more naked hostility towards Muslims both in India and abroad than has been seen or heard in the country for half a century. Even where there is no actual violence or hard-edged hostility to Muslims, pejorative valuation of Muslims and of Islam seems to have seeped into the very culture of the Hindu majority of India. This is the dangerous context of the developments discussed in the present chapter. The specific argument here is that powerful elements within India have used the direction of world affairs since September 11 in ways that tend to undermine that strand of the Indian constitutional order that constitutes the libertarian tradition. Opportunistic authoritarianism threatens to work with other developments (such as the increasing criminalisation of politics) so as to undermine some of the fragile supports of Indian democracy. But there have been more heartening developments over recent months. Against virtually every prediction, the BJP won fewer seats in the national election of 2004 than did the Congress party, and the latter has now formed a coalition government in New Delhi. Congress fought the election on a platform of 'secularism' and has proceeded to rescind the most draconian of the anti-terrorist legislation enacted under the BJP government. While it is to be doubted that there has been any deep turning away from anti-Muslim feeling in the country, the election and its aftermath have given new hope to opponents of the drift in national affairs sketched above.

II. The Constitutional Back-Drop

India has an intensely conflicted Constitution. On the one hand, as still perhaps the longest constitution document in the world, it represents a mid-twentieth century flowering of some of the finest constitutional norms.[6] It contains a bill of judicially enforceable Fundamental Rights, guaranteeing the classic civil and political liberties first enunciated in late eighteenth century France and America. It also declares unlawful certain deeply objectionable aspects of historical India, such as untouchability (Article 17) and forced labour (Article 23). Of greater novelty, the Constitution of 1950 goes on to enunciate certain 'Directive Principles of State Policy', not judicially enforceable but designed to guide the government in developing a society fit for the newly independent nation. For example:

> The State shall, within the limits of economic capacity and development, make effective provision for securing the right to work, to education and to public assistance in cases of unemployment, old age, sickness and disablement, and in other cases of undeserved want. (Article 41).

There are to be 'just and humane conditions of work' and 'maternity relief' (Article 42). Indeed, workers are to be paid 'a living wage' (Article 43). The state shall 'endeavour' to provide 'free and compulsory education for all children until they complete the age of fourteen years' (Article 45).

The Constitution also lays down the basis of a democratic order, marrying (after the Canadian and Australian examples) the principles of Westminster-style responsible government with US-derived federalism. In addition to specifying the powers and procedures of Parliament and of the (essentially powerless) President, the Constitution establishes a strong Supreme Court. This constitutional basis has enabled the Court to become clearly the most distinguished court in Asia. These, then, are some of the 'progressive' elements of the Indian Constitution. But there is also another tradition of government reflected in and perpetuated by the Constitution. This tradition can be called 'colonial authoritarianism'.

The most basic manifestation of the latter approach to government is the capacity of the President (in effect directed by the Prime Minister of the day) to establish a 'state of emergency' throughout the country. Article 352 authorises the President, if satisfied that the security of India is threatened 'by war or external aggression or internal disturbance', to proclaim an emergency. During its pendency the government can suspend the Fundamental Rights (including freedom of speech and association, and protection against arbitrary arrest) (Article 357). No elections need be held during the emergency (Article 83(2)).

Even without a national emergency being declared, the central or Union government can set aside the democratically constituted government of any state (Article 356). During the period of 'President's rule', the federal principle is suspended and all functions of government are directed by the centre through whichever channels it seeks to use. Clearly, then, in the basic design of the Constitution there is sufficient suspicion of the democratic principle to allow for its suspension in difficult times.

This suspicion that democracy may not always be maintainable is clearly rooted in the colonial experience of government and is not limited to providing for the total suspension of democratic principles at particular times. One of the key devices of British rule was preventive detention, anathema to any modern order that embodies a conception of 'due process'. It was often the Collector, the head official of a District, who exercised the power to detain persons deemed to be a threat to order. The Collector doubled as both head of administration, responsible for the maintenance of order, and District Magistrate, thereby confounding any modern conception of the separation of powers. While the framers of the Constitution knew the arguments about where that conception should lead them, they contented themselves with including the goal of separating the judiciary and the executive in the non-enforceable 'Directive Principles of State Policy'. So Article 50 lays down that 'the State shall take steps to separate the judiciary from the executive in the public services of the State'. The higher judiciary and the body of lawyers have taken the principle of the separation of powers seriously, particularly following Indira Gandhi's Emergency of 1975–77, and there has been progressive separation of the lower judiciary from the regular administration. As to preventive detention, however, this has continued to flourish following Independence.[7]

III. The Dialectic between Libertarianism and Authoritarianism in Independent India

The internal dialectic of the Constitution in the matter of liberty has been reflected in the constitutional experience of India over more than half a century since Independence. Perhaps unsurprisingly, the darkest periods of authoritarianism have spawned the most vigorous libertarian backlash. India now has a particularly strong civil liberties movement served by lawyers, journalists, academics and a whole range of concerned citizens.[8] Some of these activists direct their activities towards the classic political and civil liberties—speech, association, conscience, due process of law—while many others are concerned with what Isaiah Berlin called the 'positive liberty' of decent standards of living, a clean environment, abatement of sexual oppression, and so on.[9] It is doubtful that any nation has more NGOs than does India. Most of these date back no more than 25 years and the whole phenomenon of the rights movement can be seen as a conversation with what has come to be known as Indira Gandhi's State of Emergency of 1975–77 or simply as 'the Emergency'.

Indira Gandhi's Emergency was the first such proclamation to be justified on the basis of 'internal disturbance', as prescribed in Article 352. Previously, Prime Minister Nehru had initiated an emergency proclamation in 1962 in the context of the war with China. Despite the brevity of that war Nehru's emergency lasted six years, and was finally ended only in 1968 by his daughter Indira Gandhi after setbacks in the election of 1967. The explanation for the long duration of this first emergency was that the government had become addicted to the authoritarian powers the device afforded it, particularly under the Defence of India rules. These rules made preventive detention far easier than under other legal instruments. Indira Gandhi again used the device of proclaiming an emergency in 1971, during the war with Pakistan, which led to the separation of Bangladesh as an independent nation. This emergency overlapped with her 1975–77 Emergency and was not ended until after the election of 1977, which Indira Gandhi lost.

The 1975–77 Emergency had far more drastic consequences than the two earlier emergency periods. It led to censorship of the press, widespread imprisonment of political opponents, suppression of organised opposition, the implementation of authoritarian programmes such as compulsory vasectomies and brutal slum clearances.[10] The government had justified its declaration of a state of emergency by the strength of extra-parliamentary opposition to the regime, in particular the movement led by (the non-violent) Jayaprakash Narayan. Whatever the truth as to the 'indiscipline' of Indian political opposition—a favourite refrain of Mrs Gandhi—her proclamation of a constitutional emergency was clearly a desperate response by a Prime Minister who had become embattled on many political fronts.

During the Emergency the Parliament passed the 42nd amendment to the Constitution, which operated to strip the Supreme Court of much of the power it had either been given by the Constitution or won for itself in battles during the first quarter-century following Independence.[11] Above all, the 42nd amendment purported to prohibit the Court from deliberating on the validity of amendments to the Constitution made by Parliament. Here was a classic contest of executive and judiciary in the context of a regime busy re-making itself in the image of left-wing authoritarianism.[12]

When Indira Gandhi lifted the state of emergency in 1977 and held an election she was swept from power. The new Janata government swiftly moved to repeal the 42nd amendment and generally to restore democratic norms. Although the Janata government soon fell apart and Indira Gandhi returned to power in the election of 1980, her Emergency has remained an object of denunciation among the political and civil elites. In the years following the Emergency a great raft of organisations sprang up to expose and challenge arbitrary power in India—the women's movement, for example, is a creation of this era. One of the great arenas of this activity was the courts, above all the Supreme Court of India. 'Public interest' or 'social action' litigation was now positively welcomed by the Supreme Court.[13] Despite being chronically over-burdened with litigation, some of it decades old, the Supreme Court now proved itself willing to accept petitions under the Constitution from citizens protesting against their oppression. Sometimes the petitions were written on the meanest scrap of paper. Through its activism—strong in the 1980s then waning for much of the 1990s and renewing itself late in that decade—the Supreme Court reinvented itself as something quite distinct from its early incarnation in the 1950s as a conservative supporter of agrarian property.

The Supreme Court's reinvention of itself over the second quarter-century of its existence has been nothing less than central to the maintenance of the Indian constitutional order and with it a form of liberal democracy. The Court's new jurisprudence has complemented the greatest political achievement of post-Independence India, which is the conduct of competitive elections at national, provincial and even local levels throughout a vast, poor and profoundly unequal country. These elections have on many occasions unseated governments at national and state levels and in the process produced a measure of accountability. Over the same period, however, institutional decay has set in, with habitual lawlessness and violation of due process on the part of officials, the regular infliction of violence on ordinary citizens by police and army personnel, environmental degradation, and the notorious enrichment of many officials at the expense of everyone other than their superiors. The problems have not abated with the now rapid economic development of India—indeed, arguably, deep and rapid change has tended to corrupt and break down government in India. This is the condition that has provided the Supreme Court with its opportunity.

The novelty of the Supreme Court's contribution over the last quarter-century has been to fashion a jurisprudence for a society profoundly different from the nations of the West. To give a simple example, the Court has been asked to consider the interests of a pavement-dweller in the great city of Bombay in the face of the Maharashtra State government's concern to clean up the streets of India's commercial capital. In the case of *Olga Tellis and Others* v. *Bombay Municipal Corporation and Others*[14] the argument was that certain pavement- and slum-dwellers were entitled to remain on their patch because they were protected by Article 21 of the Constitution: 'No person shall be deprived of his life or personal liberty except according to procedure established by law.' There were technical arguments as to the lawfulness of methods employed by the Bombay Corporation but the central proposition was that the right to 'life' necessarily encompassed a right to 'livelihood'. The argument was that the pavement- and slum-dwellers should not be seen as voluntary immigrants and unlawful squatters but as impoverished citizens of a vast and poor country who had no options in life. If they were deprived of the capacity to inhabit the pavement or government land, they would be deprived of the capacity to sustain life itself. The Court accepted this argument. So a 'right to life' in Article 21 became by extension a right to sleep on the pavement, if there were no alternative to this.

The early years of public interest litigation were dominated by issues brought by, or on behalf of, the poor or under-privileged.[15] There were a number of cases, for example, about the rights of women and children, bonded labourers, prisoners, detainees in psychiatric institutions and sex workers. In the 1990s the strongest flow of cases was on the physical environment, a set of issues that affected everyone. In the late 1990s the Court was even prepared to enter the politically dangerous territory of official corruption, going right up to the highest levels of government. Indeed, the Supreme Court had a procedural part to play in the most spectacular case of judicial confrontation of political corruption at the end of the 1990s. On 29 September 2000 a special court convicted former Prime Minister Narasimha Rao of having taken bribes while Prime Minister and sentenced him to three years gaol. Although Rao ultimately won an appeal on 15 March 2002 in the Delhi High Court on the ground that the conviction was unsafe, the case remains a potent symbol of judicial independence in India.

The Supreme Court's activism and its probity amid the increasing corruption of Indian institutions had by the end of the twentieth century invested it with the status of being the most trusted institution in India.[16] It had become a kind of last repository of morality and decency, though there was also a prominent group of objectors to the Court's strong (and, it was argued, undemocratic) activism.[17]

IV. Terrorism and the Constitutional Order

The new threats to the Indian constitutional order are considerably different from those of the 1970s under Prime Minister Indira Gandhi. Her political problems were those of a declining Congress Party and growing anti-government mobilisation in the cities of north India, and her response was to assert the power of the executive against both the courts and the westernised middle class who placed a high value on civil liberties. Present circumstances are quite different. There is no political, let alone constitutional, crisis in India today. India appears less fragile in the first decade of the twenty-first century than in any previous decade since Independence. Politics in India now takes the form of an intensely competitive multi-party democracy. The system is neither 'one-party dominance', as it was termed at the height of Congress power,[18] nor is it the two-party system that has evolved in a number of the Western democracies. For a time in the late 1990s and the first years of the present century it appeared as if the BJP had become the pre-eminent Indian party, albeit that it had not become so dominant as Congress was in the early years after Independence. After two brief periods as Prime Minister, Atal Bihari Vajpayee was able to form a government in October 1999 that lasted until the scheduled election in May 2004. This BJP-led government, like its two unstable predecessors, was a coalition rather than a unitary BJP administration, but the party appeared so secure in its grasp of power that virtually every pollster and commentator in the country predicted that it would win the 2004 election. But it was a sharply revived Congress under Sonia Gandhi, widow of Indira Gandhi's son Rajiv, that won marginally more seats than did the BJP, so Congress was able to form a coalition government in May 2004. Sonia Gandhi, controversial by virtue of her Italian origins, stepped aside in favour of Dr Manmohan Singh as Prime Minister. What was impressive about the election was its relative peacefulness and the calm and maturity of the political bargaining that led to the formation of a new coalition government.

If India has developed a distinctive but at least for the time being quite settled political process, this democratic maturity masks political developments of great concern. India now appears less tolerant of difference, particularly religious difference, than at any time since Independence. It has become fashionable to celebrate the death of 'secularism', which for decades has been the term used to describe the religiously uncommitted character of the Indian constitutional regime. And relations between India and Pakistan are in a highly fragile state. In 1999 the two nuclear states fought a border war in Kargil, and in 2002 hundreds of thousands of troops were mobilised on both sides of the border. Within India, during the period of BJP rule in New Delhi, public discourse was full of the simple identification of Indian Muslims with an allegedly rampant Pakistan. The idea of Indian Muslims as a Pakistani 'fifth column' is not new but this view has never had the legitimacy that it enjoyed during the period of BJP power. More generally, the events of September 11 have played into the hands of those who proclaim the virtues of *Hindutva*, a view that insists that Indian civilisation, and therefore the Indian state, is essentially Hindu and that all policies must be brought into alignment with the country's essentially Hindu nature. Such a doctrine is necessarily anti-Muslim, since it discounts any beneficial effect of Muslims on Indian society and development.[19]

A. The Indian Experience of Terrorism

In the Indian case, as elsewhere, it is often difficult to arrive at an objective identification of 'terrorism'. Insurrectionary or separatist movements in India, and even non-political gangsters, have often employed violent tactics that can easily be called 'terrorist'. The validity of such labels depends upon the political position of the parties to the contest. The closer one is to the position of those practising a particular kind of political violence, the less likely it is that one will accept 'terrorist' or any other pejorative label for their activities. Supporters of a movement may identify it by a descriptor which also conveys approbation. So while the 'militants' of Indian Kashmir are often identified by that name or as 'extremists' or more recently, under the influence of American rhetoric as 'terrorists', they are 'freedom fighters' to their supporters in Kashmir itself. But the organs of the state and also majority opinion, which tends to be outraged by the violence of minority groups, are generally not prepared to look behind violent means for political justifications. On the other hand, armed actions taken by the forces of the state against political minorities tend to be reflexively viewed as legitimate force rather than morally equated with the illegitimate violence of the minority. This is now a characteristic of international affairs too. So the present US-led 'war against terror' concentrates exclusively on the violent *means* of the 'terrorists', not their *ends*, while asking us to lay aside doubts about *our* violent means.

India has had a long acquaintance with armed insurrection and with 'terror' or violence as a political tool. Immediately after Indian Independence there was a strong insurrectionary communist movement in the Telengana region of southern India, and this was only suppressed with considerable force.[20] In the Himalayan region of Nagaland tribal people have conducted an insurrectionary and separatist movement from virtually the time of Indian Independence up to the present. At one stage in the struggle a favoured tactic was to blow up trains crossing the great Gangetic plain.[21] In the late 1960s a band of revolutionary Marxists influenced by the writings and experience of Mao Zedong organised violent action in the Naxalbari region of rural West Bengal. The Naxalites, as they came to be called, saw their activities as the beginning of a revolution across India.[22] Eventually, and with considerable bloodshed, this movement was put down. A decade or so later the movement was re-born in a number of districts of the neighbouring and extremely poor state of Bihar, where it has continued for some 30 years. The character and leadership vehicles of the movement have changed over time but the practice of exemplary violence has persisted. The revolutionaries—or is it 'terrorists', 'extremists' or merely 'representatives of the downtrodden castes/classes of Bihar'?—have sought to spread terror in the countryside by threatening, and occasionally accomplishing, the 'lowering of oppressors by six inches' (the nominal height of a head).[23] It is difficult not to feel a great deal of sympathy for the causes of land reform, social respect and abatement of sexual violence for which many of these people are fighting in India's most unequal and poorest state, even if the tactics seem grotesque. And it should also be pointed out that the violence practised by the other side—some of it meted out by upper caste, landed elements who are defending their hereditary dominance, some of it by the state—has been at least as great as that of the 'revolutionaries'. Indeed, much of this violence can also be seen as 'terrorist' in nature.

In the 1980s the most serious challenge to the Indian state was from militant Sikhs who wanted to establish a separate state to be called 'Khalistan' or the 'land of the pure'. This was undoubtedly a dangerous confrontation of the Indian state but it is also now generally agreed that Prime Minister Indira Gandhi's government handled the conflict very badly. The storming of the Amritsar Golden Temple in 'Operation Bluestar' caused the death of some 1,000 Sikh 'militants' (the term generally used at the time). This event cost the Prime Minister her own life, when one of her Sikh bodyguards murdered her in retribution. The needlessly bloody confrontation of militant Sikhs resonates strongly two decades after the event and also has some parallels with militant Hindu treatment of Muslims at Ayodhya in 1992 (the Babri Masjid affair), in Gujarat in 2002, and more generally for the last 15 years or so. The parallel is a core of sectarianism within the majority Hindu population. But when highly militant and obscurantist representatives of the Hindu majority practise violence in defence of 'mother Hinduism', they are not called 'extremists', 'militants' and certainly not 'terrorists'.

By and large, the Indian state has learnt to live with chronic political violence. The constantly simmering insurrection in Bihar is the longest running example of such conflict, and to a large extent New Delhi manages to ignore what is happening in that state. This is also a grave comment on the importance of Bihar to the nation's capital and on the extent to which that state's problems are taken seriously. The Sikh militancy of the 1980s was taken far more seriously for a number of reasons, including the religious character of the challenge and the proximity of Punjab to the capital.

Given the long experience of violence, the question is why the Kashmiri 'militants' have become so dominant a concern in India today. Why has their 'terrorism' (not always an unreasonable term for their political activities) been taken so seriously? Clearly the answers to these questions have a lot to do with Indian relations with Pakistan, which is identified as a prime provocateur in Kashmir and a source of support for the Kashmiri militants. In terms of the level of violence, it is highly doubtful that the conflict in Kashmir is any worse than other chronically violent situations, notably that of Bihar. The new factor over the last few years has been the advent of September 11 and all its political and military ramifications, which have been highly advanta-geous to the cause of militant Hindus associated with or supporting the present government of India. There is a high degree of political opportunism in the government of India's enthusiastic association of its own fight against terror with the worldwide 'war against terror' waged primarily by the United States.

B. The Legal Regime and Terrorists

Consistent with what has been said earlier about the authoritarian stream in Indian constitutionalism, post-Independence India was quick to enact the Preventive Detention Act of 1950. This Act remained in force until 1970 when it was allowed to lapse but for a number of years it overlapped the Defence of India rules made under the 1962 Act of the same name. The Act and rules were the legislative response to war breaking out with China, and the rules enabled preventive detention of anyone who had acted or was likely to act in a manner detrimental to public order and national security. The rules were revived in 1971 during the war with Pakistan and its aftermath, and were maintained long enough for the imprisonment of striking rail workers in 1974.[24] With an eye more firmly focused on internal distur-bances not directly linked to war, the Maintenance of Internal Security

Act (MISA) was passed in 1971. This was the principal instrument used for widespread detention of political opponents during Indira Gandhi's Emergency of 1975–77.

After the 1975–77 Emergency the newly elected Janata government pushed through an amendment to the Constitution which substituted 'armed rebellion' for 'internal disturbance' as a basis for declaring an emergency under Article 352 (though this was later reversed under the Congress Party in 1988.) The Janata government also repealed MISA, as well as the Defence of India rules. But when Indira Gandhi returned to power in 1980, the National Security Act 1980 again allowed preventive detention of anyone suspected of subverting national security, public order and essential economic services.[25] Other decidedly illiberal legislation was passed at this time, including the Essential Services Maintenance Act 1981, providing for the suppression of strikes and lock-outs in key economic sectors.

It was the Sikh situation in the mid-1980s that focused specific attention on what were now called 'terrorists'. The Terrorist and Disruptive Activities (Prevention) Act 1985 (TADA) provided a legislative basis for a range of counter-terrorism surveillance measures (wiretaps etc). It provided for the death penalty in trials which could also be held in camera. On important matters, the burden of proof was reversed. 'Review Committees' were established under the legislation which, it has to be said, did discharge a large number of detainees, as did the Supreme Court upon individual application. Overall tens of thousands of prisoners are said to have been arrested and detained under TADA, although verification of such numbers has always been difficult.[26] There has been no definitive study of the identity of these people but it appears that many of them, probably most, could not by any stretch of the imagination be called 'terrorists'. As is the nature of authoritarian instruments, they come to be used against a far wider sector of the population than was their justification for enactment. TADA allowed detention of anyone who committed or even facilitated the commission of 'disruptive activity', a term only vaguely defined. The Act was finally allowed to lapse by the Congress government in 1995, a rare instance when Congress has been responsible for removing legal instruments which run counter to due process jurisprudence.

When the impossibly fragile Janata coalition was in power (1978–79), it did maintain something of a commitment to opposing the authoritarian thrust of anti-terrorist legislation. With the rise to power of the BJP, the most actively divisive government since Independence, there was a renewed commitment to the approach best represented by MISA and TADA. The BJP proposed a new Prevention of Terrorism Act in 2000 but after sustained opposition by various political parties and the human rights movement the bill did not proceed. Following the World Trade Centre attack, a Prevention of Terrorism Ordinance was rushed through on 24 October, and this was transformed into the Prevention of Terrorism Act 2002 (POTA). When the spokesman for the US State Department, Richard Boucher, was asked to comment on the Ordinance (later Act) in March 2000, he said:

> We do think it is important for governments to take steps against terrorism, to do it in a constitutional way ... We do believe that that can be done consistent with democratic principles. We have done that. The Europeans have done that. And India seems to have done that as well.[27]

The new Act had many features in common with TADA, though in one major respect the later Act was preferable. The vague and obnoxious phrase 'disruptive activity' is not a part of the later Act, which is limited to terrorist acts (including belonging to a terrorist organisation). The punishment for such activities, if they bring about death, was sentence of death or life imprisonment. The Act expanded the range of investigations possible under the ordinary law—for example, there was virtually no limit on what property can be seized (section 7). Special courts could be established to handle offences under the Act, and the trials could be held in camera. Confessions extracted outside the ordinary rules of evidence under the Indian Evidence Act 1872 were deemed admissible (section 32). And, importantly, the burden of proof was in effect reversed if fingerprints or the possession of arms pointed to the involvement of the accused (section 53).

Given the route along which India has passed for thirty years or more, it would not be possible to erect a case on the basis of POTA that India had entered into a new and more draconian phase of legislation justified by the hunt for terrorists. The case against this legislation, as with TADA and MISA before it, was that the most radical aspects were probably not necessary. It is not clear, for example, why proceedings should have been in camera or why there should have been open slather on confessions. The latter is a positive invitation to tyrannical police officers. There were particular concerns about providing a secret regime of trial, conviction and sentence of death. Reversal of onus of proof and other relaxations of the evidentiary burden will almost certainly lead on occasion to wrong conviction. And surely it is not desirable that special courts be established, albeit that the judicial officers are sufficiently qualified. It is true that the Indian court system is inefficient and plagued by delay, and it is therefore possible to sympathise with a government that wishes to bypass these problems in its fight against terrorism. But there are also ways of expediting justice within the regular criminal justice administration without going down the path of a separate apparatus for those accused of terrorism.[28]

There was, then, a strong argument that POTA was too authoritarian an instrument, even conceding the legitimacy of the concern to combat terrorism more effectively in what is undoubtedly a dangerous political and security environment for India as well as for many other countries. It was all but inevitable, based on past experience, that if POTA had been richly employed it would quite often have been directed against people who could not by any reasonable definition be thought to be 'terrorists'. In this sense the law was an unwelcome legislative reincarnation of Indian authoritarianism that had been beaten down during the backlash against Indira Gandhi's Emergency.

Of course, India was not alone in having enacted new legal instruments that cut down on the 'luxury' of due process that is maintained, if always under challenge, during 'ordinary' times. In the immediate aftermath of September 11 the United States itself passed the Uniting and Strengthening America by Providing Appropriate Tools Required to Intercept and Obstruct Terrorism Act 2001 (USA PATRIOT Act, 2001). This Act is considerably criticised by civil liberties organisations within the United States for the loss of due process guarantees that are set aside for government agencies in pursuit of terrorists.[29] And there is a great deal of international criticism of the long-term incarceration at Guantanamo Bay of hundreds of people from a number of countries in effect declared by the United States to be guilty of terrorism, treason or unlawful warfare but almost all of whom have yet to face a judicial procedure, let alone one that will command the respect of jurists around the world. There are legitimate fears that the American system of justice is being significantly weakened by such measures. And like India, of course, the United States possesses and routinely imposes the death sentence. Australia is another country that has given new powers to its primary security agency following September 11, although the new powers are not so great as those of comparable American agencies.[30]

C. The Political Context of Indian Anti-Terror Legislation

The special issue in relation to anti-terrorist legislation in the Indian context is the extent to which it represents a symbolic contributor to the increasingly strained relations between the Hindu majority and the Muslim minority community. Again, the issue of discrimination against Muslims is not an issue confined to India. In the present inflamed world situation there has been ugly discrimination and violence against Muslims and other identifiable 'outsiders' (Sikhs with their highly-visible turbans, for example) in the United States and other western nations.[31] But the situation in India is especially difficult given the size of the Muslim population, some 130 million.[32]

India developed for more than four decades as a secular state under the Indian Constitution, its modernist first Prime Minister Jawaharlal Nehru and later leaders from both the Congress Party and ruling coalitions that included socialist elements. With the rise of the Bharatiya Janata Party (BJP), the communal landscape of India has changed quite dramatically and the country's commitment to 'secularism' has become a matter of controversy rather than a fundamental commitment. The BJP grew out of an earlier party, the Jana Sangh, which had roots going back to the nineteenth century. Its rationale is its conception of India as 'Hindutva', a land governed by the Hindu view of life in which non-Hindu elements, notably Muslims and Christians, can have only a subsidiary role.[33] This is a deeply divisive political position in a country that has a larger Muslim population than any country other than Indonesia.

The BJP Prime Minister from 1998 to 2004, A.B. Vajpayee, was presented as the moderate face of the party and its front organisations. Indeed, as a former Foreign Minister, Vajpayee knows how to steer a patient passage through the complexities of both domestic and foreign circumstances. But Vajpayee is also someone who has contributed powerfully to the reconstruction of an India that is progressively pushing

Muslims to the margins. His New Year's Message, promulgated from Goa at the turn of 2003,[34] represents the vintage Vajpayee approach to politics.[35] On the face of it, the message appeared as a strong attack on the right wing of his own party and movement and invoked tolerance in the face of the appalling Gujarat riots of 2002. But closer scrutiny of the speech revealed an approach to society that was more to the taste of his own side and far more insidious from the standpoint of the advocates of a secular India. Vajpayee was at pains to assert that there was no contradiction or even tension between Hindutva and secularism. Hindutva, he suggested, is itself secular by virtue of being tolerant, and therefore India is essentially a tolerant society. Of course, what is controversial about this statement is the view that it is Hindutva that constitutes 'India' and that the good qualities of Indian society arise from that Hindutva and from no other source. The religion of 130 million Muslims, not to mention Christians and others, is thereby pushed to the margins of irrelevance in terms of the fundamental character of Indian society. In short, the Indian Prime Minister is at the head of a party that is energetically staging a peculiarly Indian version of the culture wars that is profoundly destabilising for the sub-continent. Perhaps the sharpest of the problems faced by Indian Muslims today is the constant suspicion put about that they constitute a fifth column for Pakistan, the nation formerly part of undivided India and composed overwhelmingly of Muslims. So when bombs go off in Mumbai, as they did again on 25 August 2003, killing some 50 people, the forces of Hindutva (including the militant Shiv Sena) are quick to attribute them to 'Muslims', careless of whether they are Indians, Kashmiri separatists or Pakistanis. The object of the exercise is to assert a seamless identity between the enemy nation of Pakistan and Indian Muslims, who are 'really' Pakistanis in Indian clothing.

This, then, was the context of the new Indian security legislation promulgated in the aftermath of the World Trade Centre attack in 2001. There is no denying the existence and potent development of extremist elements among Muslim communities of the sub-continent (mainly in Pakistan, Afghanistan and Kashmir): this is a cause for legitimate concern in Indian security circles. But equally the heightening of tension and distrust between the two largest religious communities of India holds particular danger for the Muslims, who are outnumbered by about 6:1 by the Hindus. For the Muslims attacked in the

Gujarat riots of 2002, the terror was brought about by unscrupulous proponents of hatred and intolerance in the majority community. This was no simple popular response to the appalling death of Hindus on the train in Godhra, Gujarat.[36] It was an organised murder of Muslims on a truly massive scale.[37] In these inflamed circumstances, any ratcheting-up of official authoritarianism is to be viewed with suspicion and concern.

D. The Return of Congress and the Repeal of POTA

The political landscape of India has changed considerably since the victory of Congress in the 2004 election, though it is far too soon to proclaim the reversal of the drift into deeper communal disharmony. Congress ran a campaign that revolved around its claim to represent 'secularism', as opposed to the embrace of 'Hindutva' by the BJP and its allies. As noted earlier, to almost universal surprise Congress ended up with more seats than did the BJP. It is highly doubtful that the result was brought about by any sudden access of commitment to 'secularism' or new-found antipathy to Hindutva on the part of the Hindu majority. The main plank of the BJP's platform for this election was not Hindutva but 'India Shining', a reference to the new prosperity and national prestige being generated by the boom in the ICT and certain other industries. This message turned out to be far from universally attractive. The BJP had forgotten that a large part of India, particularly the rural areas which still comprise over 70 per cent of the population, had benefited little—if at all—from the urban and intensely regional nature of the economic boom. In this and a number of other ways the BJP proved remarkably out of touch with the electorate, which turned back towards Congress and even more towards a range of parties of the left in the different regions.[38]

During the campaign Congress promised to repeal POTA if it won the election. This seeming libertarianism was a newly discovered commitment for a party that had instituted all the anti-democratic emergencies, above all Indira Gandhi's Emergency of 1975–77, since Independence almost 60 years ago. The stance enabled Congress to portray the BJP and its affiliates as dedicated to both sectarianism and authoritarianism. Some four months after its electoral victory the

Congress-led government repealed POTA and introduced substitute legislation. Initially both the repeal of POTA and the new law were accomplished in the form of ordinances, and these were converted to Acts during the next session of Parliament.[39]

An early commentary on the new legislation talked in terms of 'three steps forward ... two steps back'; the article was headed 'The Reincarnation of POTA'.[40] This title was probably overstating the case. Certain key aspects of the Unlawful Activities (Prevention) Act 1967 (as amended in 2004) are demonstrable improvements over POTA. For example, POTA (s 32(1)) set aside the hitherto ruling provision of the Indian Evidence Act 1872 whereby confessions to police officers were inadmissible as evidence in court. The new Act restores the bar of admissibility of confessions to police, thereby making torture less rewarding a behaviour of gaolers and police. Under POTA a suspect could be held for up to 180 days without charge (s 49 (2)(b)), whereas now suspects must be produced before the court within 24 hours as prescribed by the ordinary criminal law. Bail could effectively be denied a suspect under POTA for a year without consideration of the court (s 49(6) and (7)), but now the ordinary provisions of the criminal law have been restored in this matter. POTA had authorised the court to draw 'adverse inference' from certain matters (including the finding of fingerprints at the site of an offence: s 53(1)(b)), thereby transferring the burden of proof from prosecution to defence. This too has been removed. And importantly, whereas it was enough for POTA that a person 'belongs or professes to belong to a terrorist organisation (s 20(1)), under the new Act the accused is guilty of an offence only if he (sic) associates himself with the organisation 'with intention to further its activities' (s 38(1)).

On the other hand, as the author of the Human Rights Features article[41] makes clear, the open-ended definition of terrorist acts persists from TADA, through POTA and into the new Act. The definition is bound to sweep up many oppositional activities that are either dubiously or not at all terrorist in nature. And there remains no procedure for the listing of an organisation as 'involved in terrorism' (s 35(1)(d)) and therefore to be included in the Schedule of the Act. Moreover, proceedings may still be held in camera 'if the court so desires' (s 44(1)).

Overall, however, replacement of the POTA with the new Act is a considerable step in the right direction. The new Congress government has translated its recently found rhetoric of civil liberties into some valuable reform of legal instruments. No doubt this process of reform was aided by the reduced intensity of political pressure from the United States, which is now embroiled in a war in Iraq widely seen to have little to do with its 'war on terror'. The United States too continues to be roundly condemned internationally and at home for its treatment of prisoners in Guantanamo Bay and its torture and mistreatment of prisoners in Iraq. The time was therefore ripe for the new Congress government to show a more civil libertarian face. Whether or not this results in more orderly and careful administration of the criminal law in relation to political opposition remains to be seen.

V. Conclusion

The broad problem of the post-September 11 anti-terrorism legislation in India, particularly POTA, was that it constituted a significant contraction of due process. Aside from the immensely worrying threats to liberty in general represented by such legislation in India, as well as in a number of other jurisdictions throughout the world, under the BJP government there were realistic fears that authoritarian legislation would be enforced in a discriminatory way. Indian Muslims held particular fears that this would be so, though evidence of practice is insufficient to make a sound judgment as to whether this has actually occurred and if so to what degree. This chapter has sketched a picture of the Indian constitutional order as conflicted, with elements of both the proper observance of human and civil rights and also patterns of authoritarianism inherited from the colonial administration and extended in the years since Independence. A positive account of some aspects of the institutional development of justice in India has been sketched here, particularly the invention of 'social action litigation' by the Supreme Court of India. On the other hand, it cannot be assumed that the Supreme Court, let alone Indian courts in general, will either systematically stand up to, or be effective against, authoritarian rule in the future. Meanwhile, and to the surprise of virtually everyone, political developments within India have to a considerable extent reversed the downward spiral into authoritarianism. Congress is re-born as the party in power at the head of a mildly left-leaning coalition, and this time round it has embraced civil liberties as never before. In the context of the increasingly inflamed character of relations between religious communities in India, this development may be of considerable value.

Notes

1. Dipankar Banerjee and Gert W. Kueck, *South Asia and the War on Terrorism—Analysing the Implications of 11 September* (New Delhi: India Research Press, 2003).

2. As with many other countries, India's position on the war in Iraq was equivocal. Prior to the war, if pressed, India declared itself to be against a military solution to the Iraq problem. India, like China and Russia, had intense ambitions in relation to Iraqi oil post-Saddam Hussein, and these ambitions were one factor limiting any Indian criticism of the American invasion. Also, the aggressively Hindu BJP would scarcely have taken the line that an attack on Iraq was an attack on Islam. Following the initial phase of the war the mildness of the Indian position even led to talk of India as a potential contributor to a peacekeeping force in Iraq. But it is also true that the government had to be careful not to senselessly outrage Muslim opinion, both within India and internationally, by its stance in relation to a nation within the heartland of Islam. Solidarity with 'non-aligned nations' like Iraq had been a cornerstone of Indian foreign policy throughout the Cold War, though such policy was now considerably less relevant than before. Ultimately India has stayed clear of any involvement in the war in Iraq.

3. This is the figure that is regularly cited, though doubts are often cast on its accuracy. For a broad collection of material and sources on the Gujarat riots, see the website of OnlineVolunteers.org, available at: http://www.onlinevolunteers.org/gujarat/reports/index.htm, last accessed 15 November 2006.

4. Concerned Citizens' Tribunal, *Crime against Humanity: An Inquiry into the Carnage in Gujarat, Vol. II Findings and Recommendations* (Mumbai: Citizens for Justice and Peace, 2002).

5. The BJP Chief Minister of Gujarat, Narendra Modi, jumped to the conclusion (still unverified) that the victims of the train fire in Godhra had been murdered by Muslims. His explanation, almost justification, of the ensuing riots throughout Gujarat was to point to Newton's third

law: 'every action has an equal and opposite reaction', *The Times of India*, (2 March 2002).

6. For an accessible account of the making of the Indian Constitution, see Granville Austin, *The Indian Constitution: Cornerstone of a Nation* (Oxford: Clarendon Press, 1966). The most authoritative commentary on Indian constitutional law is H.M. Seervai, *Constitutional Law of India* (Bombay: Tripathi, 1991).

7. Granville Austin, *The Indian Constitution*, pp. 53–63; Prasenjit Maiti, 'On Civil Liberties and Society in India', formerly available at: http://www. e11th-hour.org/security/india.society.html (as at 28 March 2003), but relocated at: http://www. poetryrepairs.com/v01/144.html, last accessed 15 November 2006.

8. One of the strongest organisations is the People's Union for Civil Liberties, formed in the immediate aftermath of Indira Gandhi's Emergency. Its website is at http://www.pucl.org, last accessed 15 November 2006.

9. Isaiah Berlin, 'Two Concepts of Liberty', in his *Four Essays on Liberty* (London: Oxford University Press, 1969), pp. 118–72.

10. E. Tarlo, *Unsettling Memories: Narratives of the Emergency in Delhi* (Berkeley: University of California Press, 2003).

11. Rajeev Dhavan, *The Amendment: Conspiracy or Revolution?* (Allahabad: Wheeler, 1978).

12. Granville Austin, *Working a Democratic Constitution—The Indian Experience* (New Delhi: Oxford University Press, 2000), pp. 370–88.

13. Upendra Baxi, 'Taking Suffering Seriously: Social Action Litigation in the Supreme Court of India', in Upendra Baxi (ed.), *Law and Poverty—Critical Essays* (Bombay: Tripathi, 1988), pp. 387–415.

14. AIR (1986) SC 180.

15. Oliver Mendelsohn, 'Life and Struggles in the Stone Quarries of India', *Journal of Commonwealth and Comparative Politics*, 29(1) (1991), p. 44; Sangeeta Ahuja, *People, Law and Justice—A Casebook of Public Interest Litigation* (Hyderabad: Orient Longman, 1997).

16. Oliver Mendelsohn, 'The Supreme Court as the Most Trusted Public Institution in India', *South Asia* 23 (2000), p. 103.

17. For example, Andre Béteille, then Professor of Sociology at the University of Delhi, wrote in *The Times of India* on 12 December 1995: 'Judicial activism often stems from the best of motives, the desire to set things right in corrupt and decaying public institutions ... But it can also be argued that in a democracy, judicial restraint is a virtue not only in good times but also in bad times.' Nani Palkhivala, one of the most successful lawyers of post-Independence India, wrote about public interest litigation in these

terms: 'The real point of issue is not whether the apex court is entitled under the Constitution to decide such issues, but whether democracy can survive this kind of shift in authority' (*The Sunday Times of India* [3 December 1995]). For a more recent view, see Arun Shourie, *Courts and Their Judgments* (New Delhi: Rupa, 2001).

18. This phrase was first used by W.H. Morris-Jones to identify the towering dominance of Congress, despite the system of free elections. See his 'Parliament and Dominant Party: Indian Experience', *Parliamentary Affairs* 17 (1964), pp. 206–307.

19. For a recent discussion of the implications of the Hindutva movement, see Marika Vicziany, 'Globalization and *Hindutva*: India's Experience with Global Economic and Political Integration', in Gloria Davies and Chris Nyland (eds), *Globalization in the Asian Region: Impacts and Consequences* (Cheltenham: Edward Elgar, 2004).

20. P. Sundarayya, 'Telengana', in A.R. Desai (ed.), *Peasant Struggles in India* (Bombay: Oxford University Press, 1979).

21. Dinesh Kotwal, 'The Naga Insurgency: The Past and the Future', *Strategic Analysis: A Monthly Journal of the IDSA*, 24(4) (July 2000), available at: http://www.ciaonet.org, last accessed 15 November 2006.

22. S. Banerjee, *In the Wake of Naxalbari: A History of the Naxalite Movement in India* (Calcutta: Subarnekha, 1980).

23. Oliver Mendelsohn and Marika Vicziany, *The Untouchables—Subordination, Poverty and the State in Modern India* (Cambridge: Cambridge University Press, 1998), pp. 44–76.

24. Stephen Sherlock, *The Indian Railways Strike of 1974: A Study of Power and Organised Labour* (New Delhi: Rupa, 2001).

25. There are a number of Websites put up by activist or revolutionary organisations that provide quite useful material on these matters. See, e.g., Amnesty International, 'India: The Prevention of Terrorism Bill. Past Abuses Revisited' (23 June 2000), available at: http://web.amnesty.org/library/index/ ENGASA200222000, last accessed 15 November 2006.

26. In 1997, two years after the repeal of TADA, Amnesty International's annual report on India cited a government source to the effect that in March more than 42,000 people were still detained under the Act pending trial (Amnesty International, *AI Report 1997: India*, available at: http://www.amnesty.org/ailib/aireport/ar97/ASA20.htm, last accessed 15 November 2006). This number had apparently declined by December 1997 to 2,000, following a Supreme Court directive ordering the release on bail of various categories of detainee.

27. *The Hindu* (29 March 2000).

28. There is a large body of literature on the problems in the administration of justice in India. For a recent view, see Marc Galanter and Jayanth K. Krishnan, 'Debased Informalism: *Lok Adalats* and Legal Rights in Modern India', in Thomas Heller and Erik Jensen (eds), *Beyond Common Knowledge: Empirical Approaches to the Rule of Law* (Stanford: Stanford University Press, 2003).

29. Nancy Chang, 'The US PATRIOT Act. What's So Patriotic about Trampling on the Bill of Rights?' (2001), available from the Center for Constitutional Rights at: http://www.ccr-ny.org/v2/reports/docs/ USA_ PATRIOT_ACT.pdf, last accessed 15 November 2006.

30. Australian Security Intelligence Organisation Legislation Amendment (Terrorism) Act, 2003 (Cth).

31. Human Rights Watch, '"We Are Not the Enemy" Hate Crimes against Arabs, Muslims and Those Perceived to Be Arab or Muslim after September 11', Report by Amardeep Singh for HRW (14 November 2002), HRW Index No G1406 (see especially Part V 'The September 11 Backlash'), available at http://www.hrw.org/reports/2002/usahate/usa1102-04.htm, last accessed 15 November 2006.

32. Although the last Census of India was in 2001, no totals for religious affiliation have been published and may not be until 2005 or later. The delay arises at least in part for political reasons: the figures will immediately become political fodder for both Hindus and Muslims, whose leadership will exploit them for their own ends. The Muslim leadership will use them to claim new facilities for the predominantly poor Muslim population, while Hindus will cite them as evidence of a dangerously rising Muslim population. For population estimates, see Syed Shahabuddin, 'Approximate Muslim Population in India (2001)', *Milli Gazette* (28 October 2003), available at: http:// www.milligazette.com/Archives/15092001/29.htm, last accessed 15 November 2006.

33. Bruce Graham, *Hindu Nationalism and Indian Politics: The Origins and Development of the Bharatiya Jana Sangh* (Cambridge: Cambridge University Press, 1990).

34. A.B. Vajpayee, New Year's Message (2002), available at: http://www. indianembassy.org/pm/vajpayee/_pm_dec_31_2002.htm (consulted 27 March 2007).

35. V. Venkatesan, 'A Secular Veneer', *Frontline* 20(2) (January 2003), pp. 18–31, available at: http://www.hinduonnet.com/fline/fl2002/stories/ 20030131005103700.htm (consulted 27 March 2007).

36. It is still unclear just who committed this act, and there are unsubstantiated accounts that point to Hindu provocateurs as the culprits. But it has to be

acknowledged that there are extremist elements among Indian Muslims, as there are among Hindus, and that these could have been responsible for the deaths in Godhra. For a collection of reports on the Gujarat massacre in general, see OnlineVolunteers.org (n 3, above).

37. The progress of one of the major murder cases stemming from the Gujarat riots suggests there is a high degree of fear among witnesses to the atrocities of that period. It is also clear that money is being employed to induce witnesses to change their testimony. In the Best Bakery case, 21 people were prosecuted for the murder of 14 people during the Gujarat riots. Witnesses gave evidence that some 500 people had attacked the bakery with petrol bombs and that many of the dead had been burnt to death. The accused were originally acquitted on 27 June 2003 by a 'fast track' court set up to bring swift justice in relation to the Gujarat riots. The court found a want of evidence after 37 of the 73 witnesses turned hostile, including a key witness named Zahira Sheikh. So unsatisfactory was this result that the BJP government of Gujarat was forced to appeal to the Gujarat High Court, and a re-trial was ordered. The tragic affair turned into something like a soap opera in late 2004, as Zahira Sheikh changed her position a couple of times again in the lead-up to the re-trial. Her community became so outraged that they are reported as having sought to expel her: http://en.wikipedia.org/ wiki/Best_Bakery_Case, last accessed 15 November 2006. For an analysis of the case, see also People's Union for Civil Liberties, 'Best Bakery Case—PUCL Demands Fresh Trial', press release (7 July 2003), available at: http://www.pucl.org/ Topics/Religion-communalism/2003/best-bakery.htm, last accessed 15 November 2006.

38. Two early academic considerations of the 2004 election are Zoya Hasan, 'Indian Election 2004: A Setback for the BJP's Exclusivist Agenda' (2004), available at: http://www.ceri-sciences-po.org/ archive/sept04/ artzh.pdf, last accessed 15 November 2006; and Gareth Price, 'How the 2004 Lok Sabha Election Was Lost', Chatham House Briefing Note (Royal Institute of International Affairs) (July 2004), available at: http://www. chathamhouse.org.uk/pdf/research/asia/BNgp0704.pdf, last accessed 15 November 2006.

39. POTA was repealed by the Prevention of Terrorism Act (POTA) Repeal Ordinance 2004 (promulgated on 21 September). On the same day The Unlawful Activities (Prevention) Amendment Ordinance 2004 was promulgated, amending the Unlawful Activities (Prevention) Act 1967. These ordinances were converted to Acts of Parliament on 9 December 2004.

40. Human Rights Features, *The Reincarnation of POTA* (New Delhi: Voice of the Asia Pacific Human Rights Network, 2004), available at: http://www. hrdc.net/sahrdc/hrfeatures/ HRF106.htm, last accessed 15 November 2006.

41. Ibid.

INDEX

ABOUT THE AUTHOR

Oliver Mendelsohn is a former Dean of Law at La Trobe University, Melbourne. He has worked on Indian law, society and politics for more than 40 years. His initial fieldwork for his doctorate titled 'Dispute Settlement in Rural India' was mainly in Rajasthan. Among his publications are an edited volume (with Upendra Baxi), *The Rights of Subordinated Peoples*, Oxford University Press, 1994; and Oliver Mendelsohn and Marika Vicziany, *The Untouchables: Subordination, Poverty and the State in Modern India*, Cambridge University Press, 1994. He was also the founding and long-time editor of the journal *Law in Context*. In recent years he has taken a particular interest in the globalization of parts of the Indian legal system.